WITHDRAWN

D0937498

## Picturing the Past

### DATE DUE

| | |
|---|---|
| MAR 2 1 2007 | |
| APR 1 2 2012 | |
| APR 1 3 2012 | |
| OCT 1 5 2014 | |
| | |
| | |
| | |
| | |
| | |
| | |
| | |
| | |
| | |
| | |
| | |
| | |
| | |

BRODART        Cat. No. 23-221

**The History**

**of Communication**

*Robert W. McChesney and*

*John C. Nerone, editors*

*A list of books*

*in the series appears*

*at the end of*

*this book.*

# Picturing the Past

## MEDIA, HISTORY, AND
## PHOTOGRAPHY

*Edited by Bonnie Brennen
and Hanno Hardt*

**University of Illinois Press**

*Urbana and Chicago*

© 1999 by the Board of Trustees of
the University of Illinois

Manufactured in the United States of America
⊗ This book is printed on acid-free paper.

Library of Congress Cataloging-in-Publication Data
Picturing the past : media, history, and photography /
edited by Bonnie Brennen and Hanno Hardt.
p.    cm. — (The history of communication)
Includes bibliographical references and index.
ISBN 0-252-02465-6 (cloth : alk. paper)
ISBN 0-252-06769-x (pbk. : alk. paper)
1. Photojournalism—History.
2. Photography—Social aspects.
3. Mass media—History—20th century.
I. Brennen, Bonnie.
II. Hardt, Hanno.
III. Series.
TR820.P555    1999
070.4'9'09—ddc21    98-58009
CIP

1 2 3 4 5 C P 5 4 3 2 1

AUSTIN COMMUNITY COLLEGE
LEARNING RESOURCE SERVICES

Every image of the past that is not recognized

by the present as one of its own concerns

threatens to disappear irretrievably.

—Walter Benjamin

　*Theses on the Philosophy of History*

# Contents

# Picturing the Past

# Introduction

*Hanno Hardt and Bonnie Brennen*

The following collection of original essays provides an introduction to the study of photographic images from a variety of perspectives that are suggestive rather than exhaustive in their treatment of the relationship between photography and history in the context of media studies. The social uses of photographs as visual expressions of a culture and constituents of a collective memory have played a minor role in considering a cultural history of communication, even though the visual is closely related to the more fundamental issues of what Martin Jay (1988) has called "ocularcentrism," or the privileging of vision in Western culture, which has occupied social theorists for some time. Maurice Merleau-Ponty (1962) has written on perception, Michel Foucault (1977) on surveillance techniques, and Guy Debord (1992) on the spectacle. Karen Newman's work (1997) on the relationship between visualizing science and contemporary "fetal politics," which traces the production and effects of specific images through history to emphasize the importance of the visual in social history, also contributes to the notion of ocularcentrism. Still other contemporary discussions often stress the historical dimension of language and the limits of visual immediacy in the production of meanings.

The contributions to this volume address the use of photographs as visual manifestations of material culture and speak to the question of representation and the process of history in the context of understanding the experience of the visual in modern media environments. The essays discuss the use of photographic images during the twentieth century and deal with producers and products of cultural labor at specific historical moments. They focus on two major issues: the difference photographs have made in the construction of a collective memory (and their place as historical markers in the culture of society) and the potential of photographs as contemporary journalistic documentation and historical evidence.

Photography is a product and witness of the industrial revolution whose consequences have marked the social and political struggles of the twentieth century. The mass production of cameras offered access to the world and reshaped popular notions of time and space when photographs provoked the imagination and, combined with new technologies of transportation, significantly enhanced the mobility of society. Indeed, with the beginning of the twentieth century and throughout the 1920s, the rise of a modern visual culture, revealed by the almost immediate impact of photography on the construction of reality, challenged the established literary culture and those whose identity and professional existence depended on the power of the word.

Until the print media finally accommodated the visual as text and language as well as illustration, there were serious discussions among intellectuals about the demise of literature in all of its forms. In fact, forms of representation—the nature of language—became a major issue with the emergence of photography (and film) and resulted in considerable debates over, for instance, the uses of photographs as appropriate forms of expression for newspapers (Hardt 1996). That debate was followed by a period of professional adjustment to a new interdependence between words and images in the reporting of events. The relationship between the consciousness of print and the consciousness of images still remains a defining characteristic of the critique of visual media.

The documentary style of the photograph, with its affinity to "the real" and therefore to the claims of journalistic objectivity or social truth, made a successful debut and retained its persuasive power in Soviet and German journalism of the 1920s and continued in the United States during the 1930s with the rise of photojournalism and magazines such as *Life* and *Look*. Because photographs were universally comprehensible, their use in the discovery of imaginary space and in the challenge of reality (expressed, for instance, in the social and political propaganda of the time, as in the work of Alexander Rodchenko and John Heartfield) was a response to the need to destroy familiar conventions about perception and the human eye. Instead, there arose new possibilities for the camera eye to teach readers an aesthetic appreciation of the visual and its potential in the context of integrating art and social practice through print or film. The deconstruction of conventional language succeeded with the aid of photographic images, photo essays, and photomontage as well as film, which replaced traditional forms of social communication as the new vocabulary of modernity to address the political, social, and cultural conditions of the world.

The central idea of the visual as an emerging cultural milieu of the twentieth century was expressed and confirmed during the 1920s. It was celebrated by the producers or practitioners of film and photography, reflected in the work of designers, and continued later in the practice of television. Its creative or experimental phase provided insights into the potential of visual communication and offered production techniques and the accepted strength of a visual language, attributing the power of facts to the image and expressing the need to create a vocabulary of visual imagery that met the expectations of audiences.

Since then, audiences have become sophisticated participants in the mediated realities of the press, whose photographic coverage occupies a central position in explaining the world, while media have gained significantly in political power and cultural status with their complex technological capabilities of disseminating knowledge and information. An understanding of their respective historical roles in the production and reproduction of photographic images may provide insights into the nature and limitations of representation.

In the United States, media technologies responded to commercial interests and turned media into the functional face of business. More specifically, European avant-garde movements were reduced to their aesthetics rather than explained in terms of their ideological foundations. Thus media, in following the function of other institutions in an urban, industrialized society, emerged in forms that acknowledged the prevalent features of an American life-style: mobility, competition, and the conditions of middle-classness. At the same time, they catered to the taste cultures of commodified audiences rather than serving specific emancipatory goals. In the popular and lucrative rush to embrace mainstream America, media marginalized the notion of cultural diversity but produced and reproduced a "mass" culture phenomenon that has led to what Herbert Marcuse (1964) once called a one-dimensional society. The production of *Life* magazine, for example, became a weekly celebration of America as a middle-class experience, comforting in its public reinforcement of moral values, patriotic in its representation of nationhood, and openly voyeuristic in its display of poverty and human misery at home and abroad. Its coverage of people and events demonstrates the workings of the dominant ideology in the picture press of the times.

The preparation of media content, particularly in photography and film, was reinforced by social and ideological expectations grounded in traditional values and the performance of an established print culture. They reflected the historical break between types of communication technologies and styles of consciousness, that is, between the consciousness of an age of typography and television. These values celebrated the nature of the documentary, which, as William Stott suggests, "imposes its meaning" and "confronts us . . . with empirical evidence of such nature as to render dispute impossible and interpretation superfluous" (1973, 14). Such a view expresses confidence in the intent of the visual narrative and the power of the authorial gaze. It also reflects the impact of a scientific spirit on privileging facts. The photograph imposes rather than creates a space for meanings, and the notion of documentary (in the 1930s) gains social and political strength from its inaccessibility.

The potential of images quickly exceeded its assigned role of illustrating or reflecting the mood of a society whose gullibility or willingness to be deceived only added to its influence. The next step involved the creation of a visual environment capable of transcending memory and reconstructing history. It required the transformation of society into a televisual culture that coincided with the technological and ideological mission of dominant political and economic forces. Thus, contemporary television emphasizes, by and large, the immediate and confuses its own presence with documentation. In fact, it plays with the notion of human existence and merely entertains. The manufactured versions of television reality collide with the rationale of a print culture and are at odds with notions of totality or historical consciousness. The selective visions of television practices are the results of technological constraints and ideological guidance. They produce a reality that anticipates the expectations of audiences and reflects the tastes of a reconstructed Western culture by privileging the signifiers of modern culture: celebrities, music, and popular movements.

The rise of a visual culture coincides with the progress of professionalism and the recognition of expert knowledge in the world of media practice. Print journalists and other practitioners in film and television, for instance, were redefined by the demands of new technologies. A lack of collective consciousness based upon assumptions about the relationship between individualism and professionalism (and a general reluctance to join organized labor) resulted, however, in a failure of media workers to determine the definition and execution of professional practices.

The professional response to photography constituted a major development affecting the face of the press. Journalists were more apt to protect their own positions than invite yet another competitor to share the meager rewards of their labor. Yet their experience with photography was real and often personal when editors demanded that they carry cameras and produce photographs on a regular basis. Journalists also observed the rise of photographs as credible and objective evidence at a time when their own activities had become increasingly suspect among readers. There was also the traditional bias of a print orientation, however, and the threat of a redefinition of newswork—defined here as the editorial process controlled and enforced by media ownership—that had accompanied each and every technological change in the newsroom. The former stemmed from the fear that the predominance of the image would eventually destroy the word culture, and the latter was based on experiences with the telegraph, the telephone, and the typewriter, which had changed the conditions of newsroom labor. Both represented a more general reaction to outside ideas that threatened the autonomy of established interests. Accordingly, photography emerged as yet another technology that would redirect the practice of working journalists, who may have felt unprepared and certainly uncompensated for carrying the burden of radical change.

In any event, the conflict between news and photography was ultimately resolved by the industrial authority of media ownership rather than by the cultural authority of journalists. In both cases, photographers offered a visual gestalt of the news, information, and entertainment that now characterize modern newspapers. They did so through an interpretive process in which the need to reflect modern life and appeal to readers became industrial priorities. The authority that insisted on change was the authority of industrialization, which used technology to communicate power, instill credibility, extend functional design, and enlarge the definition of news or information to stress the importance of being contemporary. At the same time, these developments suggested the limitations of professional media work, the specific conditions of labor, and the boundaries of intellectual or creative autonomy that have characterized the history of newswork. Thus, the appearance of images also spoke to the larger issue of industrialization and its effects on the structure of professional existence.

When images emerged as fictional or documentary narratives, they caught the eye of an audience and created a new sense of proximity that was engaging and therefore effective. At the same time, images need words, and both become inseparable in media work. They reinforce each other and offer a basis for making meanings that rests on the power of the visual experience and the authority of the word, connecting the present and the past and producing a context for interpreting the world.

This project is grounded in cultural materialism that sees all cultural practices as part of an ongoing social process that each society produces at a particular historical time and under distinct political and economic conditions.
It offers explanations of photographic truths embedded in the dominant
ideology of society and confronted by critical readings, which deconstruct
photographs as historical records, to examine their framing of issues against
the cultural experience of representation. Because photographs retain accessibility and the capacity to elicit responses, they challenge the imagination
of critical readings—aided by the familiarity of the cultural milieu, language,
and textual explanation, in particular—which provide the social, cultural, and
political rootedness of the visual experience.

The availability of photographs as products of society enables cultural
historians, media historians in particular, to interrogate the power of visual
evidence and reconstruct the historical conditions of an image-conscious
society. While the uses of photographs by the press offer insights into the
making of a mediated world, photographs of the press supply information
about circumstances and conditions of newswork, institutional environments, and relationships with the public that produces knowledge about the
workings of the press.

Thus, the following essays provide yet another opportunity for reflecting
on the status of photography. Popularized by the press and reinforced by
private uses, photographs constitute a significant cultural terrain for the discourse of society. But they are not only expressions of their time, rising to
become icons of collective experience and historical markers of a pictorial
era. They are also building blocks of specific experiences through decontex-
tualization and displacement that range from redirecting the original purpose of photographic coverage, for instance, to placing photographs in museums. While the former arrangement removes photographs from a specific
realm of potential meanings, the latter confers status on photographs as
objects of aesthetic appreciation. The location of photographs in archives
constitutes yet another example of how context effects meaning. According
to Alan Sekula, "Archives are contradictory in character. Within their confines
meaning is liberated from use, and yet at a more general level an empiricist
model of truth prevails. Pictures are atomised, isolated in one way and
atomised in another" (1991, 118).

Photographs reveal as much as they obscure, but because they reveal they
hold readers to a seductive surface quality that the culture industry exploits.
In fact, photographs become part of a pictorial (print) media strategy to
articulate an ideological position within a cultural discourse and with regard

to specific conditions of society. They reinforce the prevailing social and political perspective and celebrate the power of a visual narrative, and their production becomes less important than the process of repositioning them according to specific social, political, or cultural interests in re-presenting a different reality.

The following essays address the potential of photographs and the process of social representation. Photographic images, shaped by a struggle between the intent of the culture industry and the activities of a reading public, constitute reminders of public and private moments. They extend the possibility of sharing in the dominant interpretation that controls the public use of photographic images. They also offer readers what bell hooks has called "resistant representation," that is, the possibility for opposition (1995, 57). Thus, meanings of photographs emerge from cultural experiences; they are ideological reproductions of reality and viewed as realizations of an objective truth. They are also a source of multiple collective memories and therefore components of history as a creative process. In that sense, photographs also serve the imagination of historians and feed their creative instincts. But unlike traditional historians, who generally consider sources of evidence "particles of reality from which an image of the parts is made" (Kellner 1989, 10), a cultural materialist approach to photographic images understands that historical evidence offers a way of creating meanings from the cultural debris of society. That would include news photographs, advertisements, or family photography whose use value often exceeds their original purpose of meeting immediate demands for visual information.

This is a picture-driven society, and photographs have paved the way for a broad acceptance of a visual discourse that dominates the media. The essays in this volume cut across traditional narratives about photography that are located in technical, artistic, or social considerations to address a broad theoretical and historical concern about photographs as constituents of collective memory and historical markers. They reflect the centrality of photographic images in contemporary journalism, their importance as public language, their role in maintaining a sense of (national) community, and their ideological portability for multiple social and political purposes. They also embrace a belief in the power of the image, and therefore in the effectiveness of pictorial journalism, while raising questions about photographs as documentation of news or historical evidence.

Photographs are also visual forms of knowledge, and knowledge is related to centers of social or political power. These essays address several ideological conceptions of history— the Holocaust, war, advertising, and journalism, for instance—through photographs produced as documents by the dominant ideological apparatuses of media and government agencies. The respective conceptions serve what Foucault has called the "regime of truth" by which a society organizes its discourse and establishes its truth (1980, 133), including what constitutes fact or evidence. The essays also provide opportunities for contemplating challenges to the privileged status of photographs when the power to bestow authority on photographic representation shifts to serve different needs or institutions, revealing not only the ideological nature of photographic "evidence" but also suggesting the historical in photographs.

Thus, Hanno Hardt and Bonnie Brennen recount the rise of photographs as documents of their times and engage in a close reading of a specific photograph of a newsroom of the 1930s to demonstrate the potential of photographs as historical sources of information about the newswork environment. They argue that photographs provide thick descriptions that add detail and nuance to the reconstruction of the workplace and locate the newsworkers in relation to colleagues and editors. Their work provides an example of working with visual evidence in the reconstruction of press history and becomes the entry point into theoretical and methodological issues that are raised by the following contributions.

Robert Craig suggests that the contradictory developments in the history of journalism between factual and fictional illustrations have roots in the rise of a commercial press. He traces the process of visualization through the historical production of images by church and state to the impact of commercial interests on the creation and dissemination of advertising images.

Kevin Barnhurst and John Nerone engage in a study of newspaper presentation at a time when changes in reporting and the introduction of photographs are joined in redefining content. In tracking the rising use of photographs and the subsequent renegotiations of space and priorities between text and picture, the authors note a shift from intellect to emotions as news photographs become a personal archive of memory.

John Erickson reflects on the daguerreotype portrait of an editor, perhaps the earliest visual evidence of a working journalist in the United States, and on its construction of a professional aura of journalism in the nineteenth century.

Barbie Zelizer demonstrates how photographs of the Holocaust have resulted in shaping a specific kind of collective memory and have influenced popular experiences of other atrocities. She addresses the consequences of recycling images over time and questions the use of photographs as memory tools, when specific photographs become the last resort in efforts to regenerate memories of an experience reproduced by definitions of news and journalistic practices.

Michael Griffin recalls the development of war photography as a source of national myths and collective memories that construct history as a process of representation. He argues that photographs lose their historical specificity and become markers of a cultural belief when notions of documentation and aesthetic expression become subsumed by an understanding of photographs as ritualized symbols.

Dona Schwartz examines the fidelity of photographs as news documents and raises ethical issues related to professional practices and the struggle to uphold the viability of the profession. In an era when photographs become raw material in the production of images that fit the ideological narrative of the medium, conflicts between the technique of the producer and the claim of objectivity become a shared everyday reality of professional life.

David Spencer traces the emergence of photographs in the Canadian press and the specific use of picture postcards as yet another popular means of individual communication in the context of World War I. He analyzes the reproduction of the war as a specific visual experience that was almost entirely removed from the actual battlefields of Europe and fully engaged in propagandizing a divided country. Selective representations of military might and the war effort, in particular, suggest the limited usefulness of photographs as historical evidence.

Monique Berlier recounts the history of an exhibition as a visual medium to question the viability of photographs as historical evidence. She proposes that recontextualizing and repositioning individual photographs constitutes a new social, political, or cultural document that addresses the specifically new requirements of a given historical moment.

In the concluding chapter, Hanno Hardt returns to the use of archival photographs to suggest the potential of a historical narrative about newswork based on newspaper archives. The images also provide insight into archival rationalization and the role of photographs as objects in the process of describing and systematizing evidence. This chapter is a reminder of the inherent power of visual material in historical discourse and relates to the practice of investigating photographic sources in the reconstruction of press history. It also constitutes a return to the concerns of the opening chapter.

Together, these essays suggest that photographs are major sources of representing not only people and events but also, in a much larger sense, of defining community or nation and ultimately humankind. They are not, however, mirrors of reality. Rather, they are points of entry into an exploration of cultural experiences with "regimes of truth," or sources of power, which appropriate and shape the image to fit the social discourse. It is not the production of the photograph but the context of social relations, with its practices of making meaning and rendering interpretations, that becomes the appropriate terrain for contemporary observers. Yet individual authorship is reduced to detail work that focuses on the fragmentary. That is particularly true in a postmodern media environment in which the circulation of images belongs to a daily ritual of replacing a discourse of knowledge with increasingly self-referential visual narratives guided by the proposition that if we don't have a picture, it must not be news.

## References

Debord, Guy. 1992. *Society of the Spectacle and Other Films.* London: Rebel Press.

Foucault, Michel. 1977. *Discipline and Punish: The Birth of the Prison.* New York: Pantheon.

———. 1980. *Power/Knowledge.* New York: Pantheon.

Hardt, Hanno. 1996. "The Site of Reality. Constructing Photojournalism in Weimar Germany, 1928–33." *Communication Review* 1(3): 373–402.

hooks, bell. 1995. *Art on My Mind.* New York: New Press.

Jay, Martin. 1988. "Scopic Regimes of Modernity." In *Vision and Visualty: Discussions in Contemporary Culture 2,* ed. Hal Foster, 3–23. Seattle: Bay Press.

Kellner, Hans. 1989. *Language and Historical Representation: Getting the Story Crooked.* Madison: University of Wisconsin Press.

Marcuse, Herbert. 1964. *One-Dimensional Man: Studies in the Ideology of Advanced Industrial Society.* Boston: Beacon Press.

Merleau-Ponty, Maurice. 1962. *Phenomenology of Perception.* London: Routledge and Kegan Paul.

Newman, Karen. 1997. *Fetal Positions: Individualism, Science, Visuality.* Stanford: Stanford University Press.

Sekula, Alan. 1991. "Reading an Archive." In *Blasted Allegories,* ed. Brian Wallis and Marcia Tucker, 114–28. Cambridge: MIT Press.

Stott, William. 1973. *Documentary Expression and Thirties America.* New York: Oxford University Press.

# Newswork, History, and Photographic Evidence: A Visual Analysis of a 1930s Newsroom

*Hanno Hardt and Bonnie Brennen*

The invention of photography is credited with a variety of new ways of seeing the world, among them the ability to record and document life in great detail and with considerable precision and certainty. From the very beginning, photographers compiled a substantial visual record of their surroundings and documented explorations of places, people, and events that challenged the imagination and invited interpretation. It was a new kind of knowledge that began to infringe upon the domination of language in Western culture.

This essay addresses the relationship of photography, history, and cultural studies and explores the uses of photographs as historical evidence. It also examines a specific photographic image as a source of insights into the work environment of journalists during the 1930s.

Photography is a cultural practice, and photographs are forms of material production. Both are elements of an explicit, practical process of communication at a historically specific moment. Images play a major role in the life of society, ranging from earlier religious practices to contemporary representations of secular events. As Donis Dondis suggests, "Most of what we know and learn, what we buy and believe, what we recognize and desire, is determined by the domination of the human psyche by the photograph" (1974, 7). Photographs, like all cultural products, have conditions and contexts based on historically determined cultural conventions, forms, beliefs, and perceptions. They articulate and actively shape the practical, evolving, and lived experiences in society along with connections between individuals and the social, political, and economic structures residing within each culture (Williams 1981, 353). Thus, looking at photographs, like looking at paintings to help elucidate social history (Clark 1973, 1985; Herbert 1988), promises to reveal the details of a rich cultural life.

In particular, a history of communication consists not only of a chronology of media technology (or its ownership and uses) but also of a history of its productive forces. Photographs representing aspects of newswork may offer especially appropriate insights into the understanding of the professional self under specific social and institutional circumstances within media organizations. This topic is of great interest to social historians attempting to reconstruct a history of newswork related to the experiences of reporters, whose professional contributions to the rise of American journalism have neither been acknowledged nor approached in any detail (Hardt 1995). Instead, ideological reasons have prompted media historians to focus primarily on newspaper owners and their properties.

In addition, there has been a discouraging lack of traditional evidence concerning newswork and a reluctance among contemporary media historians to engage in oral history projects (or the use of alternative materials such as novels, memoirs, and photographs) to remedy the situation and build on existing sociological databases (Hardt and Brennen, eds. 1995). Although photographic reproductions of workplaces—that is, depictions of newsworkers, newsroom environments, and newswork—do exist as evidence to help reconstruct the historical conditions of newswork, media historians generally do not draw upon photographs in their constructions of communication history. Rather, photographs appear in media histories as illustrations and become objective, nonproblematic representations of reality.

By contrast, the use of photographs to describe social and economic conditions of society is well known in the American tradition of documentary photography. Among classic constructions of various aspects of culture, mostly guided by sociological and journalistic intent, are *How the Other Half Lives* (Riis 1970 [1890]), *Have You Seen Their Faces?* (Caldwell and Bourke-White 1937), *An American Exodus: A Record of Human Erosion* (Lange and Taylor 1939), and *Let Us Now Praise Famous Men* (Agee and Evans 1970 [1941]). These works helped shape the public image of immigration, farm labor, poverty, and migration by documenting everyday existence and creating a historical record of the social and economic situation of the working class. William Stott (1973) provides an extensive discussion of the documentary approach of the 1930s, when the use of photographs helped construct a sense of national identity.

Since that time, there has also been a critical reception of photography by cultural anthropologists, social historians, and sociologists who have found a variety of uses for it not only as a means of collecting and storing information but also as a record of historical consciousness and source of material evidence. The study of other cultures by Gregory Bateson and Margaret Mead (1942), for example, was greatly aided by photography. The application of photography was continued by anthropologists and ethnographers such as Richard Sorenson (1976), Edward T. Hall (1966), and Ray Birdwhistell (1952) and was problematized by Melissa Banta and Curtis M. Hinsley (1986) and systematized by John Collier, Jr., and Malcolm Collier (1986).

But the promise of photographs as sources of information had already been realized by the mid-1850s. In an extensive discussion of the use of photographs in American history, Thomas J. Schlereth (1980, 47) finds that the "validity of the photograph's enormous value as historical evidence, despite its necessary qualifications, remains intact." The studies of Michael Baxandall (1985), James Guimond (1991), and Alan Trachtenberg (1989) address the issue of constructing history from available photographs. Mary Panzer (1997) has demonstrated how Mathew Brady used images of famous contemporaries to construct a positive history of the Republic at a time of national crisis. Their work and the interdisciplinary nature of their activities suggest a specific context and direction for the consideration of photographs by cultural studies and critical communication studies.

A considerable tradition of film studies, enriched by a theoretical discourse involving Marxism, semiotics, and psychoanalysis (Andrew 1984), accompanies a range of Marxist and non-Marxist perspectives on photography, from the early work of Walter Benjamin (1969) and Siegfried Kracauer (1960) to contributions by Roland Barthes (1981, 1985), John Berger (1972, 1980), Victor Burgin (1982), and John Tagg (1988). Along with writers such as Günther Anders (1992), Thomas Mitchell (1986, 1994), and Paul Virilio (1984, 1994), this literature provides an intellectual context not only for the rise of cultural studies in the United States in the guise of a culture-specific fascination with technology but also as a response to the preoccupation of modernity with the visual as a privileged experience (Jay 1988). Yet less intellectual effort and analytical expertise has been invested in the discussion of photographic theory and practice within the field of communication studies than in the pursuit of film and television.

In fact, the exploration of photography as a modern form of cultural expression or the investigation of its social and political implications remain marginal activities even within cultural studies. Stuart Hall (1973) provides an early British study of news photographs, while Deborah Bright (1990), Susan Moeller (1989), and Nicolas Monti (1987) offer explorations of the role of photographs in representations of society. In addition, Malek Alloula's structuralist analysis of French-made picture postcards of Algerian women (1986) reveals the importance of photographs as historical evidence and offers an interpretation of women under specific historical conditions. Likewise, the study of Edward S. Curtis's photographs by Christopher Lyman (1982) attempts a critical examination of the role of photographs in the (staged) representation of Native Americans. Catherine A. Lutz and Jane L. Collins (1993) have demonstrated how photographs operate in producing an American worldview, particularly of non-Western societies, through a critical reading of *National Geographic.* The relationship between texts and photographs, typically discussed in critical advertising research (e.g., Williamson 1978), has also been taken up by Jefferson Hunter (1987).

Nevertheless, the desire to remain contemporary and relevant in the pursuit of theorizing technological and industrial progress provides one possible reason for the scarcity of critical media studies involving the use and application of photographs. Film and (later) television emerge in quick succession as more dramatic versions of visual practices that gather greater economic forces than the use and application of still images by the print culture, particularly by magazines and newspapers. As myriad social, economic, and political problems challenge the foundations of American society, the glamour and, more important, financial support of media research reside with television, especially in studies of its impact on contemporary society.

Yet a cultural studies perspective on media and communication analysis must acknowledge the presence of still images in the repertoire of cultural practices. Photographs constitute the historical foundation of a contemporary, technology-driven, visual tradition in American culture. They offer the first modern visual constructions of social reality and have instructed what have become widely accepted interpretations of the past. For instance, the visual explorations of the Western frontier, the conceptualization of the Civil War, or the social reportage of urban and rural life in the United States are individual or collective achievements of documentary photographers. They are also definitive historical signs of social conditions in the United States that continue to act as societal referents to experiences or feelings. Photographs are ideological markers of a specific, culturally determined relationship between visual production and consumption in which the intent of the photographer as producer dissolves into various meanings constructed by readers. Such constructions have been guided and reinforced by a culture of pictorial presentations spanning private practices at home and the public discourse of journalism and advertising.

Consequently, many still images continue to serve as symbols of society at specific historical moments and also as expressions of a collective historical consciousness. "Breaker Boys" (1911) by Lewis Hine, "Migrant Mother" (1936) by Dorothea Lange, "Flag Raising on Iwo Jima" (1945) by Joe Rosenthal, or the shooting of an alleged Vietnamese terrorist by Eddie Adams in 1968 are not only memorable encounters with twentieth-century history but also ideological constructions of people and events. They are reminders of shared experiences that contribute to a sense of national identity. Even at a time when television prevails, they remain powerful instruments of propaganda and have reproduced and strengthened dominant ideological positions as means of social and political communication. The death of Alfred Eisenstaedt, for example, provided an opportunity to celebrate the power of photographic images in the memory of a society. The "photographer of the defining moment," Eisenstaedt was remembered for photographs that frequently offered "the essence of a story in a single image" ("Alfred Eisenstaedt" 1995). His career spanned the phenomenal rise of photojournalism from Germany in the 1920s to its professional perfection and editorial success in the United States with the founding of *Life* magazine, a popular weekly celebration of society by a talented group of émigré and native photographers under the leadership of Henry Luce.

Since the founding of *Life,* social, cultural, or political conventions have been reinforced by the presence of photographs in everyday life. The subsequent success of fast films, instant photographs, and one-way cameras suggests the continuing popularity of photographic images as personal documents. The rise of family photographs (Hirsch 1981) indicates personal involvement in the making of a visual culture in which possessing a camera represents ownership of the means of production beyond access to the photograph as product. Control over the process of reproducing reality, however, is accompanied by increasing access to the professional conventions of advertising and news photography. Both influence and provide guidance for constructing a visual representation of the family.

There has also been a crossover effect, as Judith Williamson (1978, 125) observes, and "the ideologies incorporated into domestic photography—democracy, choice, fun, leisure—are reproduced on a large scale in public photographs which . . . can more easily tap family values" and create a public spectacle. Thus, the aesthetics of the private realm serve commercial interests in their exploitation of family values. Too often a personal desire for fame and immortality is combined with an active participatory photography that celebrates the visual presence of an individual and reifies individualism. The photographic display of studied postures, popularized by advertising and reproduced in the personal spheres of society, obscures the borders between public and private visions of family and individual identity. The result is a merger of private preferences and commercial cultures of taste in a reality dominated by sales campaigns.

The production process of private images also invites public surveillance with the help of the industry; it has become as easy as the old Kodak slogan that generations ago promised "you push the button, we do the rest." When Kodak focuses on the creation of family history in a series of Christmas advertisements produced between 1904 and 1910, for example, it locates itself inside the family, encouraging exposure for the sake of happiness. Thus, a text of a December 1910 magazine advertisement invited readers to "make Kodak your family historian. Start the history on Christmas day, the day of home gathering and let it keep for you an intimate pictorial history of the home and all who are in it. Make somebody happy with a Kodak this year—the pictures will serve to make many people happy in the years that follow" (Strasser 1989, 104–6).

Such happiness "with a Kodak" comes at a price, however. Photography lab employees who scrutinize pictures frequently discover "pornographic" images in batches of personal photographs, a find duly publicized in the media, suggesting the widespread nature of societal surveillance and problematizing the status of the private photograph. An advertisement in *Shutterbug* (1997), for example, acknowledges the problem by offering "uncensored custom photofinishing."

Nevertheless, the trading of conventions across private and public spheres also contributes to an increased sense of readers knowing and understanding photographic images. Consequently, an understanding of photographs as social documents has been strengthened, and their historical value confirmed, by the increased popularity and credibility of visual expressions. It has also been aided by the sheer quantity of photographs made each day in an almost universally acknowledged effort to capture the realities of private and public lives. Even during times of intensive technological development in video and computer technology or experimentation with film size, for instance, the concept of the still image survives and the camera remains a popular and indispensable instrument of documentation for laypeople and experts alike.

The production of photographs occurs under the cultural, political, and technological constraints of a specific historical period and results in specific representations of people or events. A photograph taken during the first decade of the twentieth century expresses the technical limitations of film and cameras. The era's use of cheap paper and ink as well as other technical problems slowed the use of halftones. There were also political and cultural issues involving censorship and aesthetic (taste) judgments that defined the social boundaries of photography in the early twentieth century. Whatever issues may have existed, it was, after all, the eye of the observer, the cultural perspective of the camera operator, including professional conventions, that shaped the photographs that revealed the world. Photographic documentation is determined by a tradition of seeing and an experience of observing whose roots extend beyond the invention of photographic processes or customs to the beginnings of visual representation. It is a time when specific visual perspectives begin to be culturally defined, accepted, and transmitted.

The rise of photography, for example, challenged the hegemony of painting as visual expression, and that relationship has determined both traditions in terms of composition and style. Central to discussions among artists and proponents of the "new technology," particularly during the nineteenth century, was the question of realism, the enemy of art and the friend of photography. Aaron Scharf (1986, 13) observes that after the appearance of photography, "painting and drawing styles became noticeably more tonal." It "was not surprising, during an age in which the efficacy of the machine would appear to be one of the essential virtues, that the authority invested in a machine by which nature could take her own picture would impinge on art in the most fundamental way." Portraiture is an example of that relationship between art and photography. The rise of the daguerreotype as a form of democratizing the process of visual expression is considered an important first step in the history of photography. Its success reflected public enthusiasm for a new technology that produced an affordable image reliably fast and therefore appealed to the working class and helped popularize photography, not only in the United States but also in many other Western and non-Western societies.

Similarly, photographic depictions of the workplace expand the repertoire of appropriate topics for a camera operator beyond the view of domesticity and leisure time, primarily among the middle and upper class, and confirm the legitimacy of everyday life as a theme of photography. The rise of a documentary tradition in photography and film and the increased uses of press photography are related to social and political developments of the 1920s and the resulting rise of realism in literature and the fine arts. The documentary films of Dziga Vertov, for example, including his newsreels as well as an emerging photojournalism in the Soviet Union, focus on the reality of the revolution and cater to the public need for facts in an unstable social and political environment. Similarly, during the early 1930s the Workers Film and Photo League in the United States advocated engagement in "photographing events as they appear to the lens, true to the nature of the revolutionary medium" (Alexander 1981, 57). The league also promoted the use of documentary film and photography by the working class to help break the illusion of a classless society and educate a class-conscious readership. Consequently, the discovery of the photographic image as a powerful tool of political propaganda in both the Soviet Union and the United States inspired great photographers and produced memorable images for the cause of socialism and democracy.

The power of documentary work rests in the abilities of its authors to raise the familiar to the noteworthy and imbue the obscure with the aura of spectacle. Press photographers, however, work with definitions of news that rule the life of newsworkers. Their photographs reflect the value of newsworthiness and construct the day's events by combining texts and images to confirm, question, or refute the fact while corroborating the experiences of readers. Together, they help perform the functions of a middle-class institution called upon for precise observation and objectivity in their reconstruction of societal life. For these reasons, any designation of a photograph as a mirror of the world is a superficial explanation that ignores the cultural and political dimensions of seeing and constructing reality. Yet photography is frequently understood and appreciated by the belief that photographs can explain society and contribute to its progress.

Reporters, searching for the facts of the day, realize the competitive nature of photographs to reproduce reality and provide an interesting if not accurate reflection of people and events. Alas, the camera's eye competes successfully against the imperfection of reportorial observation, and its rapid success may explain the hostility of journalists toward photojournalism. During the 1920s and 1930s, reporters generally considered photographers "the rogues and boors of the business, uncouth, unkempt and uncontrollable" (Sontheimer 1941, 231). Although reporters recognized the usefulness of photographs, they often focused on their potential to "mislead," "misrepresent," and "lie"

(241). Consequently, tension between the culture of the printed phrase and the culture of the image became part of the practice of journalism in the 1920s. In Germany, despite the immense popularity of picture magazines, even publishers defended the sanctity of the text and remained highly suspicious of photographs (Hardt 1996). The growing public acceptance of photographs and their frequently debated effects on readers could, after all, undermine the status of the word. As a result, cameras represented a new technology of reporting that produced anxiety about change and fear that the traditional reportorial process could be redefined and reorganized under the impact of visual experience. When newspaper reporters in the United States were handed cameras and required to take pictures, professional practice was affected, as it had been with every technological change in the newsroom since the telegraph and the telephone.

During the course of privileging observation, photographic images rise beyond their significance as representations, allowing photographers, joined by writers or reporters, to provide insights into the working lives of individuals, including those of colleagues. The depiction of the workplace, although ordinary enough, has been a controversial undertaking when identified with labor's attempts to gather evidence or cause unrest. The pioneering work of Soviet photographers and the contributions of worker-photographers during the late 1920s and early 1930s in Germany, as well as the success of the *Arbeiter-Illustrierte Zeitung* as an outlet for this type of political surveillance of the workplace, provide early historical evidence of the role of photography in the description of work environments (Hardt 1989; Ohrn and Hardt 1981).

The depiction of the workplace either by social or worker photography is less frequent and was often severely restricted. Industrial photography, public relations, and advertising photography, representing commercial or industrial interests in the workplace, provide the most common and recurrent sources. Yet both involve documentary approaches; the former represents the effort of workers to describe their workplace and the latter features an institutional perspective. Both focus on the human factor in the world of labor defined by the conditions of work, the relationships between practice and environment, and the consequences of various forms of industrialization. Yet a documentary photograph offers not only a description of evidence but also an argument in its representation of facts. Examples of these activities range from the efforts of Jacob Riis, Walker Evans, and worker photography in Germany and the Soviet Union (Hardt 1989) to the photographs of Sebastião Salgado (1993), who attempts to capture a global notion of workers and the conditions of labor. In that context, efforts of photojournalists to depict their newsrooms are of particular interest. They reproduce a subjective, even critical, gaze of the insider, potentially informed by the conventions of celebratory, industrial photography or socially engaged documentation.

The intensity and quality of a daily encounter with photographs is defined by procedural skills of reading and the observer's assumptions about the photograph, harking back to the rise of a visual understanding. Jonathan Crary (1991, 150) has traced the "reconfiguration" of vision during the nineteenth century and projects the consequences of vision becoming "relocated in the subjectivity of the observer," leading to "all the multiple affirmations of the sovereignty and autonomy of vision" and to "the increasing standardization and regulation of the observer . . . towards forms of power that depended on the abstraction and formalization of vision."

Thus, reading photographs, as a process of reconstructing history, is a complex negotiation between what people know and what they see. Readers draw on prior knowledge or experience to identify people; they speculate about the authenticity of the photograph as a depiction of reality and introduce an assumption of literalism into their interpretation. A black and white photograph reveals the facts as it signals its documentary intent, while the frequency of placement or the location of photographs in media spaces may suggest notoriety and confer credibility.

Depiction of editorial space and relations among newsworkers becomes the subject of informed inquiry into the general context of establishing photographs as historical records made by photographers or constructed by readers. This essay constructs a reading of a specific photograph depicting the work environment of the *New York Daily News* editorial room in 1930, a pivotal period in newsworker history. It is based on understanding the differences of intentions involving the production and consumption of photographs and the pertinent historical explanations of newswork.

During the 1920s and 1930s technological changes encouraged the dissemination of news on a scale that had never been available. For the first time, millions of people had access to a daily urban newspaper, and telephones, radios, films, photographs, and automobiles were also available to vast numbers. Those inventions appeared to be advancements that made communication more accessible, effective, timely, and relevant. Dependence on new technologies, however, also influenced the decline of individualism and encouraged critics to question the impact of the inventions on contemporary society. Writers argued that "with the coming of standardized and commercialized pictures goes the word and with it the possibility of genuine thought and reflection" (Susman 1984b, 109). Many feared that no "real" communication was possible in a time of endless communication. With the invasion of new "public" technologies, it was frequently suggested that a sense of community was being destroyed (Susman 1984a, xxix).

By the early twentieth century, industrialism and urbanization had fueled the growth of the cities, and increasing numbers of immigrants joined a growing urban industrial workforce. By the 1920s, more than half of the population lived in urban areas, and the agrarian life-style had begun to decline. Individuals, lured to cities because of employment opportunities, frequently expected an improved standard of living, many new and exciting experiences, and cultural diversity. Yet for many, their visions of excitement contrasted with "a harsher reality of sweat shops, mind-deadening and back-breaking industrial routines, long hours, and short pay" (Murphy 1984, 56).

Although the 1920s have generally been seen as prosperous times, economic indicators forecasted critical problems in U.S. society. As machines influenced every aspect of industry, workers became increasingly tied to technology. A correspondingly smaller number of people were needed to run the machines, and by 1928 approximately four to five million U.S. workers were unemployed. An economic study by the Brookings Institute determined that in 1929 the majority of American families still earned only subsistence wages. In 1929 approximately one-third of all nonfarm family incomes were at or below the $1,550 poverty line (Stricker 1985, 291). Yet the pressures of contemporary capitalism encouraged people to consume a growing number of continually advertised material possessions.

The 1920s brought an excessive disparity between the wealthy and the poor. The wealthiest 1 percent of the population earned as much as the combined income of half the working families in the United States. After the October 1929 stock market crash, more than five thousand banks closed, industrial production was cut in half, and by 1933 approximately one-third of U.S. workers were unemployed. While people starved, food sat in warehouses or rotted in the fields because it was not profitable to transport or to sell it. "There were lots of houses, but they stayed empty because people couldn't pay the rent, had been evicted, and now lived in shacks in quickly formed 'Hoovervilles' built on garbage dumps" (Zinn 1985, 378). In *Hard Times,* an oral history of the Great Depression, Studs Terkel tells how many blamed themselves rather than society for being out of work:

> True, there were hunger marches and protestations to City Hall and Washington, but the millions experienced a private kind of shame when the pink slip came. No matter that others suffered the same fate, the inner voice whispered, "I'm a failure."

True, there was a sharing among many of the dispossessed, but, at close quarters, frustration became, at times, violence, and violence turned inward. Thus, sons and fathers fell away, one from the other. And the mother, seeking work, said nothing. Outside forces, except to the more articulate and political rebels, were in some vague way responsible, but not really. It was a personal guilt. (1970, 5)

Although unemployment, starvation, and homelessness were facts of life for millions of Americans during the depression, it is important to remember that the very wealthy survived the period relatively unscathed (Meltzer 1969, 93).

A repressive lack of tolerance emerged during the 1920s. The Ku Klux Klan was revitalized, and African Americans returning from World War I encountered race riots, lynchings, and intensified discrimination. Marcus Garvey lead the first black nationalist movement and preached black pride and racial separation to more than a million followers (Meltzer, ed. 1984, 191). Socialists were dismissed from universities and congressional offices, loyalty oaths were administered, and many immigrants with uncertain loyalties were deported during the Palmer Raids at the height of the Red Scare. Attempting to stop the flood of immigrants, Congress passed laws setting quotas: "No African country could send more than 100 people; 100 was the limit for China, Bulgaria, for Palestine; 34,007 could come from England or Northern Ireland, but only 3,845 from Italy; 51,227 from Germany, but only 124 from Lithuania" (Zinn 1985, 373).

The labor movement lost ground during the 1920s. Membership declined from more than five million in 1921 to 3,443,000 in 1929. Anti-union campaigns promoted the open shop as a technique against collective bargaining, and many employers blacklisted active union members and used discriminatory hiring practices. "It was the old story of intimidation and coercion, and when trouble developed in spite of all such precautions, strong-arm guards were often employed to beat up the trouble-makers while incipient strikes were crushed by bringing in strike breakers under the protection of local authorities" (Dulles 1966, 247).

Consolidations, mergers, and buyouts confronted U.S. businesses. At the beginning of the twentieth century, a variety of consumer products were being produced by an abundance of companies. The profusion of brand names encouraged an illusion of diversity and choice, however in most instances competitors manufactured virtually identical products. Yet some who owned larger businesses were not satisfied with a small share of the market and sought to eliminate competition.

Newspapers also faced pressures of standardization and chain journalism. As a result of consolidation, competition was significantly reduced, and by 1930 nine hundred cities were one-newspaper towns (Leab 1970, 26). Even though there were significant gains in population and advertising revenue, the number of morning daily newspapers dropped from 500 to 388 between 1910 and 1930. Chains controlled 10 percent of press circulation in 1900. By 1935, however, they represented 41 percent of daily press circulation (Sloan, Stovall, and Startt 1989, 251). The content of daily newspapers became increasingly standardized as individual chain newspapers shared story material, and press associations and syndicates supplied many newspapers throughout the United States with identical news and feature information (Bleyer 1927, 390). Although the number of daily newspapers declined during the 1920s, those that did survive generally had expanded circulation and increased advertising and were extremely profitable. By the end of the decade, daily newspapers in towns of fifty to one hundred thousand were appraised at $1 to $2 million (Leab 1970, 27).

Radio challenged newspapers' position as the dominant communication medium when it emerged as a cost-effective and efficient means of public communication. During the 1920s, radio broke through technological barriers that previously restricted the dissemination of news and began to broadcast information, advertising, and entertainment to millions of Americans. Nonprofit "pioneer" stations, along with those intended to profit and primarily owned and operated by newspapers and other private businesses for publicity purposes, battled for control of the airwaves (McChesney 1993, 223–24). By 1929, 50 percent of U.S. households owned radio sets, and millions more gained access to programming in stores, taverns, restaurants, and other public places (Meehan 1993, 206).

The makeup of the press underwent significant changes with the introduction of photographs. Robert Taft reports that the "year 1897 really marks the advent of half-tone illustration as a regular feature of American newspaper journalism." But it took a number of years until "the photograph . . . the most literal, the most factual, the most readily and rapidly obtained" visual form was regularly used by newspapers (1964 [1938], 446–450). The growing number of press photographers quickly became a nuisance. By the mid-1930s the *New York Times* was complaining, "'Give us a smile, Einey,' addressed to Professor Einstein, may seem very 'American' and 'waggish,' but is nothing less than the worst of bad taste and bad manners" ("News Photographers" 1935, 18).

Half-size newspapers, known as tabloids, became extremely popular during the 1920s. Distinguished by large headlines and an extensive use of photographs, they focused on human interest and entertainment. Certainly, the *New York Daily News*'s page-one photograph of the execution of Ruth Snyder, taken with a miniature camera smuggled in by a *News* photographer, helped design a specific understanding of the news. As Warren Susman explains, "The emergence of new ways of knowing . . . stood in sharp contrast with old ways of knowing available in the book and the printed word. It was a significant break for a culture that had taken form under Bible and dictionary" (1984b, 111).

Although the actual adoption of the printing technology was slow, photographs became a more important source of news reporting with each subsequent decade. The equipment necessary for producing photographs was adapted to meet and master additional, challenging circumstances, which led to different kinds of photographs. By the late 1920s, for example, flash photography produced images of interiors. The handheld Speed Graphic, a large-format press camera, offered sturdiness, portability, and even accommodated movement, and the emerging 35mm camera added greater speed and flexibility. For years, the use of the Speed Graphic was synonymous with photojournalism in America, and the photographs of Weegee (Arthur Fellig) are classic representations of the genre (1945). Because it recorded great detail and allowed for a close viewing of the captured images, the Speed Graphic was also used in police work to secure and describe crime scenes. In that sense, the use of a Speed Graphic camera suggests accuracy or reportorial quality and conveys a grasp of professionalism in the execution of assignments. Photographers enthusiastically endorsed the introduction of the miniature 2¼ by 3¼ Speed Graphic in the late 1930s. Gannett photographers, for example, found that it did "a far better job than 4 by 5 cameras" and recommended it highly (*Bulletin* 1940). After World War II, Speed Graphics were gradually replaced by more efficient Japanese versions of the Leica-format camera. The practices of *Life* and *Look* magazines were heavily influenced by the versatility of the smaller 35mm format, which changed the aesthetics of photojournalism for good.

During the 1920s and 1930s, newsworkers, including photographers, confronted poor working conditions, low wages, and long hours. Newspaper offices were dirty, littered, disordered, crowded, and confused; reporters put in extremely long and irregular hours and were required to work as long as needed, often fifteen-hour days. Salaries were extremely low, and in many cases reporters earned less than factory workers. Newsworkers confronted strict deadline pressures, excessive expectations, and rigid news-writing conventions, and are often treated as expendable products—their job was to get the news—all the news—no matter how difficult doing so might be. Jobs were rarely secure; reporting was seen as primarily a business for the young. Competent reporters were fired if they became a liability in any way. Those who had trouble keeping up with the hectic pace were frequently told they were no longer welcome in the newsroom. As the seasoned journalist Morton Sontheimer writes in *Newspaperman*, a trade book, salaries were "so low that, even if a man could hold up his head in spite of them, he couldn't keep his feet properly shod. The hours were so long you'd wonder when newspapermen had a chance to get drunk, until you realized they did it on the job. Overtime was expected of you. To work thirty-six hours at a stretch on a big story was not unusual, and sometimes there'd be forty-eight hours steady going under pressure. There might be a bonus for this but there probably wasn't" (1941, 322).

Reporters frequently perceived of themselves as outcasts and considered themselves somewhat tainted by their reporting tasks. Although women's experiences were similar to those of their male counterparts, they faced additional problems, constraints, and pressures. During the 1920s and 1930s they battled continually to prove their value as newsworkers while enduring the burden of being token females on an otherwise all-male staff.

By the early twentieth century, new technologies, including the telephone and typewriter, divided the news-gathering and news-writing aspects of the journalistic process and had significant impact on the jobs of newsworkers. In many cases, it now took two individuals to produce a story. Reporters in the field ("legmen" or "district men") rarely ventured into the newsroom. They would often telephone in information they had gathered to individuals generally referred to as "rewrite men," who wrote the final stories. Most journalists who gathered the news and interacted with members of the community did not receive bylines and were generally underrecognized for their work. Those who wrote the stories and received the bylines in reality were obtaining secondhand information and had limited actual access to the news. This departmentalization may be seen to contribute to inaccuracies as well as to influence a sense of routine in the crafting of stories. It also contributed to the depersonalization of the industry (Brennen 1995).

These historical conditions provide the context for analyzing one particular photograph and its potential as a source of historical evidence regarding newsroom environments. This context helps identify the historical evidence embedded in the photograph and helps overcome a conventional surface reading of images. At the same time, the photograph represents a construction of the everyday world of newsroom journalism. Although it projects the presence of a variety of discernible individuals and objects and their physical relations as a "slice of time," it also produces a specific worldview. The photograph (fig. 1.1) is not a conventional image of an editorial staff but rather a distinct visual statement about the newsroom as a symbolic space of human labor that challenges preconceived notions regarding newswork. It was taken at a time when society's increasing self-consciousness resulted in a cumulative practice of defining itself through images. That is why the photograph attracts attention and beckons to be read. Such reading is not only informed by a recognition of contemporary historical circumstances, most gained through biographical, eyewitness accounts, but also by an ideological/theoretical perspective that recognizes the importance of observing the productive forces as a site of historical development. Finally, it should be understood that the "reading of public photographs is always, at bottom, a private reading" (Barthes 1981, 97).

The photograph reveals the nature of urban journalism during the 1920s and 1930s, when writing as mass production occurred under conditions of anonymity and availability and therefore under the threat of replacement. It is a group portrait that does not reveal the identity of its subjects but stresses the machinery of journalism, in which individuals become part of an industrial process. In that sense, the photograph reproduces the style of early industrial photography that features the role of technology by depicting the machine rather than an individual in control of technology and at the center of progress.

The picture speaks to the nature of producing a newspaper rather than to the importance of individuals by constructing the newsroom as a crowded but distant place in which the process of production remains the key to understanding journalism. Its purpose is unclear. It seems to be a candid image, hardly staged for publicity purposes, yet there is some posing and perhaps knowledge of the project, particularly on the part of the copy editors. But such demeanor could also signal recognition of the photographer's intent at the moment of exposure. Journalists remain hidden in their work. Although they are part of the work environment, their faces are turned away and their bodies are lost in the rhythm of the workplace. Few seem aware of the photographer.

More than thirty reporters and editors sit, stand, or wander about, in addition to a switchboard operator whose station is located along the lefthand wall, behind a man in a vest and tie. Because the photograph was taken from above a row of desks, the individuals look small and insignificant under a pressed-tin ceiling. The bleakness of the windowless expanse is accentuated

*Figure 1.1. New York Daily News* editorial room. (Library of Congress Prints and Photographs Division)

by rows of commercial lighting fixtures that hang well above newsroom traffic. Several silent metal fans are mounted on top of wooden partitions and against walls. The former are switched on for night work, and the latter suggest the stench of cold cigarette smoke hanging over rows of battered, wooden desks despite a "no smoking" sign on the back left wall. The view is from the center of the room onto the writing process and beyond into the departmentalized spaces of the editorial office. The eye of the camera accentuates the spatial arrangement, making the room look larger than it is and generously hiding the proximity of people and objects.

Two rows of desks face each other and divide the length of the room. Their wells hide well-worn typewriters, and their tops are cluttered with papers and carelessly dropped hats and coats. There are no telephones on the desks. The scene suggests self-inflicted chaos, improvisation, and filth as well as the preoccupation and concentration of those who sit poised on wooden chairs in front of these desks, their images filling the lower half of the photograph. These reporters seem to work from notes and refer to old newspapers, because no other resources except for colleagues and editors are visible. They have returned from their beats for a desk space, if only for a short time, to complete their assignments and give life to the newsroom atmosphere in a passing manner.

One female reporter shares the desk space, and another stands, involved in a conversation with a male colleague. Her dress suggests the street clothes of a working female reporter, perhaps a society reporter, with a regular beat and one of the few women working outside the newsroom. But all the workers are too absorbed in their respective tasks to pay attention to the photographer and his camera on top of an adjoining desk. The fact that the reporters sitting closest to the camera are out of focus conveys movement and anonymity and heightens the feeling of work in an obscure environment.

Along the righthand wall is a glassed-in, partitioned space, perhaps a protected entryway hiding a door to the outside. Arranged against it are more unoccupied desks covered with papers, and the floor reveals trash thrown underfoot, suggesting vacancies and disregard for the work environment. The sight reinforces the lack of personal claims over space or expressions of taste; indeed, the sparse and impersonal atmosphere confirms the transient nature of the reporting process and the production of news. These are not permanent office quarters or the setting for intellectual labor but rather stop-over locations for men and women who must drop by periodically although their business lies elsewhere. They wear street clothes, and their hats, always within reach if removed at all, are signs of mobility and readiness to face the outside world—the world of the reporter.

There are signs of intense work. Men who wear dark suits and gray hats are located on the outskirts of the work area and look like copy editors returning from errands. Reporters, having thrown off their coats and hats, lean into typewriters and pay no attention to their surroundings. Only copy editors seem comfortable. Coatless, their dark vests buttoned and shirt sleeves rolled, they occupy the same space at desks that continue down the middle of the room but are separated from reporters' stations by a small passage. Several copy editors wearing glasses confer with each other or with reporters wearing lighter suits and ties and standing at their desks. One carries a book across the room, in possession of knowledge however obscure. They seem relaxed. Several return the inquisitive look of the camera, and their gaze expresses confidence and authority. It is obvious that the copy editors are the permanent residents of these quarters. Their desktops appear cleaner than the reporters' and hold stacks of newspapers or copy paper and telephones, indicating the nature of their work as well as their status.

The copy editors' desks are located toward the back of the room and extend to within reach of the editor's desk or series of desks. These desks, on a raised platform near darkened windows under a large clock indicating ten past nine, are framed by a heating duct that runs across the ceiling and pneumatic tubes that carry copy into the composing room. A reporter's glance in that direction ascertains the source of daylight and time of day or night but fails to recognize the face of authority. The presence of the editor in the same room, however, only accentuates and reinforces the sense of distance to management and positions the reporter as a worker firmly within the organizational structure of the newspaper.

There is no other alternative for locating reporters—and the process of writing—under these conditions except at the margin of the enterprise, still within the range of power but without direct access to editorial decisions except through the space of copy editors. The ordering of space is deliberate and insists on replicating a hierarchical setting that ranges from the open, anonymous, and unprotected desks of reporters to the ordered and designated accommodations of the editor in the most desirable space within the room. Such an arrangement helps socialize employees and serves as a reminder of the condition of work under the eyes and within the reach of management. The concept of work space is guided by practical considerations of access and availability. In practice, however, it supports issues of power and reinforces notions of inequality, however subtle, which define relationships among editorial staff members.

The photograph provokes a strong feeling of the industrial production of culture, locating the site of constructing reality along a line of desks that imitate the efficiency of conveyer belts, where editors and reporters use an anonymous technology of typewriters, tubes, and wires to produce what many of them no doubt view as the greatest newspaper of the city: the *New York Daily News.*

The photograph provides a rare opportunity to observe and interpret the actual conditions of the past and, in light of our knowledge, confirms its usefulness as a historical document. Its reading reveals several details about the conditions of work, the demeanor or positioning of individuals in the work space, their attire as symbols of a particular role in the production process, and their spatial relationships. The photograph also yields many details relating to the material conditions of the work environment, from the type of equipment there, to the desks and their arrangement, to the space itself and its furnishings. It seems equally important, however, to allow the collective impression of these details to determine the general reading of the image. Together, they provide a complete and powerful statement about the way reporters functioned in a particular situation at a particular time. The photograph provides not only historical evidence of their presence but also a biographical explanation of their work through the eyes of an anonymous staff photographer documenting his own view of the newsroom.

According to the visual evidence in the photograph, newswork in 1930 was not an isolated, individual effort. Although it may have reflected the results of intellectual labor, it also reproduced the impact of industrialization on a redefinition of the professional sphere. Newsworkers shared the success of technology, which created not only specificity in the production of news or entertainment but also confined them to specific spaces in the physical order of the newsroom and the execution of routinized work schedules. As the distance between the interests of ownership and the process of newswork decreased, freedom became defined by assigned roles rather than intellectual inclinations. The fragmentation of editorial labor in particular is a visible phenomenon whose consequences affect the concept of news. That concept changes from being the result of an individual encounter with sources or events to being the creation of a manufacturing process based upon mass appeal. As a result, the accepted need of readers to know and understand the events of the day falls victim to the commodification of information in which newsworkers produce for purposes of consumption rather than enlightenment.

The accessibility of visual evidence such as staff photographs not only promises an encounter with newsroom conditions but also completes the historical record by contributing to knowledge about specific conditions of work. Photographs confirm and reinforce historical evidence; they also provide details and connect the mysterious or ambiguous with the transparent or obvious. For instance, photographs effectively address the notion of space and distances between people and objects. They also reflect the social or professional understandings of how to occupy and protect a spatial dimension of labor. The visual documentation of spatial relations offers additional information about the work environment, where the importance of distance and placement of newsworkers and editors in relation to each other and to the technology of news production contribute to an interpretation of the newsroom milieu. Thus, the experience of space is a cultural expression of domination or suppression that is also inscribed on the reading of photographs.

But photographs of working conditions among newsworkers also remind the field of journalism education that the study of newsworkers enhances its educational mission and is a service to the profession. Specifically, those being prepared by universities and journalism programs to become newsworkers need to understand the history of their profession. It is barely conceivable that professional training programs have existed for more than one hundred years without accounting for those individuals whose labor promoted the idea of the press and contributed to its commercial success. Equally important is a need for self-knowledge and the recognition of a biography of labor among newsworkers, whose historical consciousness remains restricted to experiences in newsroom situations. In that context, the reading of photographs is a process of sharing a specific moment. As Susman concludes in writing about the 1930s, "The whole idea of the documentary . . . makes it possible to see, know, and feel the details of life and its styles in different places and to feel oneself part of some other's experience" (1983, 229).

There is no shortage of information available to media historians. In order to help establish and verify the position of newsworkers in history, they may rely on a variety of sources that range from the writings of newsworkers themselves to accounts in novels and films and to compilations of oral histories. The use of photographs, collected for decades in press archives, in the reconstruction of the workplace is yet another contribution to these efforts to understand newsroom practices of the past.

At the same time, however, the incorporation of photographs as historical evidence should include a critical evaluation of these elements of material culture. The digital manipulation of photographic images that became possible during the 1990s, for example, suggests that shared representations of culture may no longer have any connection to the reality of lived experience. Because photojournalism seems to shift quietly "toward pictures as ornamentation or entertainment rather than reportage" (Lasica 1995, 139), the bias of the spectacle introduces a different response to the need for documentary evidence and demands reflexivity to uncover the unconscious of photographic practice.

Still, photographic images remain concrete elements of culture that articulate particular relationships between individuals and society at specific historical moments. Their critical examination remains an important task: to provide not only a historical dimension to understanding the means of communication but also address the ideological conditions of seeing the world, making meanings, and representing reality.

## References

Agee, James, and Walker Evans. 1970 (1941). *Let Us Now Praise Famous Men.* Boston: Houghton Mifflin.

Alexander, William. 1981. *Film on the Left: American Documentary Film from 1931 to 1942.* Princeton: Princeton University Press.

"Alfred Eisenstaedt, Ninety-six, Photographer of the Defining Moment, Is Dead." 1995. *New York Times,* Aug. 25, A13.

Alloula, Malek. 1986. *The Colonial Harem.* Minneapolis: University of Minnesota Press.

Anders, Günther. 1992. "Die Welt als Phantom und Matrize." In *Die Antiquiertheit des Menschen: Über die Seele im Zeitalter der Zweiten Industriellen Revolution,* 99–211. Munich: Beck'sche Reihe.

Andrew, Dudley. 1984. *Concepts in Film Theory.* New York: Oxford University Press.

Banta, Melissa, and Curtis M. Hinsley. 1986. *From Site to Sight: Anthropology, Photography, and the Power of the Imagery.* Cambridge: Peabody Museum Press.

Barthes, Roland. 1981. *Camera Lucida: Reflections on Photography.* Translated by Richard Howard. New York: Hill and Wang.

———. 1985. "On Film," and "On Photography." In *The Grain of the Voice: Interviews 1962–1980,* 11–24, 353–60. New York: Hill and Wang.

Bateson, Gregory, and Margaret Mead. 1942. *Balinese Character: A Photographic Analysis.* New York: New York Academy of Sciences Special Publication.

Baxandall, Michael. 1985. *Patterns of Intention: On the Historical Explanation of Pictures.* New Haven: Yale University Press.

Benjamin, Walter. 1969. *Illuminations.* New York: Schocken Books.

Berger, John. 1972. *Ways of Seeing.* London: Penguin Books.

———. 1980. *About Looking.* New York: Pantheon.

Birdwhistell, Ray L. 1952. *Introduction to Kinesics.* Lexington: University Press of Kentucky.

Bleyer, Willard Grosvenor. 1927. *Main Currents in the History of American Journalism.* Boston: Houghton Mifflin.

Brennen, Bonnie. 1995. "Cultural Discourse of Journalists: The Material Conditions of Newsroom Labor." In *Newsworkers: Toward a History of the Rank and File*, ed. Hanno Hardt and Bonnie Brennen, 75–109. Minneapolis: University of Minnesota Press.

Bright, Deborah. 1990. "Of Mother Nature and Marlboro Men: An Inquiry into the Cultural Meanings of Landscape Photography." In *The Contest of Meaning*, ed. Richard Bolton, 125–42. Cambridge: MIT Press.

*Bulletin.* 1940. Jan. 11, 5.

Burgin, Victor, ed. 1982. *Thinking Photography.* New York: Macmillan.

Caldwell, Erskine, and Margaret Bourke-White. 1937. *Have You Seen Their Faces?* New York: Modern Age Books.

Clark, Timothy J. 1973. *Image of the People: Gustave Courbet and the Second French Republic, 1848–1851.* Greenwich: New York Graphic Society.

———. 1985. *The Painting of Modern Life: Paris in the Art of Manet and His Followers.* New York: Knopf.

Collier, John, Jr., and Malcolm Collier. 1986. *Visual Anthropology: Photography as a Research Method.* Albuquerque: University of New Mexico Press.

Crary, Jonathan. 1991. *Techniques of the Observer: On Vision and Modernity in the Nineteenth Century.* Cambridge: MIT Press.

Dondis, Donis A. 1974. *A Primer of Visual Literacy.* Cambridge: MIT Press.

Dulles, Foster Rhea. 1966. *Labor in America: A History.* 3d ed. New York: Thomas Y. Crowell.

Guimond, James. 1991. *American Photography and the American Dream.* Chapel Hill: University of North Carolina Press.

Hall, Edward T. 1966. *The Hidden Dimension.* New York: Doubleday.

Hall, Stuart. 1973. "The Determination of News Photographs." In *The Manufacture of News*, ed. Stanley Cohen and Jack Young, 176–90. Beverly Hills: Sage.

Hardt, Hanno. 1989. "Pictures for the Masses: Photography and the Rise of Popular Magazines in Weimar Germany." *Journal of Communication Inquiry* 13(1): 7–29.

———. 1995. "Without the Rank and File: Journalism History, Media Workers, and Problems of Representation." In *Newsworkers: Toward a History of the Rank and File*, ed. Hanno Hardt and Bonnie Brennen, 1–29. Minneapolis: University of Minnesota Press.

———. 1996. "The Site of Reality: Constructing Photojournalism in Weimar Germany, 1928–33." *Communication Review* 1(3): 373–402.

Hardt, Hanno, and Bonnie Brennen, eds. 1995. *Newsworkers: Toward a History of the Rank and File.* Minneapolis: University of Minnesota Press.

Herbert, Robert L. 1988. *Impressionism: Art, Leisure and Parisian Society.* New Haven: Yale University Press.

Hirsch, Julia. 1981. *Family Photographs: Content, Meaning, and Effect.* New York: Oxford University Press.

Hunter, Jefferson. 1987. *Image and Word: The Interaction of Twentieth-Century Photographs and Texts.* Cambridge: Harvard University Press.

Jay, Martin. 1988. "Scopic Regimes of Modernity." In *Vision and Visualty: Discussions in Contemporary Culture 2*, ed. H. Foster, 3–23. Seattle: Bay Press.

Kracauer, Siegfried. 1960. "Photography." In *Theory of Film*, 3–26. New York: Oxford University Press.

Lange, Dorothea, and Paul Schuster Taylor. 1939. *An American Exodus: A Record of Human Erosion*. New York: Reynal and Hitchcock.

Lasica, J. D. 1995. "Photographs That Lie." In *Impact of Mass Media: Current Issues*, ed. Ray Eldon Hiebert, 135–41. New York: Longman.

Leab, Daniel. 1970. *A Union of Individuals: The Formation of the American Newspaper Guild, 1933–1936*. New York: Columbia University Press.

Lyman, Christopher M. 1982. *The Vanishing Race and Other Illusions: Photographs of Indians by Edward S. Curtis*. New York: Pantheon.

Lutz, Catherine A., and Jane L. Collins. 1993. *Reading* National Geographic. Chicago: University of Chicago Press.

McChesney, Robert W. 1993. "Conflict, Not Consensus: The Debate Over Broadcast Communication Policy, 1930–1935." In *Ruthless Criticism: New Perspectives in U.S. Communication History*, ed. William S. Solomon and Robert W. McChesney, 222–58. Minneapolis: University of Minnesota Press.

Meehan, Eileen R. 1993. "Heads of Household and Ladies of the House: Gender, Genre, and Broadcast Ratings, 1929–1990." In *Ruthless Criticism: New Perspectives in U.S. Communication History*, ed. William S. Solomon and Robert W. McChesney, 204–21. Minneapolis: University of Minnesota Press.

Meltzer, Milton. 1969. *Brother, Can You Spare a Dime? The Great Depression 1929–1933*. New York: Knopf.

———. ed. 1984. *The Black Americans: A History in Their Own Words, 1619–1983*. New York: Harper Trophy.

Mitchell, W. J. Thomas. 1986. *Iconology*. Chicago: University of Chicago Press.

———. 1994. *Picture Theory*. Chicago: University of Chicago Press.

Moeller, Susan D. 1989. *Shooting War: Photography and the American Experience of Combat*. New York: Basic Books.

Monti, Nicolas. 1987. *Africa Then: Photographs, 1840–1918*. New York: Knopf.

Murphy, James E. 1984. "Tabloids as an Urban Response." In *Mass Media between the Wars: Perceptions of Cultural Tension, 1918–1941*, ed. Catherine L. Covert, and John D. Stevens, 55–69. Syracuse: Syracuse University Press.

"News Photographers." 1935. *New York Times*, Dec. 17, 18.

Ohrn, Karin, and Hanno Hardt. 1981. "The Eyes of the Proletariat: The Worker-Photography Movement in Weimar Germany," *Studies in Visual Communication* 7(3): 46–57.

Panzer, Mary. 1987. *Mathew Brady and the Image of History*. Herndon, Va.: Smithsonian Institution Press.

Riis, Jacob. 1970 (1890). *How the Other Half Lives*. New York: Scribner's.

Salgado, Sebastião. 1993. *Workers: An Archaeology of the Industrial Age*. New York: Aperture.

Scharf, Aaron. 1986. *Art and Photography.* Harmondsworth: Penguin.

Schlereth, Thomas J. 1980. "Mirrors of the Past: Historical Photography and American History." In *Artifacts and the American Past*, ed. Thomas J. Schlereth, 11–47, 240–50. Nashville: American Association for State and Local History.

*Shutterbug* advertisement. 1997. *Shutterbug* 26(3): 228.

Sloan, William David, James G. Stovall, and James D. Startt. 1989. *The Media in America: A History.* Worthington, Ohio: Publishing Horizons.

Sontheimer, Morton. 1941. *Newspaperman.* New York: Whittlesey House.

Sorenson, Richard. 1976. *The Edge of the Forest: Land, Childhood, and Change in a New Guinea Proagricultural Society.* Washington: Smithsonian Institution Press.

Stott, William. 1973. *Documentary Expression and Thirties America.* New York: Oxford University Press.

Strasser, Susan. 1989. *Satisfaction Guaranteed: The Making of the American Mass Market.* New York: Pantheon.

Stricker, Frank. 1985. "Affluence for Whom?—Another Look at Prosperity and the Working Classes in the 1920s." In *The Labor History Reader*, ed. Daniel J. Leab, 288–316. Urbana: University of Illinois Press.

Susman, Warren. 1983. "The Thirties." In *The Development of an American Culture*, ed. Stanley Cohen and Lorman Ratner, 215–60. 2d ed. New York: St. Martin's Press.

———. 1984a. "Communication and Culture: Keynote Essay." In *Mass Media between the Wars: Perceptions of Cultural Tension, 1918–1941*, ed. Catherine L. Covert and John D. Stevens, xvii–xxxii. Syracuse: Syracuse University Press.

———. 1984b. *Culture as History: The Transformation of American Society in the Twentieth Century.* New York: Pantheon.

Taft, Robert. 1964 (1938). *Photography and the American Scene: A Social History, 1839–1889.* New York: Dover.

Tagg, John. 1988. *The Burden of Representation.* Amherst: University of Massachusetts Press.

Terkel, Studs. 1970. *Hard Times.* New York: Pantheon.

Trachtenberg, Alan. 1989. *Reading American Photographs: Images as History, Matthew Brady to Walker Evans.* New York: Hill and Wang.

Virilio, Paul. 1984. *Guerre et cinema I: Logistique de la perception.* Paris: l'Etoile.

———. 1994. *The Vision Machine.* Bloomington: Indiana University Press.

Williams, Raymond. 1981. *Politics and Letters: Interviews with* New Left Review. London: Verso.

Williamson, Judith. 1978. *Decoding Advertisements: Ideology and Meaning in Advertising.* London: Marion Boyars.

Weegee [Arthur Fellig]. 1945. *Naked City.* New York: E. P. Dutton.

Zinn, Howard. 1985. *A People's History of the United States, 1492–Present.* New York: Harper Perennial.

# ■ 2

## Fact, Public Opinion, and Persuasion: The Rise of the Visual in Journalism and Advertising

*Robert L. Craig*

During the late nineteenth century U.S. industrialists began placing visual images in the mass media to create and promote nationally distributed brand-name products. The advertising and marketing strategies behind the image advertisements, which at first were illustrated and later employed manipulated photographs, violated the value Enlightenment thinkers had placed on the role of the press in encouraging rational deliberations about political and social policy. Advertisers began to understand that images could be designed to sell products by making irrational appeals to consumers' needs and desires.

At the same time, the ideology of journalistic objectivity began to emerge and eventually limited the kinds of images that appeared in the press. Art illustrations, whose rhetorical qualities could editorialize as well as report, were relegated to the status of editorial cartoons. Natural photographs—that is, those that appeared not to be manipulated, retouched, or set up or those that set out to code referents "faithfully"—became accepted as factual. Illustrations came to be regarded as opinion despite having a long history of use as realistic and factual in cartography, science, and journalism.

The dividing line between journalistic photography as factual and illustration as constructed persuasion has continued despite academic criticism of the theory of objective journalism and photography and investigation of the ideology of advertising images (Craig 1994; Schwartz 1992). In this essay, these contradictory developments in the history of visual communication will be placed within the context of the decline of the political party press and the rise of commercial journalism. The commercial press has truncated political rhetoric in journalism while allowing advertisers to use highly rhetorical imagery to sell products and spread consumer ideology. By eliminating illustration as a form of discourse and replacing it with so-called objective photography, the press reduced the range of media available for communicating political ideas, opinions, and criticism. At the same time, advertisers developed a style of using highly distorted imagery to promote products and a consumption-oriented, psychosocio-cultural complex (Craig 1992; Ewen 1976; Lears 1983).

The press allowed industrialists and advertisers to establish a communication code of advertising based on irrational appeals to readers, which subverted the press from its Enlightenment function of debating the merits and policies of a good society. These economic interests were essentially industrial but can be traced to the factionalism of the Revolutionary War and post-Revolutionary era. The process of business shaking itself free from the rationalist ideals of the Enlightenment and creating a society conducive to its own interests was somewhat slowed by the Civil War but developed relentlessly thereafter.

Throughout history, those in power have used images to establish and maintain authority. The iconic character of images leaves them open to the inventions of power. On the one hand, they are representational. Their mode of coding meaning replicates, in some stylized fashion, their referent. This representational mode codes pictures in a way that connects them to the real world and makes them familiar. That is why they become an easy form of address to viewers. On the other hand, although readers decode meaning from representational images' visual relationship to their referent, they also infer meaning from the selection of that image (rather than others that could have been chosen) and from its context (that is, from all the signs with which the image is juxtaposed in a message). Much of the political power of images comes from how they engage viewers' subjectivity and allow a certain degree of free association in the process of interpretation. The fact that individuals bring their own biography, mood, feelings, and dispositions to the inferences they make leaves them with the ideological sensation of having understood images. That sensation is called ideological because viewers, unless trained to examine the images and motivations of their creators and sponsors critically, often interpret them in ways creators prefer (Craig, Kretsedemas, and Gryniewski 1997).

Preferred meanings are powerful because one prerogative of power is to saturate culture with images that reiterate ideologies favorable to elite groups. It is the ritualistic appearance of images at every turn that constitutes iconography's contribution to social reification. Just as people are born into a society with language ready-made and approach the world through it, so, too, are they born into a ready-made visual field that they must learn. The visual field may be composed of all manner of visual symbols and codes, including facial expressions and gestures, styles of dress, hair and body decoration, calligraphic and typography styles, architecture, graphic design, art forms, ornamentation, photography, cartoons, television, and film. Visual fields also include the ways visual symbols and media are culturally inscribed through their classification (e.g., as in sacred or profane art or in art history) and by their conventional use. Visual fields mark all forms of identity from membership in civilizations, nations, cities, communities, ethnic groups, tribes, religious groups, families, and subcultures. They may change slowly or dramatically, but individuals are born into them and must learn to read these visual fields to function in society. Like language, this visual field is highly codified and conditions new images and their interpretations.

Even if viewers are critically predisposed, images must first be interpreted through the visual code of powerful elites who set the parameters of discourse within the symbolic realm. Conditioned by the familiarity of the visual field, viewers learn to interpret images at a glance without deep critical reflection, making initial interpretations powerful (Craig, Kretsedemas, and Gryniewski 1997). Establishing and controlling the visual field is a strong form of socialization. Elites may use coercion or legislation to control behavior, but power is most insidious when naturalized by managing constructions of what is and what can and should be. The aesthetics of visual fields, then, should be examined as flowing from social structures.

The ability to make and display images in public has been particularly important to the exercise of power by those who control the political economy and culture. Although this model might be traced through the visual fields of Egyptian, Assyrian, Classical, and other social formations, this essay will begin with short references to the visual fields of the Middle Ages and of Renaissance, Reformation, Baroque, and Enlightenment periods.

In creating a historical framework for the analysis of advertising it should be made clear that assigning any visual artifact—whether drawing, graphics, painting, sculpture, architecture, photography, or film—to a visual field is a process of considering it within the context for which it was made and viewed. Although images may, of course, be viewed privately, my concern is with the social aspects of viewing and how images are either presented and viewed as public communication or as communication to a public. Because older art objects are usually viewed within the confines of fine art and museum culture, it is easy to forget how such art was conceived and how it functioned as a mode of public persuasion that often rationalized and reified existing social structures. The production of public art is tied via wealth to power through sponsorship. Articulating image production within specific historical sociopolitical formations sets a framework for understanding advertising art. What is particularly troubling about advertising imagery is that the rationale for using it runs counter to (and undermines) the Enlightenment project of establishing a rationally organized society. Before examining advertising imagery, it is useful to examine the ideological role of images in other societies.

Vestiges of the medieval visual field continue to remain powerful in religious practice. In its time, it was a visual field of religious iconography that was hegemonic, flowing from the political economy of the feudal system. It was against this hegemony that the Enlightenment was formed as an attempt to break the power of aristocratic and religious elites and reformulate society along the lines of bourgeois democratic ideals.

Early Christians rejected their Judaic, iconoclastic heritage and began to use religious imagery to adorn rituals and architecture, making the Catholic Church a major sponsor of the arts in Europe. The church created an expansive visual field of images, sculpture, artifacts, and architecture. From eastern icons to Gothic, Renaissance, and Baroque ornamentation, religious images and symbols adorned the exterior and interior spaces of Europe's churches and cathedrals. The church, wealthy aristocrats, and merchants sponsored these images as symbols of their prestige, wealth, and power and also as ways of teaching and reminding people of the Bible stories central to Christian faith. As John Berger has forcefully shown in his film and book entitled *Ways of Seeing* (1973), the images and the buildings that housed them were the sites of the rituals of adoration and worship that situated people as subjects within the political and religious order of feudalism.

One of first cracks in the feudal order was the development of the printing press. As an early instance of mass manufacturing, it used a combination of human power and die-cast machinery (type) to produce identical multiple copies of a commodity that would be sold. The press thus presaged the age of manufacturing, when profit through capital investment, manufacturing, and commercial sales would create bourgeois wealth and power to overwhelm the land-rich but capital-poor aristocracy. Reformation and Enlightenment leaders used the press ideologically to spread Protestantism, establish the public form of scientific inquiry, disperse scientific knowledge, and foment the eventual overthrow and political realignment of the aristocracy. Meanwhile, the church and aristocracy tried to control the press and continued to produce imagery to secure their social positions. Yet in the end, they could control neither the alternative textual or visual fields that spread rapidly via the press.

Protestant iconoclasm ended the role of the church as the sponsor of art in northern European Protestant countries. It also created a new social space for a visual field independent of religion. Freed from religious subject matter, painters pursued subjects that had interested them since the Renaissance. Although Renaissance paintings mostly depicted religious themes, these artists also expended considerable effort to painting detailed backgrounds that included landscapes, cityscapes, seascapes, the interesting light of sunrises, sunsets, and storms, and still lifes. Isolated from the Renaissance's overtly religious context, these subjects became the focus of Enlightenment art and its visual field.

During the Counter-Reformation, the Catholic Church used the decorative style of baroque art and architecture as propaganda to win back Protestants. Later, rococo artists rejected complex baroque forms and replaced them with simpler, more naturalistic ones. But rococo art remained idyllic, pleasurable, and elitist. Like the baroque, rococo was propagandistic in that it emanated from well-established positions within the political hierarchy (Levey 1966, 121–25).

With the ascension of William and Mary in 1688, the rationalism of the Enlightenment began to take hold. Although the printing press had been invented early in the Renaissance, no technology was so central to the coming Age of Enlightenment and modernism. Elizabeth Eisenstein (1983) has pointed out that the growth and spread of publishing since the Renaissance created the social conditions necessary for the rapid advancement of modern science. The ideology of a rational, ordered universe was propagated through the publication and dissemination of scientific propositions, which had supporting facts for argumentation and falsification. No single fact, right or wrong, was as important as this new weltanschauung, aptly labeled by Jürgen Habermas as the "bourgeois public sphere." Addressing propositions to a larger community of scholars differentiated the public sphere from other forms of communication in which subjects and conditions of address were arbitrarily, ideologically, politically, religiously, and existentially constrained by central powers. Public communication or publicity is the sine qua non of modern science.

The scientific model of open public communication had profound implications for the feudal political order. Mercantile and manufacturing economies empowered the bourgeoisie and inspired national revolutions that replaced religious feudal governments with parliamentary ones founded on democratic principles. Open public communication was the most essential quality of democracy.

Being the most economically advanced, Britain developed the most advanced forms of public political expression (Habermas 1989). Patterns of immigration, governance, and trading between Britain and the United States created strong cultural and political ties. Colonial America's visual field flowed directly from British tastes. As J. H. Plumb (1976, 18) has noted, "At all cultural levels, from the breeding of flowers or horses to natural philosophy, literature and the arts, the two countries were almost as one." Before the eighteenth century there was little fine art in the United States. Art historians have pointed to the lack of disposable income, the difficulty of daily life, the irrelevance of European history painting, and the iconoclasm of Protestant Puritan settlers as major reasons for the evolution of an indigenous folk art rather than the importation of a fine art tradition (Andrews and McCoy 1967, 24–41).

The increased prosperity of the wealthy during the latter part of the eighteenth century widened the social and cultural gap among merchants, artisans, and workers; between planters and independent farmers; and between the urban North and the rural South. These growing inequalities were compounded by poor people's lack of a political voice. The rising American upper and middle classes increasingly turned to British portrait painting, which became a social marker that distinguished the wealthy from the lower social classes. By the end of the eighteenth century, portraits had become the main visual form of colonial fine art. "For the colonial merchant or planter a portrait served a functional end as decoration in his sumptuous house, as a record of himself and his family, and as an acceptable symbol of his position in society" (Brown 1977, 90).

Critical and satirical art, literature, and journalism emerged. Meant to stir public opinion, they addressed political and moral questions of the day in an attempt to shape individual behavior and public policy. The political art of the Enlightenment differed from previous political art in that it "seemed to be committed to participating in the making of policies by serving as a vehicle for the expression and formation of public opinion itself" (Phillipe 1980, 94). Earlier political art only promoted or sniped at positions that had already been taken at the center of power and did not engage the formation of those policies publicly. "Whether the truths it [the political art of the Enlightenment] depicts are physical facts or the psychological facts of the human heart, it concentrates upon truth," Levey observes (1966, 124). "The artist takes his place in society therefore not as ministering to its dreams of pleasure but as an educator. Art recovers a definite purpose, attaching itself to morality and science as it had earlier served religion."

At the founding of the United States, Revolutionary leaders recognized that the new democratic republic had to make a political and cultural break with Europe in order to survive. It had to create values and sociocultural rituals that would end the arbitrary and capricious practices of privilege and power vested in Europe's class system, religions, nationalities, and ethnic groups. The U.S. political establishment tried to ease these tensions. Elected government brought an end to the aristocracy and its hereditary claims to power, arbitrary taxation, and market controls. Religion was separated from the practices of the state, and Deists such as Tom Paine argued that it should be an individual rather than institutional or governmental matter.

The innovative enfranchisement and protection provided by the Constitution freed the press from governmental restraint, creating a fourth, permanent seat of power alongside the administrative, legislative, and judicial branches of government. What resulted was an innovative institution whose cultural, political, and ritualistic functions—either as an extension of political parties and their electioneering activities or as an independent critical voice leading to the formation of public opinion—became a major vehicle for public discourse about political and governmental action.

As political parties began to institutionalize political opposition during the early years of the Republic, they subsidized newspapers to publicize their legislative platforms. Because both parties were focused around opposing business interests, however, their newspapers presented a fairly narrow range of opinion. The ideal of a democratic press and the practice of dealing with free, critical opinion were two different matters.

Despite the vitriolic qualities of the debates and the Federalists' attempts at censorship, political discourse in the American Revolutionary and post-Revolutionary periods furthered developments that had occurred in the British public sphere and authenticated the Enlightenment's drive toward engaging citizens in public affairs. In that sense, the U.S. political party press institutionalized the practice of political commentary and publicity, which sought to galvanize public opinion and shape public policy. The fact that dominant business interests of the day narrowly framed U.S. debate did not diminish its standing as an institution of the public sphere. If emphasis is placed on the term *bourgeois* (as in Habermas's concept of the bourgeois public sphere), the U.S. party press was decidedly political rather than commercial and may be considered similar to institutions in Britain, where elites argued the merits of their proposals (Baldasty 1992).

The post-Revolutionary visual field continued to be dominated by painted portraits of wealthy elites. To create a sense of national identity, however, painters including Charles Willson Peale, Joseph Wright, Gilbert Stuart, and Joseph Silfrede painted Revolutionary War heroes and important government leaders such as Washington, Jefferson, Franklin, and Hamilton. For those who could not afford paintings, engravings were available. Art historians have distinguished approximately nine hundred distinct engravings with more than six hundred variations of Washington from this period (Montgomery and Kane, eds. 1976, 136).

By the mid-1820s the increasing number of working-class people in the United States, especially in the West, gave rise to a populist movement. Under the leadership of Andrew Jackson, who had broken from the Whig Party to be the new Democratic Party's candidate for president, issues of concern to immigrants and workers were brought into politics. In 1828 Jackson defeated John Quincy Adams, the representative of the old, moneyed interests of the Federalists, and commenced a series of Democratic presidents who held office for most of the next thirty years.

The American penny press developed during this period as a response to industrial growth, urbanization, and a growing working-class population, forces that combined to create a "democratic market society" (Schudson 1978, 60). Penny papers became "spokesmen for egalitarian ideals in politics, economic life, and social life through their organization of sales, their solicitation of advertising, their emphasis on news, their catering to large audiences, and their decreasing concern with the editorial." Although there had been sporadic attempts at forming a labor press, the penny press offered average people a cheap newspaper that was relatively disinterested in political discourse and that tended to report sensationalized news. "The raw product of the press was also changed by the newspaper of the masses. When the *views* paper became a *news* paper, the style of the writer also changed. Editors were less interested in opinion and were more concerned with reporting straight news. This was less a development toward objectivity than it was a shift away from political partisanship" (Emery and Emery 1978, 145).

Here, another child of Enlightenment science—objectivity—was born. The new journalism was meant to cover news from outside political parties. As a result, the press became popular and egalitarian. Without funding from political parties, however, it also became openly commercial and relied on advertising and subscription revenues. Content was tied less overtly to a party agenda, but advertisers' control of content was to become as insidious as governmental restraints (Soley and Craig 1992). In the end, the impact of commercialization and sensationalism pushed content away from party politics, diminishing its relevance as a voice of enlightenment. That coincided with major developments in the visual field, photography in particular.

In 1839 Louis-Jacques-Mandé Daguerre invented the daguerreotype (photography on silver or silver-coated copper plates), and William Henry Fox Talbott invented paper photography. Highly popular from its beginning, photography had a profound impact on the visual field. While painted portraits had been the province of the elite, photography introduced a surge of portraits and other visual artifacts. Its mimetic qualities made photography a curiosity, and its inexpensive price made it easily available. The photographic style was not completely new, however. Artists from the Renaissance onward had employed lens and camera technologies (Coke 1972; Galassi 1981). Even before photography, the visual field was photographic. Lenses aided in the development of linear perspective drawing, which created the illusion of three dimensions on a two-dimensional surface while correlating distance and scale. The camera obscura and camera lucida, two popular pre-photographic devices, not only stylized art but also conditioned artists to see and draw as lenses imposed. Early in the Renaissance, lens-based codes of linear perspective and single point of view became ideologically synonymous with objectivity and realism and provided a starting point for a code of photographic representation.

Galassi and Coke demonstrate that art and photography influenced each other after the invention of photography. In fact, many early photographers were also artists. Daguerre himself was an accomplished painter. Mixing art and photography was common. For instance, the photographic process provided more people with the opportunity to have their images made, but photographers continued to pose subjects in front of painted backdrops.

Even some survey photographs, long considered straightforward naturalistic reproductions of the American West, were highly manipulated for dramatic effects by artist/photographers. Timothy O'Sullivan, for example, cropped photographs and even rotated his camera to create dramatic visual effects when he saw that the horizon line would be hidden behind rocks and could not be seen in a shot (Klett, Manchester, and Verburg 1984). Henry P. Bosse, who photographed the Mississippi River for the Army Corps of Engineers to show how its dams affected the river, also painted in romantic clouds for artistic impact (Craig and Neuzil 1996). Art photographers such as Henry Peach Robinson and Oscar Rejlander combined multiple photographs to create large composite images to fit the aesthetic of oil painting. Although some of these early attempts at photomontage were pictorial and superimposed people sentimentally in nature scenes, others fit into the Enlightenment tradition of raising questions about social issues.

Photography's entry into the visual field was dramatic. It quickly became an immensely popular form of art that democratized and commercialized the ability for self-presentation. Its heightened mimetic qualities were a powerful draw because society demanded more and accurate representations. But photographs that were set up, manipulated, or displayed in groups also had powerful rhetorical effects. They could inform, insult, cajole, persuade, and even move people to action. The popularity of photography soon created a demand for illustrated newspapers and magazines as well as for illustrated ephemera such as advertising trade cards, calendars, and packages. These commercial and rhetorical prospects caught the eye of the commercial press.

That the first photographs, daguerreotypes, were one-of-a-kind images was no chance occurrence. Daguerre had carried on the work of Joseph Nicéphore Niepce, the French physicist credited with making the prototype for the first photograph in 1827 (Rosenbaum 1984). Niepce was trying to discover a way to transfer images directly onto metal printing plates for commercial printing. He thought of photographs as printing plates to be engraved and mounted on a press so thousands of copies could be published from them without paying an artist to spend days, weeks, or even years handcopying images onto a printing plate. The solution to Niepce's goal of mass printing from photographic plates was decades away, however. The first halftones appeared in the *New York Daily Graphic* in 1880, but it was not until 1897 that the *New York Tribune* became the first publication to reproduce halftones daily.

Throughout the nineteenth century, publications continued to be illustrated, albeit in the style of photographic realism. Even if based on a photograph, every illustration in a publication had to pass through the hands of an artist or engraver who might either render it as faithfully as possible or embellish it to create a variety of visual and rhetorical effects.

The *Illustrated London News*, the first successful illustrated news magazine, began publishing on May 14, 1842. *L'Illustration* and *Illustrirte Zeitung* followed in France and Germany the next year. In the United States, *Frank Leslie's Illustrated Newspaper* appeared on December 15, 1855, and *Harper's Weekly* followed in 1857. They were the most widely read news publications of the day (Taft 1964 [1938], 420), and they printed wood engravings and lithographs of important events and people, usually focusing on European news.

During the Civil War, *Harper's Weekly* carried illustrations of major battles, many of them copied from photographs. Yet the style and content of Civil War photographs taken by Matthew Brady, Alexander Gardner, or Timothy O'Sullivan are very different than *Harper's Weekly* illustrations. To be sure, in some instances the illustrations are uncannily similar to the original photographs. But photographs were limited to recording the stillness and immediacy of a moment: portraits of soldiers at rest, battle preparations, the dead on the battlefield, and the injured resting at field hospitals. Illustrations, although not as graphic, communicated even more: panoramic scenes of whole armies on the move; soldiers charging up hills; smoke rising from canon fire; flags fluttering in the breeze; miners working with picks and shovels deep underground; the explosion of the walls of a fort; citizens cheering at a raucous celebration as a steamboat opens the Mississippi River at New Orleans; the building and burning of buildings, bridges, and pontoons; soldiers on guard duty, trudging through knee-deep snow at night in a blizzard; soldiers dragging artillery over the mountains at night; and ships battling and sinking at sea. Such images used linear perspective and were factual, yet they were all interpretations of experiences that transcended actual moments in time. They stood for honor, glory, camaraderie, compassion, hard work, and the awe and terror of the new machinery of war. They also left little doubt that *Harper's* supported the Union war effort.

This style of interpretative imagery was also found in newspapers. Tuesday, March 4, 1873, marked the first edition of the *New York Daily Graphic,* America's first illustrated daily newspaper. Three-quarters or more of the eight tabloid-sized pages were illustrations. Anticipating television, the *Graphic* only covered stories that had a visual component. Its news was highly political, presenting opinions about local, national, and international events. Its decorative nameplate displayed a camera on a tripod and a printing press in front of a sun that radiated light. The emblem signified the *Graphic's* belief that photographers and artists were integral to illuminating the day's events. Sometimes text was included, cartoon-style in a balloon, as a cutline, or as part of a separate explanation or story. Examples of image-stories published in the *Graphic* included:

—Gen. U. S. Grant driving a team of horses up Pennsylvania Avenue.

—A full page of illustrations of the Vienna Exhibition of 1873.

—Portraits of businessmen who were important from the ideological perspective that "leadership in business as in politics is to be a shining mark for the artist or editor."

—A series of twelve sketches of shanty life in upper New York City that presaged the *How the Other Half Lives* photographs by Jacob Riis twenty years later.

—A critical image of political corruption in New Jersey, where railroad monopoly henchmen used greenbacks to blind justice.

—A full-page illustration of "Cephalopod or Terrestrial Devil Fish—A Monster of Centralization," showed an octopus, whose tentacles are railroad tracks, devouring a flag-draped female clutching a rolled-up U.S. Constitution (an argument that railroad monopolies were hurting the nation).

—Jonathan (Uncle Sam) and Ivan (Russia) grasping parts of the globe (that is, imperialism seeking profits).

—A full-page cartoon, "The Question of the Day," in which a miner, a New Yorker, a western farmer, a consumer, and Columbia (yet another flag-draped female) have a conversation. Miner: "I get only fifty cents a ton for mining coal." New Yorker: "And I pay $6 a ton." Western farmer: "I get only fifteen cents a bushel for corn." Consumer: "And I pay a dollar a bushel for my corn meal." Columbia: "Mr. Railroad Monopoly, you charge entirely too much for your services. If you cannot do it cheaper, I must try my hand at running the railroads" The explanation: "The government should see that the railroads are run in the interest of the masses instead of the monopolist."

—"Justice and the Striking Workers" (favorable coverage of workers striking against the gas company for better wages).

—A skeleton (death) herding poor European emigrants onto an unsafe boat in one illustration of a group. In another frame, a second skeleton swings a lantern to lure the boat and its passengers to their deaths on a rocky coast.

—Death beckoning to a passerby while dead poor children look on from the clouds (an attack on the Street Cleaning Bureau for ignoring unsanitary conditions in New York City).

The *Daily Graphic* continually crossed the line between aggressive political commentary and sensationalism. It reported and commented on events that were important and controversial, and it took political stands on most issues. More important, the *Graphic* shows how illustrations could create powerful critical narratives by caricature, by juxtaposing related but disparate events and people, by creating imaginary conversations between social groups and or symbolic types, and by using multiple images to create narrative and mix factual with speculative images.

Thus, even to the end of the nineteenth century, illustrations in the press maintained an Enlightenment ideal of commenting on public events and stimulating public opinion about social ends and public policy. Ironically, when the *Daily Graphic* is discussed in journalism history books (Emery and Emery 1978, 235), the emphasis is on the fact that the first halftone in a daily newspaper appeared in its pages on March 4, 1880 (Rosenblum 1984). The histories often laud that date as a milestone, yet do not discuss how halftones changed the *Daily Graphic*. The fact was that the halftones were so poor that they had no discernible effect on content, and interpretive illustrations dominated *The Graphic*.

Illustrations did not give way to photography in illustrated publications until the advent of quality halftones in 1897 solved technical difficulties previously encountered in printing photographs. Still, it is important not to invoke a technologically deterministic perspective. The major rhetorical differences between "natural" or point-and-shoot photography and illustration should not be overlooked. It would appear from looking at *Harper's* Civil War illustrations and the illustrations in the *New York Daily Graphic* that both publications consciously used the rhetorical qualities of illustrations and photographs to frame political propositions. Engaging in discourse was, after all, the constitutionally protected Enlightenment function of journalism.

Nineteenth-century illustrations and photographs were oriented by science, art, and the Enlightenment ideal of public discourse. In some regards it is difficult to discern the differences between these two media, because both could be factual or overtly rhetorical. Attempts were made in naturalistic illustration and photography to capture the subject faithfully for the purpose of identification and classification. But rhetorical qualities often overpowered the facticity of naturalistic imagery. Illustrators, painters, portrait photographers, photomontage photographers, and engravers who reproduced photographs also created interpretive visual propositions and statements. Often, naturalistic and interpretive works were published alongside each other.

Naturalistic photographs had an advantage when it came to images that relied on harsh authenticity, yet they also had severe limitations. They could not stop action, needed long exposure times, and could not be directly reproduced on the press. Their usefulness was particularly limited when it came to capturing the "decisive" moment. As a result, illustrators recreated crucial moments, including those they saw or imagined as well as some that never occurred (Taft 1964 [1938], 420). These artists chose, arranged, and ideologically and aesthetically tempered every element in their images to make political statements.

Illustrators and naturalistic photographers began to embrace two fundamentally different conceptions of time. Naturalistic imagery concerned itself with facts and documented what was standing still before an artist at a specific moment. Illustrations and some photographs continued, as art had done for centuries, to idealize and demonize its subjects, creating narrative illustrations and series of illustrations that depicted critical moments in the sweep of unfolding time, imagined pasts, and futures. They even constructed images to project cause-and-effect relationships.

The mimetic characteristics of naturalistic illustration and photography made them useful for documentary and scientific applications. Photography was found especially useful for surveillance in criminology, cartography, and anthropology. It was also applied to zoology, astronomy, biology, medicine, geography, and other scientific fields in which individual images were clearly part of the Enlightenment project of classifying nature. Still, in science the facts of naturalistic images had to be situated in an intellectual context, such as a classification scheme, for public consideration. The facts and their context were debatable propositions.

The objective journalism that arose during the mid-nineteenth century, however, began to construct news reportage and photography in ways that repressed the fact that they were rhetorical propositions. Editors ignored that what they reported and photographed was debatable as either facts and contexts or as being relevant to the social responsibilities of the press in a democratic society. In this sense, the facticity or objective style of reporting and photography of newspaper journalism came to be opposed to the polemical nature of the party press, specifically to that of the engaged political image (Craig 1994; Schwartz 1992).

Dan Schiller (1981) and Gerald Baldasty (1992) have shown that the Enlightenment ideal of the press as a central component of the American public sphere was undermined economically within seventy-five years of the writing of the U.S. Constitution. The new manufacturing and consumer economy needed advertising to promote its products, which, in turn, led to a highly profitable commercial press. By the end of the nineteenth century, the American political party press had been run out of business. The commercial press, not wanting to alienate readers, maintained one aspect of the Enlightenment—the striving to report truthful information (the facts)—while dropping its mandate for fomenting debate about issues of the day. In doing so, its role in the public sphere changed, and it was diminished as a forum for stimulating public debate. The late nineteenth century was also a period of growth for American magazines, and many were started solely to attract advertising revenue.

Schiller and Baldasty document the slide of the American press from an agent of public opinion formation to a passive reporter of public events, a role that better fit the commercial needs of advertisers. Both Schiller and Baldasty have considered how newspaper reportage changed during the nineteenth century, and Schiller in particular has examined how differences in the use of visual imagery contributed to depoliticizing the American press. He argues that the integration of photography into journalism was intimately related to the rise of positivism and science. In studying the rise of the concept of objectivity in U.S. news, he notes that daguerreotypes seemed to provide the ultimate evidence of an objective truth to nineteenth-century readers. "The uncanny ability of photography to re-present reality—to depict apparently without human intervention, an entire world of referents—bolstered the apparently universal recognition of it as a supreme standard of accuracy and truth. . . . Photographic realism insisted and seemed to confirm that the only form of true knowledge was non symbolic 'reflection' of an objective world" (Schiller 1981, 92–93). Schiller concludes that the scientific aura cultivated around the invention of photography contributed greatly to the cultural myth of an objective world that grounded the ideals and ideology of objective journalism. From the very beginning of photography, daguerreotypes were considered to be so realistic that they not only supported the notion of objective reality but also helped undermine overt political partisanship in news.

Photography became practical by 1839 and was immediately popular with the public. The quickness with which it was appropriated to support the ideology of press objectivity is remarkable considering that halftone reproduction was still fifty years in the future. The *Police Gazette* photographs that Schiller discusses were not photographs at all, but rather pre-halftone graphic copies in which an artist or engraver's hand had intervened. Contemporary editors did not consider reproductions of photographs to be "photographs." They were seen as graphics and labeled as having been made "from a photograph" or "from an ambrotype." Yet the claim to authenticity provided by photographs was strong enough that even a graphic representation of a photograph—being "from a photograph"—carried powerful connotations of the real, the truthful, and the objective. Having the truth on one's side was, of course, a valuable commodity in a competitive market.

As the ideology of objectivity formed, editors began to separate photography from illustration. Photographs were defined as factual, whereas illustrations became polemical. Because the commercial press tried to create the impression that it had eliminated the polemical in favor of the rational, illustration had to be replaced by the more naturalistic photograph. By the twentieth century, illustrations had all but been eliminated from journalism, surviving primarily as editorial cartoons.

That was not the end of illustrations, however. There was a resurgence of demand for them, first in magazines and then in newspapers. By the mid-1920s a specific industrial need arose for highly sophisticated, retouched photography that would promote advertised products. Ironically, commercial newspapers were eliminating rhetorical illustration as industrialists were creating some of the most sophisticated visual rhetoric ever. Once again, art had come to the service of the powerful. Although editors supposedly eschewed the rhetorical image, they ignored (and publishers encouraged) the influx of highly misleading, persuasive images in their advertising columns. Industrialists embraced illustration and manipulated photography because they needed the rhetorical power of images.

Until after the Civil War, advertisements in U.S. publications rarely used illustrations. Sophisticated illustrated advertisements first appeared on trading cards, which were printed in full color on lithographic presses. The illustrations, typical Victorian-era ephemera, depicted sentimental pastoral scenes featuring women, children, flowers, and playful animals. Often, the products being advertised were not shown. With the exception of large department store promotions, newspaper and magazine advertisements were generally small, more like today's classifieds than large-space, illustrated advertisements. Most were to the point and provided information about products, where they could be purchased, and at what price. Until the 1870s, there were few brand-name products. Then, as brands proliferated and brand competition began, manufacturers tried to attract attention to products through visual rather than textual strategies (Craig 1992).

The first attention-getting phase of advertising had three aspects. First, some manufacturers used typographic contrast to make advertisements stand out. They reiterated text type that took up columns or even pages of space; used multiple typefaces, underscores, script handwriting, initial letters, and decorative display type; and even ran type sideways or upside down. Second, manufacturers used small engraved images of products. The illustrations remained within the textual-informative mode of advertising and were merely a small picture of the product. Finally, many manufacturers employed superlatives and hyperbole to make claims—not always honest—for products. Doing so undermined Enlightenment ideals of rational public discourse. For the sake of advertising profit, the press began to allow manufacturers to exaggerate claims in an effort to persuade consumers to buy goods (Craig 1992).

Between 1875 and 1900, thousands of new brands were introduced, and manufacturers began to rely more heavily on large illustrations to attract attention. The images no longer just showed the product, but rather embedded it in a narrative image that showed the product in use (fig. 2.1). Advertisements became semiotically loaded with meaning, juxtaposing images of products and idealized people, places, and things. The amount of type in these advertisements decreased dramatically; it was the illustrations that were meant to be "read." Owning and displaying the latest consumer goods were construed as leading to an idealized life. Buy the product and become something else—wealthy, beautiful, handsome, debonair, athletic, and a member of the leisured class, middle class, or upper class. Anything anyone desired became fodder for advertisements. In that sense, they were not about products but about readers and readers' desires (Craig 1992).

If the claims of these images had been made in writing, they would have been absurdly exaggerated. They were not, however, and narrative illustrated advertisements became extremely powerful. The strategy behind them demanded a kind of hermeneutic participation by readers, who had to "discover" the meaning of the advertisement. Without text, readers were com-

*Figure 2.1.* An early narrative advertisement from *Youths Companion* (Dec. 21, 1882) uses fashion and setting to present a moral tale: "With a Waterbury watch children will learn to be on time and prosper." Note the shadowy figures in the background. They are late, presumably because they do not own watches. The advertisement also contains a woodcut that "represents the watch two-thirds its size." This double advertisement is rare because it both describes or shows the product and indicates how owning the product would transform a consumer. The holly surrounding the watch denotes the holiday season. (Periodical Collection, University of Wisconsin-Madison)

pelled to use inference to solve the meaning. Advertisements were meant to be a dramatic scene that implored readers to change. They attempted to persuade people to enter an imaginary world where human needs were fulfilled through the purchase of goods.

In barely 150 years, modernist, Enlightenment, and American ideals of people rationally building a new society gave way to the stuff of fairy-tales. Products had become magical. Industrial manufacturers used the media for anti-Enlightenment ends. Instead of trying to make people think about the world in critical ways and engage in opinion formation, manufacturers launched massive campaigns to "educate" consumers about products and the ideals, values, and behaviors of the consumer culture. They employed science to make advertisements more successful. Research programs were designed to discover which communication strategies most effectively helped readers remember advertisements. Recalling the advertisement or the product, it was presumed, led to consumption.

The theory of behavior behind these experiments was explicitly anti-Enlightenment. Thus, Walter Dill Scott, one of the first to research the psychology of advertising, attacked the idea that human action is based upon reason. He suggested that individuals rarely act rationally but instead respond to suggestion. Scott compared advertisements to hypnosis and mob behavior. When people participate in mob behavior, he explained, they are no longer deliberating rationally. And mob behavior was connected to advertising: "We think we are performing a deliberate act when we purchase an advertised commodity, while in fact we may never have deliberated upon the subject at all. The idea is suggested by the advertisement, and the impulsiveness of human nature enforces the suggested idea, hence the desired result follows in a way unknown to the purchaser" (1913, 83).

Scott's method of using suggestion to affect consumer behavior relied heavily on pictorial images. Readers were to feel "sympathy" for people depicted in photographs that express a desire, motive, or instinct. How something "appears" or "feels" or "seems" became a critical aspect of the ideology of appearances undergirding the relationship between commodities and social identity in consumer culture:

> I have a certain amount of sympathy for all humanity but I sympathize most with those of my own set or clique, with those who think the same thoughts I think. After those of this inner circle of acquaintances, my sympathy is greatest for those whom I might call my ideals. If I desire to be prosperous, I *feel* keen sympathy with the man who *appears* to be prosperous. If I am ambitious to be a well-dressed man, I *feel* sympathetically with those who are well dressed. If I

desire to attain a certain station in life, I *feel* sympathetically with those who appear to have attained my ambition. (1913, 39, emphasis added)

Like earlier persuasive illustrations from religion, manufacturers mixed signs of cultural value with what was being sold. The fulfillment of modern values, needs, and desires was linked symbolically to products. Advertisers hoped readers would infer that purchasing their products would lead to the desired ends. As Harold Burtt (1938, 279) explained communication inference, "An automobile advertisement shows a picture of a private swimming pool with cars parked at one side and attractive people in bathing costumes disporting themselves. The obvious lead would be that in this type of car one can have a good time and mingle with people of this sort."

Manufacturers continued to use illustrations long after the halftone had been invented because "drawing [had] an advantage in that the artist may idealize the subject" (Burtt 1938, 282). Retouched photographs became more and more popular, perhaps because they could "also produce confidence because the reader *feels* that he sees the product exactly as it is" (283). The key word, "feels," indicates the power of objective photography to dispel a reader's doubt about the authenticity of an image, thus reducing the chance for a critical engagement.

The problem of quality in reproducing early halftone advertisements is shown in a Mennen's Baby Powder advertisement (fig. 2.2). The crude mixture of photography, illustration, and montage was far less attractive than had only illustration been used, although illustrations could be photo-realistic. Burtt's use of the term *retouching* is somewhat misleading; photographs were completely reworked.

From a routine studio photograph (fig. 2.3), for example, an elaborate image could be created by adding meaningful signs: polished tile floors, shining pots and pans, the latest clothing styles, and a tree-lined, middle-class neighborhood out the window (fig. 2.4). Such idealizations had become standard practice by the 1930s.

The early literature addressing the psychology of advertising indicates that industrialists reconceptualized the public not as rational or as having the capacity for engaging in rational discourse through social institutions. They believed that people were either irrational or subject to irrational appeals through the mass media. Advertising illustrations saturated the public consciousness as religious iconography had centuries before. Industrialists began to use image appeals to subvert the process of a rational, thoughtful, and scientific approach to modernity. In that way, advertising, science, and the mass media were oriented by the ideology of consumer capitalism.

*Figure 2.2.* The clumsy insertion of a product into the baby's hands makes it evident that this Mennen's Toilet Powder advertisement from the *Youths Companion* (July 28, 1910) is composed of a combination photograph. Also note the crude outline of the baby's head and the illustrated petticoat-blanket and crib. The unnatural and clumsy image is an example of why illustration was preferred to photography—illustrations could be idealized. (Periodical Collection, University of Wisconsin-Madison)

Images have always been connected to the center of power. Enlightenment artists held out hope that images might be used critically to help people understand abuses of power, see differences in political viewpoints, and find their own interests within the political process. In the United States, the constitutional protection of the press was precisely to help make a ritual of public involvement in the political arena. The American Revolution was a bourgeois revolution, primarily benefitting merchants, farmers, and industrialists. The ideals of Enlightenment discourse on human rights were powerful support for the revolution and shaped a national ideology. But as soon as middle-class power bases were solidified, critical rhetoric became dangerous, especially that which might ask in whose interests capitalism was being developed.

The nineteenth-century commercial press developed sensationalized coverage that turned crime and entertainment into a cultural fetish. Politics, in text and image, became increasingly less important. Where political parties had been masters of the press, now the invisible hand of commerce developed a more insidious form of control. That business had a profit motive and the press catered to advertisers was masked by a new rhetoric of facticity and

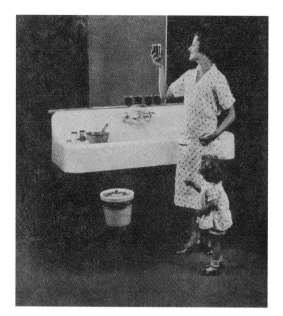

*Figures 2.3 and 2.4.* By 1927 the arts of photoengraving and manipulating photographs had improved to the point where a photograph could be completely retouched. Here, meaning is illustrated into the product (a kitchen sink) semiotically by juxtaposing the sink with known cultural symbols: curtains, an outside window that reveals a middle-class neighborhood, shiny reflections on the sink and bucket, bright tiled walls and floors, a solid stool for visual balance, and polished, modern pots and pans. (Flader 1927)

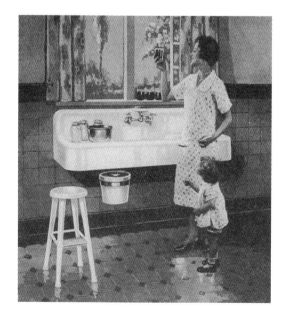

objective journalism. Objectivity was a value that emanated from science, a tool to help create a basis for the public expression of propositions and truth claims. In journalism, the idea of the objective photograph became a metaphor for a science of irrefutable facts. Most of all, what could not be challenged was the relevance of these particular facts to the fate of the Republic. The debate was closed. The public was not invited to participate as an equal. Now, news, when it is political, is a discourse of experts chosen from a small cadre of elites.

Yet advertisers were free to sell products in any way they saw fit. The written lies of patent medicine advertisers and the hyperbole of emerging competitors in the consumer goods market gave way to visually persuasive rhetoric. Because written claims for products could be tested, industrialists employed visual claims to make consumer goods appear to fulfill every conceivable human need and desire without making explicit claims.

During the Enlightenment, the ideal of critical reason, creating publicity to engage citizens and shape public opinion, arose for a brief moment. Yet in the end, business interests quickly overwhelmed the ideal, and the press abandoned its Enlightenment mantle in favor of commercial profits through the sale of advertising. The creation and reification of a consumer culture were accomplished primarily by creating a new, all-pervasive visual field in which irrational visual messages were scientifically developed to anchor the fulfillment of needs and desires in ways commensurate with industrial imperatives: to sell goods and make money.

Enlightenment ideals were an ideological episteme that masked burgeoning capitalist interests. The middle class was in power, and it had little need for a critical public that showed some signs of turning on capitalism in the 1870s (e.g., in such newspapers as the *New York Daily Graphic*). Business interests found that an apolitical but entertained public interested in consumer goods was far more useful than a critical public. To achieve that, irrational visuals pounded the human psyche.

Some doubt that human reason can be applied to the formation of a rational society. But with industrial art persistently sewing the seeds of irrational behavior, is it really surprising that people, culture, and society should become irrational? Rather than guard the use of the media closely for democratic and rational purposes, the media and their arts were allowed to serve the ends of business—even if they promoted irrational thought and behavior. By the twentieth century, the power to draw, illustrate, and display ideas had been passed from Enlightenment democrats to a new ruling class: manufacturers of consumer goods. The rhetorical function of a commercial visual field, buoyed by the ideologies of photographic realism and an objective press, constituted a massive assault on Enlightenment values and ideals.

A vigorous, politicized press and an active public sphere were useful, even necessary, during and after the Revolutionary War to create, structure, and stabilize a new nation. Such political activism, however, soon became a political threat to the establishment of capitalist hegemony. Accordingly, the press was denuded of its open political role, and the rhetorical forms of illustration and photography were made central to the development of strategies to sell consumer goods and promote consumerist ideology.

## References

Andrews, Wayne and Garnett McCoy. 1967. "The Origins of Native American Art." In *The Artist in America,* compiled by the editors of *Art in America,* 24–41. New York: W. W. Norton.

Baldasty, Gerald J. 1992. *The Commercialization of News in the Nineteenth Century.* Madison: University of Wisconsin Press.

Berger, John. 1973. *Ways of Seeing.* New York: Viking Press.

Brown, Milton W. 1977. *American Art to 1900.* New York: Harry N. Abrams.

Burtt, Harold E. 1938. *Psychology of Advertising.* Boston: Houghton Mifflin.

Coke, Van Deren. 1972. *The Painter and the Photograph: From Delacroix to Warhol.* Albuquerque: University of New Mexico Press.

Craig, Robert L. 1992. "Advertising as Visual Communication." *Communication* 13(3): 165–79.

———. 1994. "Universal Pragmatics: A Critical Approach to Image Ethics." In *Visual Literacy in the Digital Age,* ed. Darrell G. Beauchamp, Robert A. Braden, and Judy Clark Baca, 61–72. Blacksburg, Va.: International Visual and Literacy Association.

Craig, Robert L., Philip Kretsedemas, and Bruce Gryniewski. 1997. "Picturing African-Americans: Readers Reading Advertisements." *Visual Sociology* 12(1): 28–58.

Craig, Robert L., and Mark Neuzil. 1996. "The Photography of Henry P. Bosse." Delivered to the Association for Education in Journalism and Mass Communication, Anaheim, Calif.

Eisenstein, Elizabeth. 1983. *The Printing Revolution in Early Modern Europe.* New York: Cambridge University Press.

Emery, Edwin, and Michael Emery. 1978. *The Press and America: An Interpretative History of the Mass Media.* Englewood Cliffs: Prentice-Hall.

Ewen, Stuart. 1976. *Captains of Consciousness.* New York: McGraw Hill.

Flader, Louis. 1927. *Achievements in Photo-engraving and Letterpress Printing.* Chicago: American Photoengravers Association.

Galassi, Peter. 1981. *Before Photography: Painting and the Invention of Photography.* New York: Museum of Modern Art.

Habermas, Jürgen. 1989. *The Structural Transformation of the Public Sphere: An Inquiry into a Category of Bourgeois Society.* Cambridge: MIT Press.

Klett, Mark, Ellen Manchester, and JoAnn Verburg. 1984. *Second View: The Rephotographic Survey Project.* Albuquerque: University of New Mexico Press.

Lears, T. J. Jackson. 1983. "From Salvation to Self-Realization: Advertising and the Therapeutic Roots of the Consumer Culture, 1880–1930." In *The Culture of Consumption: Critical Essays in American History,* ed. Richard Wightman Fox and T. J. Jackson Lears, 3–38. New York: Pantheon.

Levey, Michael. 1966. *Rococo to Revolution: Major Trends in Eighteenth-Century Painting.* New York: Praeger.

Montgomery Charles F., and Patricia E. Kane, eds. 1976. *American Art, 1750–1800: Towards Independence, Essays on American Art and Culture.* Boston: New York Graphic Society for Yale University Art Gallery and the Victoria and Albert Museum.

Phillipe, Robert. 1980. *Political Graphics: Art as a Weapon.* New York: Abbeville Press.

Plumb, J. H. 1976. "American and England, 1720–1820: The Fusion of Cultures." In *American Art, 1750–1800: Towards Independence, Essays on American Art and Culture,* ed. Charles F. Montgomery and Patricia E. Kane, 14–21. Boston: New York Graphic Society for Yale University Art Gallery and the Victoria and Albert Museum.

Rosenblum, Naomi. 1984. *A World History of Photography.* Edited by Walton Rawls. New York: Abbeville.

Schiller, Dan. 1981. *Objectivity and the News: The Public and the Rise of Commercial Journalism.* Philadelphia: University of Pennsylvania Press.

Schudson, Michael. 1978. *Discovering the News: A Social History of American Newspapers.* New York: Basic Books.

Schwartz, Dona. 1992. "To Tell the Truth: Codes of Objectivity in Photojournalism." *Communication* 13(2): 95–109.

Scott, Walter Dill. 1913. *The Psychology of Advertising: A Simple Exposition of the Principles of Psychology in Their Relation to Successful Advertising.* Boston: Small, Maynard.

Soley, Lawrence, and Robert L. Craig. 1992. "Advertising Pressures on Newspapers." *Journal of Advertising* 21(4): 1–9.

Taft, Robert. 1964 (1938). *Photography and the American Scene: A Social History, 1839–1889.* New York: Dover.

# ■ 3

## The President Is Dead: American News Photography and the New Long Journalism

*Kevin G. Barnhurst and John C. Nerone*

In the past century, the daily American newspaper remade itself and in the process redefined journalism. Victorian newspapers were arbitrary, sometimes chaotic, jumbles of brief items; the import of each item went unremarked by its reporter; and the overall newspaper was loosely organized and arranged with little hierarchy. By the 1920s newspapers were beginning to array themselves according to topic and priority so that their visual appearance amounted to a map of the social world.

The transformation in presentation did not occur without a corresponding change in reporting style. Traditionally, the job of reporters was authorial. They presented a visually specific account of events, emphasizing the who, what, when, and where of the news. After the turn of the century, however, they traded in the role of author for that of expert. They began to concentrate more on the why of the news, sloughing off detailed visual description in favor of interpretation.

Although not usually viewed from this perspective, the entry of photography into newspapers occurred in parallel with that overall shift in newspaper form and meaning. We propose a close examination of news reports and pictures over time to show whether photographs, just as reporters turned away from detailed visual description, began to take over that function. Our study explores the role of news photography from these two perspectives. It tracks the various trends and phases in the introduction of pictures and examines the mutual redefinition of picture and text as one aspect of the development of the new journalism of interpretation.

## Previous Studies

In our previous research we identified shifts in news design as an aspect of changing journalistic styles and meanings of the newspaper (Barnhurst and Nerone 1991). Newspaper design moved through three distinct periods, beginning with the Victorian form already mentioned, passing through a period of experimentation, and finally reaching its modern form as a social map. The late nineteenth century corresponded to the era of Victorian newspapers, the period of transformation was well along in the early decades of the twentieth century, and the fullness of modernism had arrived by the 1940s (Nerone and Barnhurst 1995).

Over the same period, journalistic styles moved to longer and more explanatory formats (Barnhurst 1991). This new long journalism was the trend in news reporting away from the description of events and toward what various scholars describe as analytic, interpretive, or thematic coverage (Graber 1993; Hallin 1994; Iyengar 1991; Patterson 1993; Schudson 1982; Steele and Barnhurst 1996). Observers have noted the change for television as well as newspapers in both long- and short-term studies. They have also measured the phenomenon in newspaper reporting on a variety of topics, not only politics (the coverage most often studied) but also crime, employment, and accident stories (Barnhurst and Mutz 1997).

Long journalism shifted the emphasis to groups instead of individuals and relied more on the authority of outside experts. Journalists became less concerned with reporting an event itself than with explaining it by referring to other periods, most often historical. The geographical purview of stories expanded, referring less often to a particular place such as a street address and more often to larger regions. News emphasized the how and why over the who, what, and when of events (Barnhurst and Mutz 1997).

The evolving newspaper also was a prime site in the invention and emergence of news pictures. The history of photojournalism has had many retellings, principally by photojournalists themselves and also by art historians and critics and as a footnote to larger histories of photography. These have been summarized elsewhere (Barnhurst 1994).

The most common account underlines technology, the slow progress of inventors and scientists toward two creations: the portable camera and the halftone. A small camera capable of working at high speed with ambient light became the prime tool of photojournalists. The halftone, as a physical means to translate the continuous tones of a photograph into solid blacks and whites, became the tool of newspaper publishers. In this story, all roads lead to the modern form of photojournalism. The visual side of the press goes largely ignored before the two technologies emerged; prephotographic visual reproduction is viewed as a stunted or embryonic stage of photojournalism.

In its more sensitive telling, the history identifies three periods. The first was typographic culture, in which newspaper editors misunderstood pictures as versions of paintings and resisted their entry into news pages (Hicks 1952). To be reproduced, photographic images first had to be remade by engravers, who inhabited a stratum below painters in the hierarchy of pictorial art.

The second period accompanied the emergence of the graphic newspapers, such as the *Mirror* in London, the *Daily Graphic* in New York, and *ABC* in Madrid, around the turn of the century. Journalism of the era established a sort of apartheid in which text and pictures coexisted as separate but (perhaps) equal content (Baynes, ed. 1971). During this period halftones became a practical reality, although the pictures usually could capture only a single shot of static scenes or people in stiff poses (as the large cameras and explosive flashes required). For publication, pictures were corralled into their own neighborhoods by mounds of frothy lines, borders, and decorations.

Modern photojournalism, the third period, emerged by the 1930s as pictures gained the status of content, fully integrated into the journalistic enterprise. Newspapers bragged about their pictures, the latest and newest, in the same way they trumpeted their other scoops. New cameras allowed candid photography to capture action and emotion, the primary values of news pictures (Szarkowski 1966). Photographs gained respect as seemingly objective documents, and editors would no longer permit retouching or decorating an image.

The emergence of modern photojournalism thus paralleled the emergence of streamlined modern press pages. As front pages came to feature fewer, longer stories that were more often in an explanatory mode, the pictures in a newspaper also increased in size and narrative impact. And as reporters effaced themselves in objective news accounts, pictures also acquired an aura of objectivity, as if they were unauthored.

We might speculate, then, that the emergence of long journalism and the development of photojournalism were mutually dependent. Photojournalists came to depict events in apparent immediacy, depriving reporters of much of their authorial function and freeing them to become experts and explainers.

This study seeks to explore this relationship between text and image. Did verbal descriptions of scenes, actors, and events decline as news photography emerged and acquired the capability to show persons and places in action? Through what forms and styles of presentation did pictures evolve in relation to the changing mission of journalism?

## Methods

News photography developed in newspaper markets where two broad categories of newspapers reigned. Typically, photography was introduced into a particular market by an innovative newspaper, often a start-up and often part of a chain (the Hearst newspapers were especially important). These photographic pioneers were often more demotic in character than their older competitors. The competitors would respond to the invasion of the market by adopting some of the techniques of the invader and adjusting some of their other practices. They might, for example, begin to use photographs and then slowly adjust their reportage.

To observe both sides of journalism over time, we selected one daily newspaper from each: the inevitable *New York Times* and the more interesting *Chicago Daily News*. The period began during the late nineteenth century. The *Times*, which used to be even grayer, was throughout the period notable for the completeness of coverage as well as for stylistic conservatism. The *Daily News*, although somewhat less voluminous, was more innovative, especially in its illustrations. It was demotic, whereas the *Times* aimed for an elite readership. Any patterns of change common to these contrasting newspapers likely occurred throughout the news media.

Our study examined news coverage of presidential deaths in office, an opportune choice because such events occurred at regular intervals: James A. Garfield in 1881, William McKinley in 1901, Warren G. Harding in 1922, Franklin D. Roosevelt in 1944, and John F. Kennedy in 1963. Unlike inaugurations and other political or state occasions that have been studied, presidential deaths come closer to the core definition of news: the unexpected and startling as against the routine.

Although the old, event-centered journalism was imaginative and engaging, reporters did not hold modern notions of objectivity based on facts. They sometimes told stories as if they had witnessed them when they had not. There was little attention to sources, attribution, and the notion of verifiability in a Victorian newspaper. Choosing to examine the deaths of presidents avoided the difficulty of truthfulness and reliability in reports. Journalists were confronted with events of great historical moment, much too important to treat lightly or with too much invention regardless of their practices for less important stories.

The death of a sitting president, the biggest news imaginable, inspires the most comprehensive reporting by the best available correspondents, reporters, and artists who cover developments in the greatest possible detail. At the same time, the deaths occur on what might be described as a beat—and the most important one at that. The news media are sure to be there ahead of time, resources in place to cover events fully.

In another sense the death of a president in office might seem a counterintuitive example for examining change. The oldest, most senior staffers would also be the least likely to adopt new styles and definitions of reporting. Subject matter of such weight and seriousness would tend to dampen innovation, encouraging reporters to resort to the tried-and-true. As news events, the deaths provide the most understated, conservative estimate of the process of change.

The reporting of presidential deaths is highly comparable over a long period. Events follow a standard story line. Each death, whether by assassination or by natural causes, features similar characters: a grieving widow, a team of doctors, a cabinet, and a successor. Each puts these characters through similar paces: the swearing in of the successor, an elaborate funeral, and the journey to a final resting place. Each death motivates reflection on the past, on the dead president's career, and on previous presidential deaths, as well as on the anticipated changes in the personnel and policies of the federal government. Each offers the occasion for a representation of the people: the people in the business districts of cities, hearing and telling the news; the people bordering the streets to witness the procession; the people lining the railroad tracks to watch the funeral train go by; and the people pausing in the middle of their daily routines, stunned by grief, eager to touch greatness, morbid with desire to see the presidential corpse.

In sum, the death of a president is shocking and devastating. It happens at the epicenter of journalism, raising all sorts of fears and doubts about the security of society and the continuity of the nation. It demands a seriousness and thoroughness from journalists, who record each detail as faithfully as possible, fully conscious of history. The event follows consistent dramatic tableaux. It is unmatched as a moment to contemplate the meanings, purposes, and definitions of journalism.

Our study focuses narrowly on the life of the story, from the first report that a president is in danger to the "final resting place." In the case of Garfield, that was too long. Months of inept doctoring intervened between his shooting by disgruntled office-seeker Charles Guiteau and his actual death. Fortunately, as newspapers became thicker and more fulsome, the story's life became briefer. FDR and JFK died suddenly and were buried quickly.

Even in a study limited to two newspapers over relatively short periods at roughly twenty-year intervals, a mountain of coverage remained. Our final analysis included more than a thousand pages of text and hundreds of images. We entered the material from two perspectives, through the text and through the images. Through the images, we examined the trajectory of form over the period and its presentation of the emerging stock narrative of events. That perspective revealed the ways pictures interacted with surrounding text. Through the text, we examined recurring visual motifs in the stories themselves. Those motifs led back to images as the relationship of text to pictures changed over time and between newspapers.

## The Verbal Reports

Within the overall shift from the authorial to the expert voice, reporters began to deemphasize some forms and adopt others. Nothing disappeared absolutely from their repertoires, at least in the case of so important a story. In fact, the ritual and momentous nature of a presidential death seemed to inspire journalists to look toward the past and dust off older forms of reporting. Nevertheless, clear patterns of change are apparent.

At the outset, the variety of description and relation was all relatively lay. The reporter aimed to describe events so readers could place themselves at the scene of the action. Reporters tended to notice things a reader would notice and find significant, and they tried to conveyed the emotional force of these significant details. Reports of presidential deaths emphasized dramaturgy, demeanor, and visual detail. Long narratives were frequently constructed like scenes from a novel, with extended descriptions of the faces and emotional states of key figures and lengthy catalogs of, say, those present at a scene or floral arrangements around the catafalque. One particular way of relating detail, "walking description," gave an account of the visual impact of a scene as told by an observer strolling around it. This form was used to describe scenes of mourning in city streets, for instance.

Over time, much of this initial repertoire fell into disuse. Long verbal descriptions of floral arrangements became redundant in the age of the photograph, as did descriptions of the emotional state of the widow. Dramaturgy and walking description, along with the stance of the author, declined as well.

These narrative modes did not advance the role of expert analyst that reporters adopted.

For a time, breaking news became formless. By the turn of the century, in
some *New York Times* reporting and much of the *Chicago Daily News* coverage, breaking stories consisted of a pile of Associated Press bulletins arranged
in reverse chronological order. One example that entered into the lore of the
*Times* concerned an overnight report on McKinley's "sinking spell" put together from AP dispatches by night clerk Tommy Bracken, who worked in
the newsroom long after the reportorial staff had left the building: "Tommy
and the composing room and the pressroom crews worked until daylight,
adding A.P. matter as fast as it came in. They put out three editions, all told,
before sunup" (Berger 1951, 141). The anecdote illustrates a relatively unedited
manner of reporting breaking news, a raw updating that disappeared into
television coverage in the 1960s as newspapers yielded the function of alert-
ing the people.

Instead, reporters increasingly used the form of news analysis. They probed
the implications of events surrounding the death of the president, usually by
means of quoting experts or officials. Such news often used the future tense
and typically ran under a byline. The story engaged readers not by putting
them at the scene of action but by supplying the tools necessary for imagin-
ing the truth behind the facts, the structure underlying action. In consequence, certain tasks redounded to the photographer: providing raw physical description, conveying emotional states, and supplying dramaturgy. These
all share the present tense. In addition, photography took on much of the
news's memory function. Photographs not only relate past events through
the mere act of reprinting but also crystallize and abbreviate current news
for memory.

## The Visual Reports

Photography of the period changed in several dimensions. The scale of the
images grew over time in relation to page size and columns. The number of
images grew dramatically as well. The images became more timely, both in the
sense of the age of the image and in the sense of the delay to publication. The
immediate context given the photograph also changed with the growth of captions, the rise of photographer and agency credits, and the emphasis on the
photograph as a photograph. The decoration around photographs increased
and then vanished altogether as other contextual cues emerged. With the numbers of pictures increasing, relations among photographs also became more
complex and elaborated. Finally, shots generally shifted toward close-ups.

These changes emerge most clearly in portraits ("mug shots") of the deceased presidents. The two newspapers studied follow a similar pattern, with the *New York Times* lagging (usually by one president) behind the changes at the *Chicago Daily News*. For simplicity's sake, this section describes only the *Daily News* portraits of presidents. At the time of Garfield's death his portrait appeared several days after the event, paired with the picture of his successor. No other images of any sort ran in the subsequent coverage. In contrast, McKinley appeared in the same stock picture three times. Harding's image ran on the first day of coverage and continued to appear in various shots. Each president thereafter followed the pattern of Harding: appearing in portrait on the first day the story broke and taking the primary position at first, with his picture higher, larger, or closer to page one but with the passage of news days losing importance relative to images of the new president.

The numbers and sizes of portraits grew gradually. Garfield appeared only once, in a picture smaller than two square columns. By the end of the period, Kennedy appeared in five portraits, the largest running across four columns. The type of image entering the stream of coverage also changed. Early portraits were stock pictures of the same sort used routinely as campaign icons, much like the souvenir engraved portraits that street hawkers sold of the dead president. Harding's coverage began a pattern of showing portraits of the president as a young man. That trend reached its apotheosis in the *Daily News* in 1944 with a series of eight mug shots illustrating how Roosevelt had aged. By FDR's death the pictures had taken on a different quality and appeared more as personality studies than as generic icons.

Photography took the foreground as the *Daily News* emphasized the freshness or exclusiveness of its coverage. This first appeared after the death of Harding, when the *Daily News* announced that its portrait of the president in youth was "previously unpublished." With Roosevelt's death, the newspaper ran the "Last Picture of F.D.R." and did the same again with Kennedy's death. In both cases the newspaper advertised on page one that its interior included full pages of pictures. The Kennedy coverage included a remarkable photograph in which school children are gathered before a teacher and a page of the *Daily News* bearing a portrait of Kennedy. The teacher instructs the young to mourn through the mediation of the newspaper.

Beginning with the side-by-side portraits with Garfield on the left and his successor on the right, *Daily News* photography took on greater narrative work. The ordering and placement of the two pictures suggested the passage from time before to time after. McKinley appeared on page one whereas his successor, Theodore Roosevelt, followed on page five. By the death of Harding, the *Daily News* added a younger portrait along with a more recent one, and these ran with shots of the president in various settings and poses typifying his life. Here the representation invited viewers to examine the before and after in light of the president's life record—an elaborate narrative task. The full pages of pictures used in the Roosevelt and Kennedy coverage surrounded the portrait (usually quite large) with even more images from specific stories relating the events of the death, the events of the funeral, or the highlights of the career. Photography then carried a replete narrative load.

In sum, the portraits from the *Daily News* illustrate several moves: from small to larger, from posed and static to active and "candid," from artsy-decorative contexts to journalistic ones, and from simple to complex and detailed narratives. The tasks the photograph undertook were by and large those left off by the textual report. To the timeless portrait and label, pictures and their captions added other elements drawn from the present tense of breaking news. At the same time, photography also adapted in ways parallel to the text. They both contributed to the overall redefinition of news, expanding its purview to include history, memory, and complex narrative relations that implied an interpretation through juxtaposing images. Photography began the period as another item in the newspaper cornucopia. It ended elsewhere, occupying a firm place in the map of news content and differentiated from text in essential ways but also bearing a family resemblance to other components of the modernist newspaper.

## Visual Motifs in Text and Pictures

The process of change did not occur independently in either the text or the image but emerged from the interaction of the two. Reading the photographs together with the accompanying text made several motifs immediately apparent.

One motif is the cross-country train ride. The tradition began with Lincoln and continued for all but one of the deaths in office. Garfield and McKinley died after being shot and doctored in Washington and Buffalo, respectively. They had funerals in Washington and then went by train to northern Ohio to be buried. Harding, also an Ohioan, carried the train ride to extremes. He died in San Francisco, trained to Washington in a cross-country marathon, and then on to Ohio. All three took the same route from Washington through the mountains and mining country of West Virginia into the manufacturing region around Pittsburgh and then into the rolling cornfields of Ohio. Roosevelt died in Warm Springs, Georgia, had a quick ceremony in Washington, and then took the train ride to New York State, to be buried in

Hyde Park. Kennedy, breaking the tradition, flew directly to Washington and was buried across the Potomac in Arlington.

Other common motifs are the grieving widow, the team of doctors, and the body of the president. The spouse of any president automatically becomes a public figure but always of a particular kind: an icon of spousehood, required to live out the dominant notions of what a woman of her class ought to be. Especially at the point of death, the widows, although scrutinized and storified, have typically remained mute. By contrast, the team of doctors speaks with authority. Notably, the president's personal life, although always thickly populated, is often represented in death by the lone figure of the wife, whereas his lonely body is represented through the multiple voices of a medical team. The doctors insert their expert vision into the public gaze, for which the president's corpse and his widow's grief are twinned objects.

The successor's oath of office is yet another motif. In every case, the administration of the oath is dramatic, especially in contrast to the festive and elaborate ritual that typically accompanies the inauguration of a president. The fact that the oath of office in such cases is an emergency measure makes it all the more exciting. Unlike death, which must occur in presidential surroundings, the swearing in of a successor can happen anywhere. Teddy Roosevelt, who succeeded McKinley, was hiking in the Adirondacks when the news came and took the oath after a hurried trip to Buffalo. Calvin Coolidge, who succeeded Harding, was at his farm in Vermont and was sworn in by his father, who happened to be a notary public.

A final motif might be called the news of the news. In each case, the story was itself another story: the way the news spread like contagion through the public and the way the newspeople covered it. Ironically, although the observer disappeared from the news report, the newspeople made of themselves yet another story. These motifs provide opportunities for divining what tasks the news in its various manifestations was expected to perform.

## The View from the Grassy Knoll

A stricken president is always a big story. In 1881 the shooting of Garfield was told as an eyewitness account, full of dramatic detail. Similarly in 1901, when anarchist Leon Czolgosz shot McKinley, an anonymous report in the *New York Times,* typical of the reporting style in that era, described the action after the shots rang out:

> There was an instant of almost complete silence, like the hush that follows a clap of thunder. The President stood stock still, a look of hesitancy, almost of

bewilderment, on his face. Then he retreated a step while a pallor began to steal over his features. The multitude seemed only partially aware that something serious had happened.

Then came a commotion . . . ("President Shot at Buffalo Fair")

In this typical piece of reportage, the story is told like a story. It flows in a narrative from beginning to end and follows a sequence of events, at least after a brief summary lead. It is, moreover, written with the same range of observation one would expect to find in a novel. The reporter feels free to report authoritatively the mental and emotional states of not just the crowd but of the president himself. The reporter bolsters that assessment by recording details of demeanor, such as McKinley's pallor, with the confidence of a novelist on one hand and an eyewitness on the other. The fulsomeness of detail in this four-column report implies at every point a reporter physically present and near the president at the moment of the shooting.

This kind of reporting has a clear task in mind: to re-create the scene of the crime for readers. Doing so is a subjective venture; the reporter's experience of the event or events is offered for the reader's appropriation. The report could not work if reporters limited themselves to verifiable facts and

(National Archives and Records Administration)

sourced observations. No way exists to verify "a look of hesitancy" or the multitude's merely partial awareness of the gravity of the moment. The reporter is telling the reader that this is what *the reporter* observed. Giving readers a compendium of others' observations would not have re-created the event for them, although a reporter might think that he or she was supplying the raw information to do so.

By contrast, deathbed descriptions show the limitations of the fact-telling mode. Reporters actually witnessed none of the deaths, although they were always nearby and always in a pack. Here, an anonymous eyewitness tells the story of Garfield's death:

> Long Branch, Sept. 19.—At 10:35 o'clock, Dr. Boynton was sitting in the office of the Elberon Hotel talking with some newspaper men about the case. Suddenly a man's form appeared at the side-door and beckoned to the Doctor, who sprang to his feet and went outside. He returned in a minute and said, "The President is now sinking very rapidly." At the same time throwing up his hands with an expressive motion. A dispatch was instantly sent to the West End Hotel, and in less than a minute forty carriages filled with newspaper correspondents were dashing through the darkness in the direction of the Elberon. Hardly had Dr. Boynton disappeared than Capt. Ingalls, the commander of the guard, ran across the lawn. . . . In the meantime the newspaper men had swarmed into the hotel. For a short period they were compelled to remain in suspense. Then, at 10:33, Mr. Warren Young, the Executive Secretary, appeared. . . . He was surrounded by the eager crowd, whom he scattered like chaff by the announcement, "It's all over. He is dead." Back at break neck pace the carriages flew over the shockingly bad road, and in less than five minutes a hundred dispatches were flashing the news to all parts of the country and the world. ("The First News of the Event")

The story available for firsthand report consists of little more than "they told us this and we ran there, then they told us that and we ran back here so we could tell you." Their physical absence did not prevent reporters from trying to recreate the deathbed scene with the same dramaturgy as a firsthand account, but they had to rely on others for details. The same *Times* correspondent described the death scene in a verbatim transcript of the doctors' press conference and followed up with a catalog of those present, including an unattributed quotation from one of them: "Mrs. Garfield sat in a chair shaking convulsively, and with tears pouring down her cheeks, but uttering no sound. After a while she arose, and taking hold of her dead husband's arm, smoothed it up and down. Poor little Mollie threw herself upon her father's shoulder on the other side of the bed and sobbed as if her heart would break. Everybody else was weeping slightly."

Unlike stories of the initial attack, deathbed scenes did not usually succeed as dramatic accounts for two reasons. Not being present at the time, the reporters had to piece together the event from various sources and therefore had trouble conveying the experience of a firsthand observer. In this example, the source, expected to describe everyone's actions, does give a fairly compelling rendition of two of the actors, Mrs. Garfield and her granddaughter Mollie, but leaves everyone else "weeping slightly." The *Chicago Daily News* report of Garfield's death ("It Is Ended") used contrasting excerpts from the *Times* and the *New York Herald,* consisting primarily of a catalog of those present: family and cabinet members, servants and doctors. That is only the cast. When it comes time to set the cast in motion, all they do is watch.

Even physical presence may not have allowed the reporter to overcome the banality of these deaths. All death is banal, but these deathbed scenes were extraordinarily lacking in drama or meaning. The dying presidents themselves said nothing memorable. Garfield's dying words were "It hurts." McKinley, according to the *Daily News,* said, "Good-by all, good-by! It is God's way! His will be done!" before lapsing into incoherent mutterings thought to be snatches of the hymn "Nearer My God to Thee" ("Whole Nation in Grief"). Harding, who died while his wife was reading to him from an article full of praise for his leadership, uttered the unmemorable "That's good. Go on. Read some more" (Associated Press 1923). FDR, who usually rose to the occasion, managed only "I have a terrific headache" (Associated Press 1944).

In the Kennedy assassination, photographic images of the shooting along with the endless simultaneous television coverage displaced a firsthand, authored account. The moment of death was captured and conveyed first in photographs and then in stills from Abraham Zapruder's film. These canonical shots were perhaps not as lucid as one might suppose. They are not as graphic as the verbal descriptions of bystanders, for instance; nor are they as compelling as the photographic images of the various funeral observances that were to follow.

Moreover, although photographic images displaced the verbal, they did not eliminate it. Both the *Times* and the *Daily News* reports of Kennedy's death were full of eyewitness accounts from reporters as well as bystanders. These carefully label the observer's subjectivity so as not to be authorial in the old sense. The stance of omniscience was reserved for the objective report. The single most gripping piece is an omniscient, objective account of emergency room action when the president was brought in. The reporter was not in the room and did not proclaim an authorial presence but in the best tradition of objective narrative composed a story full of drama and action that culminated in the tragic moment when the First Lady bid the body goodbye:

> Electrodes from the machine were attached to Mr. Kennedy's left arm. But the green pinpoint of light on the scope did not waver the tiniest fraction of an inch. . . .
>
> Mrs. Kennedy stood up. Two White House aides stood on either side of her. She walked toward the cart where her husband lay. The aides stayed outside.
>
> At the foot of the cart, Mrs. Kennedy stopped. The President's feet were flush with the end of the cart, uncovered by the sheet that had been pulled over his face.
>
> Mrs. Kennedy reached out, touched the right foot then bent down and kissed it. Then she walked along the cart and stood by the President's right shoulder. . . .
>
> The priest turned the sheet down.
>
> Mrs. Kennedy bent over and kissed her husband's right cheek. Then she picked up his right hand, held it in both of hers, and pressed it to her left cheek resting it on her husband's chest her head on it, as the priest intoned, in Latin, the last rites. (Miller 1963)

This story is told so well because of the authority of doctors. Because the setting is medical, the aura of science provides an incontestable verity despite the story's absurdity—all the action performed on a body that all of the doctors agreed had already died before they started. The medical setting also allowed the detachment necessary to convey such intimate details.

Doctors were present as interpreters or exhibitors of the president's corpse in all these deaths. In Garfield's case, the illness was so protracted that the team of doctors, quoted on a daily basis, became well known, almost like O. J. Simpson's legal team. So naturalized was the medical discourse that it comes as a shock to read a simple eyewitness description of the corpse:

> The body is so greatly shrunken that artificial means had to be resorted to to give the clothes an appearance of fitting. In addition to the natural shrinking from his illness, the operations connected with the autopsy has left the body in an even more emaciated state. A plaster cast was taken of his face yesterday, as well as of his right hand. In taking the cast of the hand it was somewhat discolored, so that his hand will not be seen. The effect of the oil used upon the face prior to taking the cast disfigured the features somewhat, and slightly altered the color of the face, so that the appearance is very much less natural. ("The Last View")

The reports about McKinley's corpse also featured remarks on decomposition. By contrast, the presence of doctors allows one to forget that a corpse is gruesome. In the more recent deaths reporters refrained from describing the corpse. In Kennedy's case, reports repeatedly referred to his living appearance—his youth and vigor, his smile and stride. In the emergency room story, JFK is just a body made available for observation by doctors. The real drama comes from the evocative description of the very much alive Jacqueline Kennedy hailing the body as a dead person.

## The Grieving Widow

In all the deaths, reporters paid unwholesome attention to the First Widow. They anatomized her grief for the edification of the nation, applying the same values over time. She underwent scrutiny for the proper balance of emotion and self-control. Expected to grieve, even to make a display of grief, she also had to maintain composure and conduct the complicated funeral arrangements with skill and grace. Mrs. McKinley was too emotional. Weakened by a recent illness, under medical care, and thoroughly drugged, she could not fully participate in the funeral activities. Mrs. Harding, perhaps, and Mrs. Roosevelt, certainly, were too controlled. Roosevelt's obsequies were too abbreviated and Harding's too protracted for optimal grief. Anyone presiding

(National Archives and Records Administration)

over a four-thousand-mile funeral train ride with her husband's corpse would pace her grieving too slow. In the middle of a world war, FDR's corpse could not be gotten out of the way quickly enough. Jackie, though, was just right: the most beautiful, the most capable, and the most tragic of the widows.

Reporters' attention to decorum seems indecorous. In the earlier deaths, they sounded like gossips in describing the widow—not common gossips but especially pompous and disingenuous ones. Here is the *Times* on Mrs. McKinley:

> For an hour this morning she remained watching the body. . . . During that hour she gave herself up wholly to her grief. While the short funeral service was progressing in the Milburn home, although she remained in her room surrounded by members of the family and friends, her paroxysms of grief were pitiful, and her lamentations almost unceasing. . . .
>
> Secretary Cortelyou, when asked by a reporter for the *New York Times* this evening whether there was any truth in the oft-repeated statement that Mrs. McKinley had become to a certain extent mentally irresponsible through the administration of drugs and opiates, replied, "It is an infamous lie." ("Mrs. McKinley's Grief Is Uncontrollable")

The reporter asked a question on the order of the old saw: "And have you stopped beating your wife yet?" As intrusive as this scrutiny seems to today's reader, it was every bit as proper in its context as descriptions of floral arrangements and decomposing corpses and arguably less intrusive than the camera's eye.

Later reports were less moralizing and less intimate. Although one can read between the lines that reporters considered Eleanor Roosevelt too cool a widow, they clearly did not scrutinize her grief in the same way they scrutinized Ida McKinley's. Similarly, Jacqueline Kennedy was incessantly photographed and equally copiously described, with constant reference to her fortitude and dignity, and provided a conduit for the nation's grief. But the reporters did not gossip. The emergency room story gives an account of her actions that is heart-rending yet does not pry into her psyche. It simply registers a series of ascertainable facts. The pictures were the gossips, but the pictures were not as eloquent.

There appear to be six categories of pictures or picture content of the widows. The first to emerge was the portrait. Ida McKinley was first represented in portrait in the *Chicago Daily News*, once (next to his portrait) when news broke of the president being shot and then again (next to her successor as First Lady) when he died. A portrait of Florence Harding appeared once in the *Times,* alongside Grace Coolidge on an interior page. The *Daily News* also published a close-up of her that had been taken from a file news story rather than a formal medium shot in portrait style.

Portraits appear to have a conservative or traditional place as icons of the women in their official roles. Thus they disappeared from the *Daily News* but continued on in the *Times* until Eleanor Roosevelt, who on the first day of coverage appeared in a page-four studio shot—the last formal portrait of a First Widow. Thereafter, action shots in news style replaced portraits, such as the close-up of Jacqueline Kennedy at the moment she received the folded flag from the coffin (*New York Times,* Nov. 25, 1963, 3).

A second, much more important, kind of imagery showed the First Lady accompanying her husband during the events that led up to his death. It first emerged during the *Daily News* coverage of McKinley in the form of a September 13, 1901, sketch of Ida McKinley leaving the Milburn residence in Buffalo after he appeared to be surviving the assassination attempt. Such imagery became stock coverage with the death of Harding. Florence Harding appeared in the rotogravure section of the *New York Times* on August 5, 1923, in half a dozen shots of their trip to Alaska, the strain of which was blamed for his falling ill. The *Daily News* also ran two of the shots on August 3. It was by far the most extensive visual representation of a First Lady in any of the deaths until Kennedy's, after which Jacqueline Kennedy appeared again and again in pictures of the limousine just before and after her husband was shot. The photos came first from the wire services, and then a second wave were from snapshots that bystanders took. A third wave came from the home movies acquired by *Life* magazine. A scattering of pictures also recorded her at a series of political events earlier on the same day, in each case smiling with her husband or others.

The third kind of First Lady image illustrated stories of the presidents' political lives. Florence Harding appeared in shots with her husband campaigning as a candidate and also arriving at the Executive Mansion after the Inauguration (*New York Times,* Aug. 3, 1923, 3). The *Daily News* showed Eleanor Roosevelt in a family shot as the Roosevelts traveled to Chicago, where FDR would accept his party's nomination. Jacqueline Kennedy appeared in a *Times* portrait of JFK with his parents after winning the election. She also appeared in a file picture of her husband's swearing-in. Such pictures participated in the general move toward narrative in the visual side, with the wives playing the role of minor characters or props in a story about rising political stars.

The fourth, most important, pictorial coverage of the widows showed them during the various funeral rituals. This type of picture first ran in the *New York*

*Times* coverage of Harding's burial in Ohio and provided the only current shot of Eleanor Roosevelt in either newspaper. The coverage of Jacqueline Kennedy began as she accompanied the coffin to Washington. The *Times* showed her with the Johnsons; then boarding the hearse, her stockings still stained with blood; and finally with Robert Kennedy—all on the first day of coverage. In the *Chicago Daily News* such images began when she appeared on Sunday, first accompanying her children outside the White House and then kneeling at the casket in the Rotunda (from normal and bird's-eye views). The *Times* showed these images as well as pictures of her with the children during the eulogy and later upon their leaving the Capitol. The Monday funeral services and burial at Arlington saw her in various views in both newspapers, entering and leaving the Cathedral and standing at the graveside. The newspapers repeated each other, relying on images from wire services, and the *Daily News* repeated the image of her kneeling at the coffin—the first from United Press International and the second from the Associated Press.

The extent of coverage suggests the growing reliance on pictures for describing the grieving widow. The space given over to such images, which had already been seen in other newspapers, on television, and even in the newspaper's own pages, shows how central they were considered to the narrative. They also suggest that the invasive curiosity characterizing earlier reports in the text was eventually transferred into pictures. Photojournalists in their roles as paparazzi could capture every moment of Jacqueline Kennedy's grief, every gesture and facial expression, seemingly without responsibility. The picture itself swallowed any responsibility for humane treatment or respect for privacy.

A fifth, less important, type of image of the widow illustrates the personal life of the deceased president. This started late with an image of Eleanor Roosevelt at her wedding. The picture ran on page five on the first day of the *Times*'s coverage in a group of pictures illustrating FDR's life. In the case of Jacqueline Kennedy, both newspapers showed pictures of her on her wedding day. Both also published a more recent portrait of her and the family at Easter. These follow a longer tradition of showing presidents in various intimate moments, with children or a family dog, for example.

A sixth and final type of image showed the widow engaged in the political life of her husband's successor. These appeared only in the case of Jacqueline Kennedy, who figures prominently in images both newspapers ran of Lyndon B. Johnson swearing the oath of office in the airplane on the Dallas tarmac.

In general, the First Widow emerged slowly, first as an icon in portrait but quickly as an actor, present and witnessing the events leading up to her husband's death and then, most prominently and extensively, as the image of grieving. Pictorially, that role did not take on full importance until the assassination of Kennedy.

## When Lilacs Last

The funeral sequence following a president's death is always a journey through a national landscape. Usually it has been a physical journey through a geographical mosaic. In Kennedy's case there was no long train ride; still, the social mosaic was represented as a kind of metaphorical journey. Lining the route are the people, and the funeral journey always calls for descriptions and depictions of the variety of people who, although increasingly divided by race, class, region, age, religion, and political persuasion, are united by grief into one People.

In a sense, the reporting of a president's death was for a century an extended gloss on Walt Whitman's "When Lilacs Last in the Dooryard Bloom'd," written on the occasion of Abraham Lincoln's death. Here he depicts the breaking of the news:

(National Archives and Records Administration)

Now while I sat in the day and look'd forth,
In the close of the day with its light and the fields of spring, and the farmers
    preparing their crops,
In the large unconscious scenery of my land with its lakes and forests,
In the heavenly aerial beauty, (after the perturb'd winds and the storms,)
Under the arching heavens of the afternoon swift passing, and the voices of
    children and women,
The many-moving sea-tides, and I saw the ships how they sail'd,
And the summer approaching with richness, and the fields all busy with
    labor,
And the infinite separate houses, how they all went on, each with its meals
    and minutia of daily usages,
And the streets how their throbbings throbb'd, and the cities pent—lo, then
    and there,
Falling upon them all and among them all, enveloping me with the rest,
Appear'd the cloud, appear'd the long black trail,
And I knew death, its thought, and the sacred knowledge of death.

Whitman begins and ends with the observer. In between, he builds a vast and varied landscape, a large and disparate social world and a booming, throbbing economy—a naked nation with millions of stories now all interrupted by a cloud of death.

The same ingredients played in all the verbal descriptions of the presidential deaths. First, the initial news, striking like a thunderbolt, interrupts daily activity and hails everyone into the same story. With Garfield's and McKinley's deaths, newspapers were the prime media of diffusion. It was the custom for daily newspapers to maintain streetside bulletin boards where they could post the latest news. In the case of breaking news, newspapers sold issue after updated issue as extra editions. The *New York Times* places itself at center stage when describing news of McKinley's death:

> [news of the shooting] was duplicated on the bulletin board of the *New York Times,* and a few moments later on the boards of every journal on Newspaper Row. The casual passer-by glanced at it, stopped, rubbed his or her eyes, and read again. After that, like the shifting grains of sand in an eddying stream, the crowd gathered along Park Row . . . , and many hundreds hurried off to tell it to their fellows. . . .
>
> A little later and the great down-town buildings began to empty their hordes of workers for the day, and then City Hall Square became a great sea of upturned faces, shifting and eddying in a struggle to get nearer the bulletin boards. ("How the News Was Received")

Here the faces are all the same, although the anonymous reporter does note women in the crowds. They flow like water—a sea of faces, an eddying stream. But they are faces—not until the Kennedy death did we find the crowds described as ants.

Newspapers at first positioned themselves as one with the people. Just as the people mourned and wore black, so too did newspapers. With Garfield the only visual evidence of grief was the turned column rules that appeared only once in the *Daily News* and twice in the *Times,* when he died and when he was buried. The *Times* also composed some of the text, particularly the order of the funeral procession, in the shape of urns. These were very much particular or local expressions, as when an individual decided to wear a black arm band or a company draped its store front in black.

McKinley's death saw a change in the convention of turned rules. They appeared only on the first day in the *Times* and not at all in the *Daily News,* replaced by other signs of mourning. At the *Times,* the heavy rules shifted to the edges of pages, becoming a thick border with rounded corners that ran for six consecutive days. The *Daily News* turned to decoration, showing the deceased surrounded by an elaborately drawn frame carrying representations of several objects: curved lines, ears of wheat, and federal shields (the stars and stripes). The wheat symbolized ripe grain ready for the harvest, a sign of death drawn from the Bible, and the shields represented the national character of the life's service and of its mourning.

These signs of mourning slowly disappeared through the following presidential deaths. The *Daily News* used turned rules only on the day of Harding's death, and none of the decorative symbols appeared after McKinley. The *Times* likewise used turned rules throughout the edition announcing Harding's death. Since the time of Roosevelt, heavy borders appeared, if at all, only surrounding the deceased's portrait. Instead, advertisers picked up the custom. After Roosevelt died, some advertisers in the *Times* enclosed their space in heavy mourning rules. These sometimes contained an "In Memoriam" message but more often announced that the store would close on the official day designated by presidential proclamation. The custom also carried into the Kennedy era but was not universal. Many advertisements running next to coverage of Roosevelt's death announced cheery spring fashions and offers. The Kennedy coverage ran with similar advertising geared to the holidays. That sort of juxtaposition had always existed, but in the emerging social map of modern newspapers it provided a jarring reminder of an older form of news, with its unrelated elements jostling for space.

Over time, descriptions of the initial spreading of the news changed with the media of diffusion. News of Harding's death was the first heard via radio, and news of the Kennedy assassination via television. With each new medium, the spontaneous crowds of the era of contagious diffusion diminished further. In 1963 people learned of the assassination in a variety of private and semiprivate settings—in their homes and cars, in their offices and schoolrooms. That still left many non-spontaneous occasions for the people to assemble as spectators before the great national drama of mourning. Initially such gatherings were depicted as decentralized, with the rites of mourning occurring all over. With Garfield's assassination, major newspapers carried reports from every city in the nation. Over time that changed into a national audience watching events in Washington and perhaps in one or two secondary locations, and the grief of leading men replacing public expressions of mourning.

After Garfield's and McKinley's deaths, cities literally draped themselves in black, making a visible display of mourning. Verbal descriptions foregrounded the black banners on buildings through the technique of walking description. Here is how the *Daily News* described Canton, Ohio, on the eve of McKinley's burial:

> In Tuscarawas Street, from one end to the other, business houses are hung heavy with crape and at intervals huge arches, draped and festooned in mourning colors, span the route of the procession. . . .
> One of the arches is in front of the Canton high school. . . . The school is draped and in every window is a black-boarded portrait of the late president. In this thoroughfare, too, are two large churches, one of which was regularly attended by Maj. McKinley. . . . At each corner of the edifice and above the big cathedral are broad draperies deftly looped, each bearing a large white rosette. (Staff Correspondent, "Mourn in Home City")

In walking description, a visible field is set in motion by an observer who wanders around gathering impressions. This manner of reporting made a coherent and compelling visual impact. Engravings and photography do not truly accomplish the same thing. Photographs of draped buildings, especially in a black and white halftone reproduction, have little immediacy. Sketches can do better, both by highlighting appropriate details and positioning figures in didactic positions—marveling at the billowing crepe, for instance, in the engraving that accompanied "Mourn in Home City" on September 18, 1901 ("from a sketch made by a staff artist for The *Daily News*," 2), or in exaggerated postures with cartoonlike facial expressions in "All Chicago Mourns" on September 14.

Over time, mourning came to be depicted photographically, and symbols of mourning such as wreaths and floral arrangements became frequent subjects. On August 4, 1923, for Harding's death the *Daily News* showed a floral arrangement along with a shot of a draped doorway (3). The next day, a wreath being sent by the City of Chicago received its own portrait, flanked by inset mug shots of the mayor and commissioner who would convey it to Washington. A *Daily News* picture on April 14, 1945, during observances for Roosevelt showed flower arrangements piled around the casket (8), just as during the Harding rituals.

These representations of grief eventually disappeared. No draped facades or doorways appeared prominently in photographs following FDR's death, which also marked the last notable appearance of floral arrangements. In the Kennedy coverage, neither of these signs of mourning played a significant role. They appeared as background details only. Photos, although better in some ways than verbal description in depicting grieving people, make poor substitutes for many of the other standard visual images in reporting. They cannot provide walking description, for example. What photographs lack is a moving locus of subjectivity.

Over time, the occasion for motion, for walking description, became less compelling as newsworthy mourning was redefined. In the early deaths it was decentralized, and the reaction of the people was the news. The local character of even national events gave impetus to walking description. News slowly abandoned the local definition of political life in favor of larger domains, however. Gradually, mourning became defined by the official statements of prominent men, clustered at first in the nation's capital—then more often in the capitals of the world.

Increasingly, grief when an American chief executive died in office became internationalized. The deaths of Garfield and McKinley, especially, but also of Harding, inspired local stories and story angles with pictorial coverage limited almost entirely to such places as Buffalo and Canton. The rise of American international power made the event a worldwide story, but the availability of photographs may also have been influential. Plenty of international responses appeared in earlier textual coverage but moved into pictures only after Roosevelt died. The *Times,* on April 14, 1945, ran three shots in a representative cluster: Churchill in London, several gendarmes in Paris, and some "Filipino residents" gathered around a newspaper front page showing the news (3).

Mourners who merit detailed pictures have always been important people, dignitaries usually shown in full-length images (long shots) upon their arrival or during their march in procession but sometimes shown in closer images from the waist up that include more facial detail (medium shots). Such imagery began in the *Daily News* sketch art after McKinley died. Senators and cabinet members dominated the early pictures, but more international dignitaries appeared in pictures with each successive death in office.

The military increasingly played the role of intermediary in public grief. An honor guard first appeared surrounding the catafalque in front-page *Daily News* sketches of McKinley's rites on September 14, 1901. The *Times* did the same thing photographically in coverage of Harding. The presence of the military became a dominant theme in pictures of Roosevelt. An honor guard and pallbearers from military ranks were among the multiplying signs of the president's role as commander-in-chief. The most notable, a riderless horse, first appeared in news coverage when Roosevelt died during wartime. This symbol (dating from the era of Ghengis Kahn, the newspapers said) commemorated the loss of a leader in battle. The horse (at one time killed and buried, according to news accounts, to accompany the fallen leader into the afterlife) was led riderless after the bier. Its stirrups carried the boots, turned backward, of the dead man, and his saber pierced the saddle. The symbolism made sense to reporters during World War II, and perhaps the mood of garrisoned cold war encouraged the military imagery during the Kennedy coverage.

The way they deciphered this arcane historical knowledge also highlights the growing tendency of reporters to act as interpreters. The reliance on the military as the intermediary for public grieving arose as other aspects of the content in the new long journalism shifted away from the individual and toward institutions, groups, officials of every sort, and expert sources. These groupings in themselves provide a sort of interpretation, in the case of presidential deaths suggesting a nation fortified against not only grief but also the danger uncontrolled grief represents to the continuity of the state.

Pictures helped forward this practice of representing mourners in groups. The public appeared in crowds almost exclusively at first. The *Daily News* showed them on September 17, 1901, in Buffalo as McKinley's body was removed to Washington: the masses, the streetscape, the military officiating (4). Crowds appeared in Washington at the Rotunda and procession and finally at the cemetery. The *Times* picked up this approach later as it covered Harding, showing crowds in Ohio and Washington on August 11, 1923 (2), as well as along the train route on August 12 (3–4). With the death of Roosevelt, the *Times* began to show a representative mix of crowds. In one group of four shots crowds stood for geographical regions, gathered in Warm Springs,

Georgia, and Hyde Park, New York. Crowds in local coverage likewise represented places. In New York City, where Uptown and Downtown, East Side and West, differ in social geography, the *Times* selected various locations, such as a memorial service on Seventh Avenue, and sundry groups. The *Daily News* showed some of the same wire service crowd scenes as well as the usual throngs at the Capitol and along Constitution Avenue in Washington. Such shots continued without much change in the Kennedy coverage.

As verbal reporting abandoned ordinary people identified by name alone, text began identifying people by demographic affiliation. Pictures took over some of the representations of individuals but at the same time identified them increasingly as group representatives. Images of citizens mourning document that process. Although most mourning was accomplished through medium and long shots of dignitaries (setting aside for now the special case of the widow), medium and close shots of ordinary people emerged slowly over the period, beginning with coverage of Roosevelt. Newspapers sought to illustrate how the masses felt the death personally, and so in addition to showing mourning acts en masse they began to choose emblematic examples of personal loss. In the *Daily News,* those examples had two forms. The first was an April 12, 1945, picture (9) of a group of college students, but with each individual fully identified in the caption and with each face clearly visible. This form of representation, emphasizing the personal identity and grief of ordinary citizens, occurred only with the death of Roosevelt. A second form hid the identity of emblematic individuals. In the next day's coverage, after showing the crowds around the Capitol, the *Daily News* ran a medium shot of several women from the crowd (3–4). Of the two clearly visible, one covers her face with her hand and the other wears an engulfing hat. The caption did not identify either beyond the phrase "women weep openly" and a reference to the crowd. This kind of generalizing of personal grief became the norm for pictures of ordinary mourners.

The *Times* did not pick up the practice until Kennedy's death. On the first day of coverage, it showed in close-up "a woman" mourning (5), her hand over her face and no accompanying identification. On the second day it showed a Harvard student, weeping and hands over his face, on the steps before a crowd leaving the campus memorial service (11). In subsequent coverage, the *Times* ran medium shots of commuters, of black children, of nuns, and of Catholic boys—all with emblematic expressions and gestures of grieving but none identified beyond the group affiliation. The *Daily News* took the form even further, running a full column of seven pictures on the first day, all uncaptioned (5)—mostly women with their hands over their faces or comforting one another. The full column of stacked images formed a chimney of grief, bearing the headline "And His People Wept." In early coverage, the text described men weeping openly and copiously. As grief moved from text into pictures of the public, however, usually only women, children, and students appeared in the act of breaking down in tears.

The same process also occurred in verbal descriptions of people. Besides being described as crowds, they now became described also as individuals occasionally, given voices although not names. In general they remained a category:

> At a crowded bar-lunch room at State and Kinzie Streets, laborers from a nearby construction project gasped as the announcement of the death came over a radio.
>
> A husky Negro workman knocked a glass of whiskey from the bar, said "for God's sake," and rushed out the door.
>
> Women at a table burst into tears. All was silent except for the radio announcer's voice. (Special to the *New York Times,* "People across U.S. Voice Grief")

More and more, of course, reporters put themselves in the place of the public, either by writing of the reaction of the press corps (as in Tom Wicker's "Kennedy and Reporters" [1963]) or by writing about their own responses.

(Cecil Stoughton, LBJ Library Collection)

## The Circle Unbroken

The oath of office as a moment of action could not be pictured until the advent of smaller cameras during the 1920s and 1930s. That sort of candid shot did not represent any of the presidential deaths until Roosevelt. Newspapers could have shown the oath in sketch art but did not, an omission that suggests that administering the oath did not become an icon until recently.

Until FDR's death the event had been described verbally and was a preeminent occasion for dramaturgy. When McKinley died, Teddy Roosevelt, his vice president and a famous outdoorsman, was hunting in the Adirondacks. Messengers tracked him down and hustled him to Buffalo, the city where McKinley had been shot and where, after six days of counterproductive medical attention, he had died. There, in a private home, Roosevelt took the oath:

> It was in the subdued light that filtered through cathedral windows in the great front parlor of Ansley Wilcox's home at 641 Delaware avenue that President Roosevelt bowed his head and said: "I swear."
>
> There was a hush as deep as the silence of death when the ceremony was concluded and the new president, cool and calm as a statue, kissed the bible and taking up a gold-mounted pen signed the formal oath of office. (From a staff correspondent of the *Daily News,* "Roosevelt Takes Oath")

Here the reporter (under the generic byline, From a Staff Correspondent of the *Daily News*) performed like a novelist, although refraining from attributing states of mind to the various people (named exhaustively in a fairly typical catalog). The emphasis was on a combination of solemnity and confidence. The deep silence indicated the gravity of the occasion, and the coolness of the new president reassured all that the crisis was over as soon as it began. (Teddy Roosevelt, famous for his energy, was a good subject for reporters. Not so with the previous successor, Chester Arthur, who was described as almost "womanish" in his grief at Garfield's death.)

The Coolidge succession was similarly dramatic and more fully illustrated. Harding's unanticipated death found Coolidge visiting his family in New England, where his father, a notary public, administered the oath himself. The homeliness of the event rooted the stable succession in the molecular American family. The *New York Times* used two retrospective pictures of the dead president on August 3, 1923 (2–3), to frame the oath as an event: one of Harding on his way to the Inauguration and the other with his wife as they returned from the oath-taking and entered the Executive Mansion. The *Times* on August 24 (2) and the *Daily News* on August 6 (5) illustrated Coolidge's oath-taking by running a picture taken after the event, with the new president and his father at the Vermont farmhouse.

When FDR died, a picture ran in both newspapers showing Truman taking the oath. The wide shot, which became canonical, included the First Lady, the Chief Justice, and all the witnessing leaders assembled. The *Times* the same day ran a file photo of FDR's oath-taking, again with First Lady, leaders, and Chief Justice, with a prominently positioned flag (6). The pictures had a posed, iconic quality, much like a historical frieze.

Kennedy's oath-taking followed the Truman model almost exactly, except that the First Lady stood at the far left of her husband rather than immediately next to him, framing the picture on one side. The image ran inside the *Times* on the first day of the coverage, but the more pressing event, Johnson's oath of office, ran on the front page. Unlike Kennedy's formal oath-taking, this one occurred aboard the airplane in Dallas. Shot in close quarters, the picture shows only Johnson flanked by the new First Lady and several faces of witnessing leaders on one side. Jackie Kennedy stands prominently on his right, closest to the camera. The picture, from the Associated Press, appeared in both newspapers.

That image marks the completion of a shift from posed icons of a ritual event to the active dramatic moments preferred by journalism. In another sense, the use of oath imagery also followed a transformation of the act from a private or hidden, unseen ceremony (in the pictorial dimension) into a public ritual seen at close range (the LBJ picture is a medium shot). The repetition of images from wire services also reinforced the moment as a shared public memory.

## The News of the News

In all the reportage of all the deaths, newsfolk were everywhere. They turned up as crowds, in a deathwatch with Garfield in Long Branch, with McKinley in Buffalo, and with Harding in San Francisco. They filled the tightly packed cars in the Kennedy motorcade in Dallas and followed the funeral processions in swarms. They also turned up as intimates, chatting with doctors, relatives, heads of state, and, more and more often, with each other. At first they recounted what they saw. Later they recounted what they felt.

The reporters retreated as observers to the extent that photographers and then television cameras moved in. Reporters abandoned much of their descriptive function, even more so than this study indicates. Our sample features powerful events that inspire reporters to haul out and dust off old tricks.

Even the Kennedy assassination coverage included walking description, extensive fine detail, and a good deal of dramaturgy.

More and more, the reporter's tense had shifted from the present to the past primarily but also to the future. In the Kennedy coverage, reporters supplied whole volumes of retrospective and prospective material. If any type of story were to be signaled as the reporter's most important work, it would be the expert analysis, fully sourced, of the implications that change in administration might have for specific issues. That reporters were on holiday when doing dramaturgy, for instance, is indicated by the fact that they dramatized themselves, something they never would have done in analysis. That a reporter could admit grief while covering grief meant that grief was no longer the best beat and that mourning was not a weighty or momentous subject. A reporter would never, in contrast, admit to being a Republican while covering Republicans.

As reporters took to the future, they left the present to photographers and even more so to television. By the time of Kennedy's death, one of the most compelling stories concerned television. Coverage in both the *New York Times* and *Chicago Daily News* turned repeatedly to what was happening on television. The shooting existed as a shared newsreel, the primary text, upon which print journalists could comment and expound. Television news took over for four consecutive days of broadcasting on all three networks. All entertainment programming was canceled. No commercial spots ran. Newspapers reported these acts as primary events in the chronicle of the president's death. Both newspapers told the story of the public witnessing the shooting, the death, the swearing in, and the burial as the story of the public watching television. Reports spoke in glowing praise of broadcast news, fulfilling at last its promise—and tacitly eclipsing print.

## Conclusions

By deepening the understanding of how newspapers incorporated photography into their pages, this study also recasts the understanding of how newspapers responded to television. The conventional wisdom of journalistic circles would describe the changes as a result of the head-to-head competition between newspapers and television news in the late 1960s and early 1970s. The discovery of the (much earlier) origin of these shifts also critiques a naive narrative of technologically determined change.

News was transformed through two related processes. One involved the entry of pictures into the center of journalistic content, diminishing or entirely displacing some of the tasks of text. The other involved the shift of all news content away from the story-telling compendium and toward expert interpretation in the form of analysis buttressed by the evidence of history in words and images.

From the perspective of images, photography, as it grew out from the tradition of engraving, increasingly took on the values of journalism. Greater complexity emerged in the dialectic of form, that is, in the size, placement, and pose of images, as shown in the example of the relationship between the deceased president and his replacement. The period we studied also saw the growth of pictorial narrative, using collage first and then filling entire picture pages after the era of FDR. Pictorial representations shifted from static iconism to picture-as-content, as found in sources of imagery, beginning with stock campaign engravings and moving to journalist-produced candid shots.

Pictures adopted greater claims to status in the hierarchy of news values. Newspapers advertised scoops—the last picture or the latest picture. That change was accompanied by the loss of image-as-handicraft, not only the end of engraving and sketch art replaced by the supposedly mechanical photograph but also the disappearance of artists' signatures (which at first appeared within the photographs as autographs). Artists, like authors, were swallowed up in technical expertise.

Initially, textual reports performed many functions that illustrations subsequently either took over or eclipsed altogether. At the same time, new tasks were invented, especially that of prediction. Although the future tense was not absent in early reportage, it was usually confined to details of ceremonies (e.g., "the color guard of the 82nd infantry will follow the casket"). Over time, reporters began to speak confidently of a wider future, an aspect of the new long journalism.

An examination of text shows that it is too simple to say that the visual was missing until the rise of news photography in the twentieth century. Not only were there all sorts of ways of visually representing the news but there were also textual ways of presenting visions of events. Walking description, for example, incorporated imagery as well as motion.

It is also too simple to say that pre-photographic visual reproduction was technologically stunted photography. Scholars have taken the claim, almost universally advanced by early illustrated news periodicals, that photographs, even those reproduced by engraving, allow an immediate, real look at people and places, to mean that news illustrators were trying to do just that. In fact, the regime of news illustration that preceded the advent of halftone reproduction from photographic originals was itself a mature system and had its own guiding ideals. In that regime, the aim was to produce an authentic visual representation that was not only accurate but also lucid and uncluttered, and it was readily acknowledged that an artist must be responsible for that representation.

The intermediate regime explains the half-century lag between the popularization of photography and the printed reproduction of photographic images. The technological account of this development, although accurately and insightfully explaining the many chemical and mechanical impasses and solutions, assumes that all along everyone wanted halftones, when in fact the usefulness of photographs was far from obvious to most illustrated news. What journalists wanted was lucidity, pictures that spoke clearly and compellingly, the very effect most readily achieved by an artist's engraving carefully labeled "drawn from a photograph" to convey authenticity but at the same time freely adapted to make a point.

The full adoption of news photographs by the 1930s was therefore more ambiguous than is often acknowledged. It was the result of technological advance, of course, and also artistic innovation. It came about when news photographers learned how to make photographs as lucid as engravings. In that artistic sense, it meant the triumph as well as the defeat of the sensibility of the era of illustrated news.

The development of news illustration worked dialectically with the history of reporting. Illustrators and reporters worked to define and refine each others' tasks and create each others' claims to authority. After a long period of interaction, the reporter's task shifted from description to analysis, and the illustrator-turned-photographer took over the task of giving news its immediacy and emotional force. As an analyst, the reporter explains to the reader why things happen and what things are about to happen; the reporter's tenses are the past and the future. The photographer's tense is purely the present. The emergence of caption conventions, by the end of the period studied, imposed the strict use of the present tense.

Reportage has come to base its claim to authority on expertise, explaining a chain of events according to processes hidden from the casual observer. Photography bases its claim to authority on immediacy, on the conviction that nothing intervenes between a reader and a scene. In both cases the authority of the news presentation entails the effacement of the observer. Reportage—even in the most heavy-handed punditry—asserts that anyone expert enough (or "in the know") would give the same account. Photojournalism implies that a shot took itself, or at the very least that anyone present with a camera would have made the same picture. In neither case is the news person represented.

That the effacement of the observer accompanied the rise of the byline adds irony to this story. Bylines simultaneously assert authorship and guarantee that authorship does not matter. Reporters use them to take responsibility, but by signing articles they are certifying that they have not invented their reports. It is news that other professional reporters would also report. When a shooter puts his or her name to a news photo, the act does not mean "this is my vision." Rather, it means "I was there when it happened." Were it the photographer's vision, it would not be news. It would revert to art.

This study illuminates some neglected aspects of pre-photographic text and pictures and some previously unnoticed changes that photography accentuated. It also calls for a more respectful understanding of earlier news regimes. Our most compelling realization, however, was itself conventional. We found that the photographic images of the Kennedy assassination called to mind long-dormant emotions and anchored deep memories, not only for us but also for our colleagues and family members. The photographs triggered memories of a personal nature even as they bore witness to memories of a social or collective nature. The visual images were an archive of memory.

Our experience signals the trite fact that the shift to photography heightened the emotional register of the news. The early stories were moving at times but so thoroughly filtered as to render them safe, that is, unlikely to cause direct emotional distress. Even McKinley's decomposing corpse remained an icon of his office and history and therefore not a gross description. Kennedy, however, died in each citizen's living room (or in whatever intimate location). People saw the spatters of blood on Jacqueline Kennedy's leg, watched the restless three-year-old salute in his tiny jacket, and, more than any other image, saw the moment of death as if witnessing a murder of an acquaintance. Photography, and even more so television, in allowing individuals to see history in intimate settings, intertwines that history with personal memory and shifts the telling firmly into the realm of raw emotion, the filter hidden. It is little wonder that journalists fell to over-analyzing and interpreting.

## References

"All Chicago Mourns." 1901. *Chicago Daily News*, Sept. 14, 2.

Associated Press. 1923. "Death of President Comes Suddenly as Wife Reads to Him." *Chicago Daily News*, Aug. 3, 1.

———. 1944. "Last Words: 'I Have a Terrific Headache'." *Chicago Daily News*, April 13, 1.

Barnhurst, Kevin G. 1991. "The Great American Newspaper." *American Scholar* 60 (Winter): 106–12.

————. 1994. *Seeing the Newspaper*. New York: St. Martin's Press.

Barnhurst, Kevin G., and Diana Mutz. 1997. "American Journalism and the Decline of Event-Centered Reporting." *Journal of Communication* 47(4): 27–53.

Barnhurst, Kevin G., and John C. Nerone. 1991. "Design Changes in U.S. Front Pages, 1885–1985." *Journalism Quarterly* 68 (Winter): 796–804.

Baynes, Ken, ed. 1971. *Scoop, Scandal, and Strife: A Study of Photography in Newspapers*. New York: Pantheon.

Berger, Meyer. 1951. *The Story of the* New York Times, *1851–1951*. New York: Simon and Schuster.

"The First News of the Event: How the Newspaper Correspondents Got the Announcement." 1881. *New York Times*, Sept. 20, 1.

From a Staff Correspondent of the *Daily News*. "Roosevelt Takes Oath." 1901. *Chicago Daily News*, Sept. 14, 1.

Graber, Doris A. 1993. *Mass Media and American Politics*. 4th. ed. Washington: Congressional Quarterly Press.

Hallin, Daniel C. 1994. *We Keep America on Top of the World*. London: Routledge.

Hicks, Wilson. 1952. *Words and Pictures: An Introduction to Photojournalism*. New York: Harper.

"How the News Was Received in New York." *New York Times*, Sept. 7, 1901, 2.

"It Is Ended: The Death-Bed." 1881. *Chicago Daily News*, Sept. 20, 1.

Iyengar, Shanto. 1991. *Is Anyone Responsible? How Television Frames Political Issues*. Chicago: University of Chicago Press.

"The Last View." 1881. *Chicago Daily News*, Sept. 22, 1.

Miller, Bruce [UPI]. 1963. "Team of Fifteen Doctors Strove to Save Kennedy at the Hospital." *New York Times*, Nov. 30, 10.

"Mrs. McKinley's Grief Is Uncontrollable." 1901. *New York Times*, Sept. 16, 2.

Nerone, John C., and Kevin G. Barnhurst. 1995. "Visual Mapping and Cultural Authority: Design Change in U.S. Newspapers, 1920–1940." *Journal of Communication* 45(2): 9–43.

Patterson, Thomas E. 1993. *Out of Order*. New York: Knopf.

"President Shot at Buffalo Fair: How the Deed Was Done." 1901. *New York Times*, Sept. 7, 1.

Schudson, Michael. 1982. "The Politics of Narrative Form: The Emergence of News Conventions in Print and Television." *Daedalus* 3(4): 97–112.

Special to the *New York Times*. "People across U.S. Voice Grief and Revulsion." 1963. *New York Times*, Sept. 23, 11.

Staff Correspondent. "Mourn in Home City." 1901. *Chicago Daily News*, Sept. 18, 1.

Steele, Catherine A., and Kevin G. Barnhurst. 1996. "The Journalism of Opinion: Network Coverage in U.S. Presidential Campaigns, 1968–1988." *Critical Studies in Mass Communication* 13(3): 187–209.

Szarkowski, John. 1966. *The Photographer's Eye*. New York: Museum of Modern Art.

"Whole Nation in Grief." 1901. *Chicago Daily News*, Sept. 13, 1.

Wicker, Tom. 1963. "Kennedy and Reporters." *New York Times*, Nov. 24, 12.

# 4

## Reflections on an Editor

*John Erickson*

The photograph is both mirror and window declared the title of an exhibition at New York's Museum of Modern Art some years ago. Is it a "mirror, reflecting a portrait of the artist who made it, or a window through which one might better know the world?" asked the museum's then-director of the Department of Photography (Sander 1989, 9). Seeing through the photograph to some broader slice of the social or seeing instead glimpses of the person behind the camera are but two of the simulacra offered up by a photograph. When a photograph stands at some point distant in time from a viewer, perhaps the more apt metaphor would be that of the palimpsest. At one level, the photograph depicts a scene, frozen at some point in the past, and exists as a testament to a historical status of photographic technology. But the literal, physical image itself has a lived history—one that may have added layers of additional meaning along the way.

Lighting requirements and the need for subject matter to remain motionless during the prolonged exposure period in the early years of photography restricted not just what could be photographed but where. The daguerreotype (fig. 4.1), we are told, depicts an editor and was taken during the 1850s. For any more information we must ask the photograph itself. The backdrop

*Figure 4.1.* "Editor" (artist unknown). 1994.90.5. Daguerreotype with applied color (¼ plate), ca. 1855. 3¼ x 4¼ in. (8.3 x
10.8 cm). (National Museum of American Art, Smithsonian
Institution, Gift of Charles Isaacs)

and setting suggest not the editor's place of work but one of the hundreds of photographers' studios that had come to populate large and not-so-large urban settings. We cannot see the neck brace that likely helped the subject hold his head steady during the long exposure time required for the image to be fixed on the fragile glass-plate negative. A thin smile was the most frequent alternative to a strictly somber pose at the time. A more animated expression would be difficult to hold for so long.

What, then, can the photograph tell of this editor and his work? Inquiry must be made with care, and possible answers treated with a certain degree of caution. The daguerreotype, like other photographic images, is not just a mirror in the metaphoric sense. It literally produced a mirror image of its subject. The only way for a daguerreotype to depict other than a reversed image was for the photographer to shoot the desired image in a mirror—take a picture of the reflection of the object. Apparently that technique was sometimes used when photographing small objects, especially when they contained lettering that would be visible. The era of daguerreotyography is filled with accounts of consternation caused by this technical property of the medium. Care was taken to avoid elements in a picture that would cause confusion when seen in mirror image. For example, one daguerreotype of the period shows a group of soldiers pledging allegiance to the flag. The resulting picture, of course, shows all the men with their hands covering the wrong sides of their chests.

The editor in figure 4.1 is poised over proofs, pen in hand and ready to edit the copy. But in which hand does the quill reside? If the picture mirrors reality, the man is left-handed. If the man was left-handed and only appears right-handed because of daguerreotype's peculiar way of reflecting the world, then consternation would result in all who viewed the image and knew the editor. Perhaps he and photographer conspired to fool the reflected reality by having the editor pose with the quill in his left hand, thus producing the correct final impression. Can we assume this degree of self-consciousness regarding manipulating a reflected image? Perhaps not, but two things can be said. First, the picture was not taken by shooting the image of the editor as reflected in a mirror. As can be seen under magnification, the letters in the title of the volume on the table are reversed. Second, although it might be a blemish on the daguerreotype, there seem to be ink stains on the fingers of what in the picture is the editor's left hand.

Whether left- or right-handed, and to whatever degree we have been manipulated in this regard by the image-making, the working utensils of an editor in the 1850s are distributed around the young man. There is the quill rack so extra pens can be at the ready. In this case, only two extra quills are prepared, and it does not appear that the editor anticipates an extended work session. The inkwell, paste pot, proof sheets, blotting pad, and scissors all await the editor's hand—whether left or right. But what of the daguerreotype that just happens to be leaning with its image facing the camera? Where does it fit into the editor's work?

The presence of the daguerreotype atop the stacked books is reason for pause. At mid-century, the technology of printing did not allow for the reproduction of photographs in texts. For a short period that began in the 1850s, when producing photographs on paper through the collodion and other processes that had been introduced into general use, pictures were sometimes artificially inserted into texts. In 1853 the *Photographic Art Journal* bound an early paper photograph as a separate page in the periodical in order to share an example of this innovation with readers. During the next decade, book publishers occasionally would insert a paper photograph into text by pasting a picture onto a blank page of each book. There was no way, however, for daguerreotypes to be reproduced directly in print.

How then do we account for the daguerreotype being so prominently displayed in this picture? It could be there strictly for personal reasons, in which case the editor had a seriously underdeveloped sense of arranging his work space. It could be there because he was considering using it as the basis for a woodcut to be used in his publication. It also could be there because the setting is, after all, a photographic studio and there likely are many daguerreotypes around the premises. Although the state of printing technology at the time can tell us what the picture is not being used for, its precise role in the scene remains illusive. It is an image within an image that remains mute.

Just what is it that this editor edits? His clothing marks him as of the 1850s, but more likely of middle than upper class status. The soft fur hat, although fashionable, was not unusual. The added plume suggests an air or attitude that might distinguish him from the general crowd. The weighty tomes on the desk, one volume being a political autobiography, suggest that he might edit some political publication. Perhaps his voice was the American equivalent of those British leader writers who thundered regularly the vision of Victorian certainty. Maybe the plume and the pipe bespoke the editorial leadership of periodic literature for the smart set. And what do we make of the playing cards that have been allowed to remain (or are strategically placed) at the edge of the table within full view of the camera lens? We may be hard-pressed to say with any certainty what he edited, but the bits and pieces available allow the conclusion that he likely was not the editor of one of the many religious publications that had come on the scene by the 1850s.

What clues have we as to his economic status? Although the widespread development of daguerreotyography had made portraiture no longer the exclusive province of the very wealthy, it was not something that most people experienced very often. The quarter-plate shown here measured about three by four inches and easily was the most popular size of the day. It typically sold for between $4 and $5 in the early 1850s. The cost of this particular portrait would have been higher because color was added to it by hand. Because the price of the picture, without any addition of color, equaled what a skilled worker such as a carpenter or a blacksmith earned in four days, there clearly were still sharp economic boundaries on who could afford to be photographed and how often. This would seem to suggest that the editor was a man of some means, or at least was not a menial editorial worker who would have earned little more than a general clerk.

Here again, the mirror of the world is less than totally clear. How many of the items in the picture really belonged to the editor? How much might he have packed up from his office and carted into the photographic studio just to add realistic detail to the picture setting? The paste pot and inkwell would require special handling so as not to be spilled. The quill rack would be bulky, as would the books. The books would be heavy as well. Yet perhaps most of the objects already were on the premises. Perhaps the photographer shared quarters or at least the same building with some editorial venture and the editor merely worked there. Perhaps he did not set the editorial tone for his publication after all. Perhaps he was a man of no more than nominal means. Perhaps his pipe and plume testified to his aspirations rather than his station. Perhaps, in the end, he was a friend of the photographer, worked in the same building, and sat for this picture because of that association rather than his economic well-being.

Did he thunder the opinion of his age, or did he correct grammar and oversee the allocation of adjectives? To these questions our window remains dark. What we are able to glimpse, at least, is a man who does not appear beaten down by life. His eye and line of mouth hint that we may not know quite what it is we see. It is a face that encourages, maybe even teases, us to reflect on what it is we think we know.

## Reference

Sandler, Martin W. 1989. *American Image in Photography: One Hundred Fifty Years in the Life of a Nation.* Chicago: Contemporary Books.

# ∎ 5

## From the Image of Record
## to the Image of Memory:
## Holocaust Photography,
## Then and Now

*Barbie Zelizer*

One of the least understood dimensions of photography involves the ways in which photographs help the public construct, understand, and remember the past. This chapter discusses the popular reliance on photographs as a filter on the past by examining Holocaust photography and its recycling. Using published photographs of the liberation of the Nazi concentration camps in 1945 as a forum for discussing the cogency of photography over time, the chapter argues that photographs have helped create a specific kind of memory about the Holocaust that inflects both how it is remembered and how its memory shapes popular experience of other atrocities of the modern age.

The shared visual memory of the atrocities of World War II is in part a naturalized recollection whose discussion has been both vivid and sustained. While cultural critics as varied as Theodor Adorno (1973, 362), Jean-François Lyotard (1988, 56–57), and George Steiner (1969, 123) have continued to lament the difficulties in finding a way to express what happened in the Nazi concentration camps, atrocity photos have demonstrated a haunting capacity to linger long beyond the journal, newsmagazine, or newspaper that first displayed them.[1] Perhaps the best known of all contemporary statements attesting to their power was that of Susan Sontag, who first saw the visuals as a young girl: "When I looked at those photographs, something broke. Some limit had been reached, and not only that of horror; I felt irrevocably grieved, wounded, but a part of my feelings started to tighten; something went dead; something is still crying" (1977, 20).

This chapter is intended to address the mechanisms that help the public remember in a way often similar to that described by Sontag. It is an extension of the work of French scholar Maurice Halbwachs (1980 [1950]), who in the tradition of Emile Durkheim and George Herbert Mead emphasized the shared dimensions of the act of remembering. Halbwachs's premise, since adopted by many others, stipulated that memory is a fundamentally social activity accomplished not in the privacy of one's gray matter but via a shared consciousness that molds it to the agendas of those who invoke it. To quote one memory scholar, collective memory is a tool "not of retrieval but of reconfiguration [that] colonizes the past by obliging it to conform to present configurations" (Hutton 1988, 314). It acts as a kind of history-in-motion, moving at a different pace and rate than traditional history and thriving on remaking the past into material with contemporary resonance.

The shared memory of Nazi atrocities has been in large part tied up with the atrocity photos published in the U.S. and British press once the concentration camps were liberated in April of 1945, a period of dramatic changes in journalism in the United States and Britain. The rising status of the image in news was generating tension with its main competitor, the word. Although photographs had been around for nearly a hundred years, at the time of World War II they were still considered largely a feature of yellow journalism. Photographers were called "pictorial reporters" or "newspaper illustrators" rather than photojournalists, and images were seen as adjunct carriers of information that needed the intervention of journalists to make sense (Zelizer 1995a, 1995b). Yet with the camps' liberation, the press needed to establish an authoritative record of what it was seeing, and images became central in doing so. For many, pictures offered the crowning proof of what the liberating forces saw.

During the liberation the press was called upon to shape public belief, opinion, and action in a way that challenged most expectations of what had been happening inside the camps. Although there had been rumors of Nazi atrocity and horror, only when members of the press entered the camps and sent back documentation of what they found there was the distant public moved beyond skepticism. Yet were they ready to do so? This chapter argues that they were not. The press had not sufficiently thought out how to process images as news, and photographers had not yet organized standards of common practice. From the vantage point of the evolution of journalism, it was here that the record of the liberation becomes particularly interesting. Tensions between word and image, reporter and photographer, rested at the foundation of what was seen on the camps' liberation, and, by implication, they remained at the core of what is still remembered about the camps.

## Photography on the Eve of World War II

The record of the liberation of the camps was produced on the back of tremendous technological advancement clouded by considerable professional ambivalence concerning the ascent of photographs in news. Newsreels, radio, and faster and better wire service connections for reporters were co-opted in photography by faster lenses, smaller cameras, flashbulbs, and, by 1935, an improved means of transmission: wirephoto. But photographers and reporters did not process technological advancement equally. It was, said one editor, a time filled with "doubt and uncertainty" (cited in Stott 1973, 79). News organizations closed, and polls in the United States declared that one in three individuals disbelieved what they read in newspapers (cited in Marzolf 1991, 134). Photography, in contrast, was experiencing great popular appeal. The success of documentary photographers during the early 1930s; photography's co-optation in films, newsreels, and the tabloid press; and experimental picture formats of certain photographers all showed that it was possible to use the photograph for important social aims. That notion had direct bearing on news photography.

That is not to say that either reporters or photographers were very interested in the other. Photographers were curiously indifferent to the idea of accommodating images to current events. Even as World War II was enveloping more of the so-called free world, photographers remained indifferent to what they could do to join the war effort. As late as 1941, trade journals focused on joining camera clubs rather than the military and on tourist photography of Toledo and Madrid rather than documenting the Spanish civil war (Mason 1939; "Why Join?" 1941).

Journalists were also ambivalent about images. They knew that they needed them, but they also knew that images set in place another language that could ultimately undermine the authority of words. Issues of photographic representation began to be addressed at professional forums both in Britain and the United States, including the British Institute of Journalists, the National Union of Journalists, the American Society of Newspaper Editors (ASNE), and the American Association of Teachers of Journalism, and by 1938 dailies reported that the use of photographic cuts had increased 40 percent since 1931; still, it was only partial homage (Brandenburg 1938, 8).

Some reporters argued that photographs should be denounced altogether, saying that "we're on our way backward to a language of pictures, to the Stone Age of human intelligence" (Brown 1938, 404, 408). The work of photographers, said one British journalist, "is important and valuable but it is *not* journalism, and I am not prepared to receive them as journalistic colleagues" (Higginbottom 1935, 119). Other news organizations advised reporters to begin carrying cameras, and courses were set up to train them in photography ("Gannett Reporters" 1932; Price 1944b, 52). But the pictures they produced were of "chinless women, headless men, and tipsy buildings" (Blanchard 1935, 57). And while certain editors told their reporters to snap three shots of everything "in hopes that at least one could succeed," others discarded the use of certain types of cameras because they proved too complicated for reporters to handle (Blanchard 1935, 58). Still other reporters deflated the importance of photography, constructing it as a medium of record and arguing that pictures would be an "adjunct of the daily news" that would help journalists better report the news (Stanley 1937, 5). Photography, said one British editor intent on resisting suggestions that British photographers join the National Union of Journalists, was in "complete parallel with machine typesetting" and nothing more (Higginbottom 1935, 119).

So reporters in the press admitted photography but only in predetermined ways, as "fillers and story illustrations, but not a principal method of telling the news" (Kany 1947, 10). What was emphasized was photography's role in providing a medium of record that catered to its referentality, indexicality, and ability to reference a real-life object. What was undermined was the image's cogency as a symbolic tool and its universality, generalizability, and ability to position a real-life referent within a larger interpretive scheme. That meant that journalists, in inviting photographers into their midst, emphasized the former over the latter. They welcomed photographs only so long as they figured they would help denote things happening in the real world, playing an indexical role in news rather than an interpretive one. It was assumed that photography could help bolster journalism's authority for relaying the events of real life, supporting its aspirations toward objectivity and helping reporters become better journalists—or at least so went the refrain before the war.

Yet atrocity photos were produced through an inversion of that logic. Photographs became effective ways of marking Holocaust atrocities by playing less to their effectivity as referential documents of a specific camp, in a

specific place and time, and more to their effectivity as symbols of the atrocities at their most generalized and universal level.

## Photographs as Document and Symbol

The liberation of concentration camps at the end of the war came in the
middle of the birth of modern news photography. Although Russian forces
had been involved in liberating some camps on the Eastern Front in earlier
months, the involvement of U.S. and British liberating forces did not occur
until April 1945. At the side of front-line commanders went photographers
and reporters who documented what the liberating forces were seeing.

The circumstances for documenting the scenes of the camps were difficult,
however, and much photographic documentation resembled a situation of
"making do" on the part of amateur, semiprofessional, and professional pic-
ture-takers. Photographs were of varying quality, often the result of bad
weather, faulty equipment, and uneven training and experience. As Sgt. W.
Lawrie, a photographer with the British Army Film and Photographic Unit
said, "We did what [we] saw at the time" (cited in Caiger-Smith 1988, 11).
Many photographs lacked standardization and did not contain delineating
features such as captions, credits, or a precise relationship with the texts they
accompanied. That meant that the U.S. and British press often provided in-
adequate visualization of what was happening in the camps.

To an extent, the lack of standardization in news photographs of the time
mattered less than it might have in documenting other events of the war. The
press was acting within a larger mission that concerned the documentation
of atrocities. Not only did different kinds of reporters and photographers
need to cooperate with each other in order to join the war effort, as has been
argued about the reportage of World War II in general (Marwick 1982), but
the press also needed to bear witness to what it was seeing—to take responsibility for what was seen and respond. That mandate was set in place when
Gen. Dwight Eisenhower visited the camps, was horrified, and commanded
the press to "let the world see." The press complied at once, and reporters
and photographers within a hundred miles of the camps changed direction
to tour them. Bearing witness, then, imposed a moral obligation on those
recording the camps' liberation that went beyond the professional mores
surrounding either journalism or photography.

How did these parameters shape the pictures of the camps that appeared?
One spread that appeared in *Picture Post* in October 1941 conveyed the broad
boundaries by which the experience of Nazi oppression was typically depicted. Affixed to an article entitled "The Terror in Europe," the text used

eight uncredited images, none of their origins clear, to illustrate life under the Nazis. Each photograph depicted a moment of oppression and was captioned by one-word phrases such as "Starvation!" or "Hanging!" The first image was a reprint of an eight-year-old photograph of Nazi policemen on the roof of a building. "This is an old picture," the caption read. "The date on its back is 1933. We publish it just because it is a picture of 1933. For in that year, Nazis . . . began to hold down the free elements inside Germany" (Walker 1941, 7–13). The photographic image had been deployed less for its news value than for its valence as a symbolic marker.

Two other photographs in the series bear closer examination. One, captioned "Horror!," showed two weeping women (fig. 5.1). The subcaption read: "Their homes burnt. Their men killed. Their country crushed under the jackboot. These Polish women weep, as millions weep in the occupied territories."

The photograph carried no identifiable place or date, no definitive details about the individuals being depicted, and no credit or other information about the individual or agency who took the shot. It also had no direct relationship with the text that accompanied it. The lack of definitive or referential detailing created ambiguity about the reason for the pictures coming

*Figure 5.1.* Polish women weeping, October 1941. (AP/Wide World Photos)

together other than the fact that they illustrated the Germans' war machinery. The images made better sense within a broad interpretive scheme about Nazi brutality than within a tight frame documenting a specific instance of violence.

Yet another photograph in the series showed a similarly generic depiction of brutality: a close-up shot of a Nazi guard facing down a group of prisoners. The caption told readers of "The concentration camp! The rule of the rubber truncheon! The rule of the barbed wire fence. Inside the Third Reich alone, there were 100,000 victims in concentration camps in 1938. Now there are camps all over Europe" (Walker 1941, 9, 8). The image lacked referential indices because nowhere did the caption specifically mention a certain camp, a certain action, or a certain date. In retrospect its almost civilized pose of the Nazi guard and prisoners conveyed little of the horror that would soon characterize photos of the camps, yet at the time such a photograph was typical of the available documentation.

Equally important to what was presented was what was not shown. No identified place or date accompanied the photographs, there were no definitive details about the people being depicted, nor were there any credit lines. The images depicted generalized moments of suffering, but the relationship between the pictures and the accompanying text remained ambiguous.

This thrust away from the contingent details of what was being photographically depicted characterized most photographs of Nazi atrocities. Many photos lost their referentiality in face of their invocation as symbols, their connection chipped away as they became less definitive indices of a specific place or location and became more general reminders of the atrocities of Nazism. It was within the move from referentiality to universality that the pictures became particularly meaningful. Within a general story about the German war machinery it mattered little where in Germany a specific picture had been taken. What remained important was that the picture depicted life under the Nazis. Yet referentiality was what journalism was expecting photography to uphold, suggesting an inversion of what it was expected to do for journalism.

The tension between referentiality and symbolism became clearest when considering the difficulties reporters faced in recording the story of the liberation. They offered concrete narratives grounded in particular details of a camp's terrain or in the accounts of real people. These narratives, in themselves an index of referentiality, were accompanied by basic problems of credibility. Who could believe what these reporters had to tell? They began to deal with the deficiencies of their reportage by making comments that admitted insufficiencies of language, genre, and words themselves. The atrocities, said one, went beyond words: "I dare not, I cannot write the whole story" (Ditton 1945). Buchenwald was "more horrible than the printed description" said another (Hibbs 1945, 22). Reporters underscored how difficult it was for them to process what they saw into plausible narratives. Bearing witness involved concretized narratives pitched closely to the details of what was being witnessed.

It was here that images came into play. They extended the authority of the press by being used as confirmatory tools that upheld the veracity of what news organizations needed to report. The photographs that became available on liberation were too numerous and varied to be published in any U.S. or British publication at any one time. Scores of photographers, professional, semi-professional, and amateur as well as soldiers bearing cameras, accompanied the liberating forces into the camps and took snapshot after snapshot of Nazi brutality. Yet as with reporters, the photographers faced an inherent limitation on the representativeness of the images they took. On the one hand, the fact that images froze moments in time worked against their ability to represent what was happening, with photographs of the camps' liberation portraying not the Holocaust itself but rather a partial depiction of its final phase. What photographers were able to depict in the concentration camps provided only a small picture of the consequences of years of forced torture, harassment, and eventual death. Few photographs of the camps in the period before liberation had been available—fewer still of the death camps on the Eastern Front. Many images portrayed only one post-liberation moment that depicted varying configurations of life and death, freedom and depravation. As Mavis Tate, a British M.P., commented, "You can photograph results of suffering but never suffering itself" ("Europe's Problem" 1945, 25).

While journalists used words to bear witness by turning the story into a concrete and grounded chronicle of the liberation itself, photographs were used to position targets of depiction within a larger story of Nazi atrocity. Doing so derived from a recognition that images were instrumental to the broader aim of enlightening the Western world about what the Nazis had done. When Eisenhower proclaimed "let the world see," he implicitly called upon photographs to help him accomplish that aim. It was photography's aura of realism that could convey the "appropriate truth about atrocity" (Taylor 1991, 56). Like words, photographic images could help the world bear witness. Photography did so by drawing upon its dual function as carrier of truth-value and as symbol, helping the public come to grips with the meaning of the events at the same time they saw them.

Photography's role in documenting the camps immediately underscored the difference between images and words. As with words, photographs represented scenes that pushed the boundaries of representation and did not convey the enormity or extent of what had happened. "I have written [this] only because I thought I ought to," said one observer in an author's note to an editor three months after visiting Buchenwald. *"Au fond* I don't like horrors any more than you do. It probably won't be believed—even with the dozens of photographs I have taken" (Codman 1945, 54).

Pictures offered graphic representations of atrocity that were difficult to deny. Photographers, one reporter claimed, "sent pictures so horrible that no newspaper normally would use them, but they were less horrible than the reality" (Denny 1945, 9). They were "irrefutable evidence of Nazi degradation and brutality" ("Long Rows of German Victims" 1945, 8M). Photographs captured the atrocities in an explicit, and therefore potentially persuasive, manner and appeared to intervene less with the target of depiction than did words. Rather than authenticate the unbelievable details of the camps by pitching concrete accounts closely to the events they described, images constituted a device of representation that could be used to interpret at the same time that it depicted. That meant that words were most effective in telling a grounded story of liberation, but images were able to present a broader story of Nazi atrocity.

Thus, images flourished as a mode of documenting the camps, and these stark, naturalistic representations of horror became readily available in large numbers after liberation. Turning out roll after roll of film, photographers relentlessly depicted the worst of Nazism: bodies turned at odd angles to each other, charred skulls, ovens full of ashes, and weeping German civilians alongside massive human carnage. Within days of the arrival of photographers in the camps wire services were flooded with explicit and gruesome snapshots of horror the likes of which had never before been seen on the pages of the U.S. and British daily and weekly press.

The images did not often bear a definitive link to the stories they illustrated. One typical photograph was used alongside the official report compiled on the liberation of Buchenwald in April 1945. While the verbal report constituted one of the most detailed (and indexically powerful) narratives of the camps, presenting verbatim numbers, routines, death counts, and horrific procedures in considerable detail, the picture that accompanied it showed little more than three gaunt men and the caption offered little information ("Official Report" 1945, 9). There was no date, no attribution, and little identification of the objects of the camera. The public viewed the image and knew little about who the men were, where the picture was taken, or who took it. Even at the time of the liberation a different degree of detailing was expected from images and words. Pictures were set up as universal accompaniments to the boldly indexical narratives at their side. Again, it was a reversal of the role expected of photographs in news.

How else was the thrust toward symbolism achieved? First, it was achieved through captions. It is important to remember that photographers had not sufficiently thought out the ways in which news captions differed from other kinds of titles for other kinds of photographs. It was not even clear whether photographers were responsible for titling the pictures they submitted. And so captions often bore a mystical quality that left their relationship to the image unclear. One set of photos of a stack of human bodies, depicted alongside a crouching U.S. army major, appeared twice within a week in two separate U.S. publications, *Newsweek* and *Time*. The same stack of bodies was identified as being at two different camps: Buchenwald and Ohrdruf (Knauth 1945, 42; Newman 1945, 52). On the level of referentiality—that is, an image's ability to denote a specific action in a specific time and place—the caption specifying Buchenwald was wrong. Yet on the level of the image's universality, that wrong information mattered little. At a more general level the image provided proof of the atrocities, even if they were labeled as being in the wrong place.

Symbolism was also achieved through the lack of identification of either photographers or photographic agencies. Photographers throughout the war lamented the lack of accreditation they were accorded. Sometimes their pictures were given no credits, and sometimes the credits were buried at the back of a journal or newspaper. Only in rare cases did a photographer actually see his or her name published, and the best scenario for which most could hope was getting the name of their photographic agency into print. In mid-April 1945 the *Illustrated London News,* for instance, thought enough of a four-page supplement on the atrocities to detach more than twenty pictures from the journal and added a cautionary note to keep them shielded from children. Yet it did not think enough of the photos to accredit even one ("German Atrocities" 1945).

Photographers were not happy about the lack of accreditation. One even went on record in a trade journal, complaining of the second-class status they seemed to receive from news organizations to the extent that they only received credits for truly remarkable pictures (Price 1944a, 64). Throughout the war, conflicting directives circulated that called on the various military, service, and news organizations to lend credit to either photographic agencies or the photographers themselves. All of this was problematic because it helped chip away at a certain moral authority surrounding the initial recording as news. Similar deficiencies and contradictions in the original photographic record are still exploited frequently by those seeking to deny that the Holocaust ever happened.

Finally, symbolism was achieved through presentations that seemed to suggest that events depicted in the photographs could have taken place anywhere in the Third Reich and any time under its reign. In the British journal *Picture Post*, for instance, pictures were set up in ways that forced them to extend the meaning of the accompanying text substantially beyond the text itself. One six-page article appeared on May 5, 1945, under the title "The Problem That Makes All Europe Wonder" and recounted the importance of the atrocity photos: "A flood of news-pictures, a crop of unforgettable first-hand accounts of conditions in German concentration camps, have set Europe and the world asking one question: How is it possible?" (7). Yet despite the strong lead-in the images were used as accessories to text that boldly used a question-and-answer format. The pictures remained symbolic markers of the problem in its broadest form. At the top of the page were silhouettes—identified neither as individuals or groups—and readers were told nothing of the individuals' location or who was depicting them. The only information provided was that they were "Inside the Wire." The questionable linkage between picture and text was again a given rather than an aberration of the camps' coverage. Thus the photographs were invoked less as identifiable markers of specific activities and more as representative indices of general wartime circumstances. Images were pushed from fulfilling the role of referentiality to that of symbolism surrounding the war and the potential for human evil.

The image's symbolic quality was also achieved by universalizing the content of the atrocity story. Visual discourse was pushed from a specific reference to one camp or one victim to a universal discussion about the atrocities at all the camps. For instance, images generalized the territory of the camps not by tracking concrete routes to crematoriums as reporters did but by using one image of one camp to illustrate generic stories about the atrocities, thus generalizing the territory at hand. One such example involved a courtyard shot of rows of bodies at Nordhausen. The shot, which appeared in numerous newspapers, news magazines, and journals, was produced through revealing documentary patterns. Both the *Times of London* and the *Boston Globe* published it, but with no credit. The *Boston Globe* printed the picture on April 17 but said it had been taken on April 12. The *Washington Post* printed it ten days later (April 27) but did not mention that it had been taken earlier. The caption in most cases admitted that the photograph had been taken at Nordhausen, but in at least one case the same image was affixed to an article about the camp at Ohrdruf ("At Nordhausen" 1945, 6; "Bodies in Nordhausen" 1945). The *Picture Post* used it along with eleven other photographs, only two of which, both from Nordhausen, were identified by location ("Problem That Makes" 1945, 7–11). Thus images of territory created strong links between many locales of suffering under the Nazis, links partly lost in the concrete verbal reports of journalists. In that way the locale of one specific camp and action became representative of the larger terrain of the Nazi regime.

Images also presented variegated representations of the act of bearing witness. Four types of witnesses were depicted: reporters and photographers, soldiers, German civilians, and foreign officials. In each case, images stood for the many years of war in which witnesses to atrocities had come forward but were generally disbelieved. Pictures of a delegation of journalists and editors that visited the camps shortly after liberation, for example, were circulated widely following the junket (fig. 5.2).

*Figure 5.2.* American editors visiting Buchenwald, April 16, 1945. (National Archives and Records Administration)

What was odd about the image was what was not seen—whatever the reporters were looking at. The photo showed people viewing the atrocities but not the atrocities themselves. It was a way of prolonging or freezing the act of witnessing in a way not possible in the narratives of reporters, where witnessing became a part of a more chronological, ordered textual representation. In fact, the pattern of depicting witnesses and not atrocities extended to all types of witnesses. Similarly, readers saw picture after picture of people looking at pictures, whether POWs being forced to look at the photographic evidence, German citizens looking at photographs, or British nationals on the home front brought in to examine the visual evidence. Such shots not only displayed the horror of the atrocities and the centrality of the act of witnessing but also underscored the primacy of photography as a preferred tool for recording the parameters of the event.

Thus, visual representations of both witnesses and territory underscored links with broader interpretive schema by which it was possible to universalize what had happened. The same features in the hands of reporters closed interpretation by grounding the narratives in the here and now. In one, interpretation was closed off; in the other, it was opened up.

How did this relate to the original accommodation of images by which reporters marked the photographs as referential indices? In a sense, it inverted them. Because standards for using photographs had not been sufficiently thought out, the press inadvertently allowed the photograph's symbolic force to flourish over its referential dimensions. One final example illustrating the thrust away from referentiality can be found in *Stars and Stripes* ("The Pictures Don't Lie" 1945, 2). Intended as a rebuttal to lingering claims that atrocity photos had been faked or otherwise forged, the article tackled the authenticity of images. But the image it used to illustrate its claim was telling for its own lack of referential traits. The image that depicted the burned corpse of an unidentified laborer was uncaptioned and unattributed. Although the photograph, a depiction of a slave laborer, was in fact from the Signal Corps and had arrived over the wires complete with extensive documentation that said it had been taken in Leipzig, such documentation did not gain entry into the press, even in a piece on the authenticity of pictures.

If that was the case at the time of the liberation, it has persisted even more so ever since. An uneven attentiveness to the details of a given photograph at the time of its original recording has enhanced its status as a symbol over time. Memory work concerning the Holocaust has capitalized on the dimensions of photography set in place at the time of the camps' liberations.

Generalizeability, universality, and different interpretive schema have all made sense as the frames through which to remember Nazi atrocities. Atrocity photos have become particularly viable vehicles for shaping different acts of recollection. They have continued to do in memory what they did at the time of the camps' liberations—to move the atrocity story from the contingent and particular to the symbolic and abstract.

One image of liberated prisoners at Ebensee, taken on May 7, 1945, for example, has been used many times over, not the least of which in a *Newsweek* article thirty years later. The article discussed a gathering of Holocaust survivors in New York City, and the picture was captioned "Survivors on Liberation Day" (Woodward 1975). There was no mention of Ebensee or of any of the other details that had initially accompanied the image. The photo also appeared as an index of the camps' liberations under such captions as "Concentration Camp Survivors" (Adler 1983, 62); "Prisoners on Liberation Day" (Woodward 1975, 72); or, wrongly, "Death Camp Survivors" (Woodward 1980, 97). The same picture was used as the cover for the catalog to the U.S. Holocaust Memorial Museum's ongoing exhibit on the liberation of the camps. There, too, it was captioned "Liberation 1945" (*Liberation 1945* 1995, cover photo).

This rather hearty thrust toward using photographs as symbols rather than as tools of referential documentation suggests that photographs and photography entered newswork precisely along the least expected fault lines for doing so. The fact that photographs resonated as symbols not only as reportage but also as a mode of remembering suggests the need for a closer examination of the way in which they become co-opted in memory work. It is worthwhile to examine the ways in which two specific photographs have been recycled in memory: a Signal Corps photo of the Buchenwald barracks and one by Margaret Bourke-White of a group of men behind the barbed wire of Buchenwald.

## The Buchenwald Barracks Photograph

A picture of the Buchenwald barracks has been one of the most frequently recycled photos from the camps (fig. 5.3). At each instance of recycling the disjunctions between the image of record and the image of memory have become clear.

The image originally appeared in both the *New York Times* and the *Los Angeles Times* in 1945 and depicts prisoners leaning against bunks (Denny 1945, 9; "Hitler's Slaves" 1945, 3). Titled simply "Slave Laborers at Buchenwald," it quickly resurfaced appended to various other publications ("Racks

*Figure 5.3.* Survivors in Buchenwald barracks, April 16, 1945.
(National Archives and Records Administration)

for Slave Workers" 1945, 18; "Report on German Murder Mills" 1945, 8). Attributed to the Signal Corps and various press associations but not to a
specific photographer, the picture had already moved from signifying
Buchenwald's liberation to signifying the liberation in general. Readers were
told that they were looking at freed slave laborers in an unidentified camp.
It was thus not surprising that the same image turned up in later literature
on the Holocaust marking the liberation story but not Buchenwald. *Newsweek*'s cover story on the fiftieth anniversary of the liberation of Auschwitz
spoke of that camp in its text, but the picture depicted Buchenwald (Nagorski
1995, 58–59). The photograph appeared alongside Holocaust recollections by
Elie Wiesel, who appeared in the shot. The familiar discrepancy between the
place of the text and the place of the image was in this case transported into
memory.

An eradication of the original details associated with the photograph was
more often than not the case. Over time, the image moved even farther from
the scene it originally depicted as visualizing atrocities was invoked to sig-
nify a wide range of treatments of the war that included articles about Holocaust deniers, Holocaust education, and so-called Holocaust politics. One
journal repeated earlier errors of interpretation when it used the photograph
to illustrate an article on British Holocaust revisionist David Irving (Good-

man 1982, 33). While the text told of Irving's thesis that Hitler had not condoned or ordered the Jews' systematic extermination, the photograph was wrongly captioned as a depiction of "death-camp survivors." Repetition of the earlier inaccurate representation of Buchenwald, now within an article about Holocaust revisionism, underscored how little those using images in news were able to critique their own practices.

Other presentations of the photograph, similarly underscoring the problematic linkage between image and text, appeared regularly. The image was repeatedly captioned wrongly as that of "death-camp survivors" and mistakenly associated with Dachau in one publication (Gilbert 1988, 239; Woodward 1977, 77). One news item in *MacLean's* used the same emaciated bunkmates of Buchenwald to illustrate a story of a reunion of former Buchenwald prisoners. The photo was juxtaposed to a second picture that depicted four men, now in their sixties, smiling and mugging for the camera ("Buchenwald Remembered" 1979, 12). The images' juxtaposition implied that the reunited former prisoners were in fact depicted in the earlier image, although that was not the case. Rather, the image's invocation set in place an additional historical inaccuracy. The men pictured at the reunion had been incarcerated at the camp as non-Jewish Allied POWs, whereas the picture presumably portrayed Jewish inmates. Because different treatment was accorded the two groups of prisoners, the visual comparison between then and now was invalid not only on historical grounds but also on representational ones. The then and now comparison set in place a far crueler analogy between them and us, and the photograph's seemingly innocuous invocation as a piece of memory work inadvertently vulgarized at least one premise about how Nazi brutality was inflicted.

Not surprisingly, the photograph also resurfaced in other modes of representation. It adorned an advertisement for the Church of Scientology that called for increased German compensation to Nazi victims ("No Remorse, No Recourse" 1995). It also provided a reality marker of a 1993 art installation by Judy Chicago, who embroidered pastel-colored creatures atop the forlorn male faces in the barracks (fig. 5.4). Entitled "Double Jeopardy," Chicago's work addresses the issue of gender in the camps, and she juxtaposed the painted experiences of women to the "black and white photographs of male experiences: The men's activities [provide] the historical context for the women's, a metaphor for the fact that women are generally impacted by the historic events that men orchestrate" (Chicago 1993, 126).

In each case the image was used in ways that allowed its users to move beyond a simple reminder of Buchenwald's liberation. Not only did it help

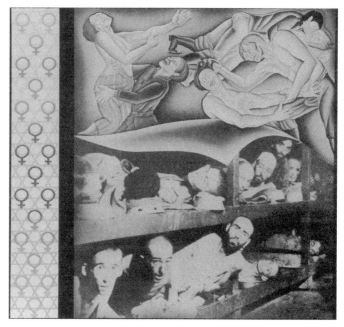

*Figure 5.4.* "Plates 7 and 8, Double Jeopardy," from *Holocaust Project: From Darkness into Light* by Judy Chicago. (Copyright © 1993 by Judy Chicago, text and original artwork. Copyright © 1993 by Donald Woodman, photographs. Used by permission of Viking Penguin, a division of Penguin Books USA, Inc.)

them recall the horrors of one camp in particular, but they also recalled the atrocities and the Holocaust in ways that fit present-day agendas. In many cases this contemporary placement signaled the surrender of the image's referentiality to its symbolic status, even in cases where that surrender consolidated old errors and introduced new ones. This was a new shape to the act of bearing witness, where the target of attention was memory and memory's invocation as a catalyst for present-day agendas.

The photograph received an additional referential life years after the liberation. Following its publication and recycling, two individuals in it took on a public identity. Wiesel and Mel Mermelstein, a Los Angeles businessperson, both identified themselves as prisoners in the depicted bunks. Mermelstein, who in the 1980s successfully challenged the claims of the revisionist Institute for Historical Review in court, was portrayed in a U.S. newsmagazine holding a framed copy of the original photograph (Beck 1981, 73). In keeping with the thrust toward using the story to mark memory, in the more recent image the original photograph's attribution and captioning were both displaced to accommodate those of the more recent shot.

What do such uses of the Buchenwald barracks photograph tell us? Like other cases, perhaps less illustrative but no less central, each twist underscores memory's fundamentally variable nature. Memory worked in unexpected ways as well as in many temporal directions at once. A repository of photographic images reflects a fashioning of their re-presentation, not necessarily because certain images supported the original photograph's presentation but because they helped launch new rhetorical arguments. Photographs have spawned a simultaneous before-and-after life as memory tools, invoking recollections of the atrocities of the Holocaust on many levels. Yet in an age in which the media cogently recycles historical information at will, that raises questions about the use of photographs as memory tools. Underlying the recycling of the Buchenwald barracks photograph was an event that over time has come to resemble less and less its re-presentation in memory.

## The Buchenwald Barbed Wire Photograph

Similar patterns of recycling characterized the uses over time of a Margaret-Bourke White photo entitled "Survivors behind Barbed Wire, Buchenwald 1945." The shot depicts scores of male prisoners clutching the camp's barbed-wire fence, newly neutralized of its electric current (fig. 5.5). The photograph had apparently not been published at the time of the liberation, however, and appeared for one of the first times in a *Time-Life* retrospective more than a year following liberation (Goldberg 1991, 37). Yet it has since become one of the most widely circulated photographs of the camps.

The photograph has likely appeared more often than any other individual atrocity photo, underscoring the degree to which visual documents that worked less effectively in the original record have easily resurfaced as vehicles of memory work. It has been recycled in dozens of Holocaust retrospectives; in anniversary issues of journals and magazines; and in overviews of photojournalism (Life *Celebrates 1945* 1995, 30–31; Life: *Fifty Years* 1986, 192; *1945: The Year of Liberation* 1995, 10; *150 Years of Photojournalism* 1989, 47). It has appeared in features as wide-ranging as a 1960 retrospective marking twenty-five years of *Life* ("Moments Remembered" 1960, 100) and in an overview on the photography of World War II that appeared in the mid-1990s (Voss 1994, 40). In that case it was used ironically to signal a chapter entitled "Putting the War in Focus: The Photographers." It was also reproduced in numerous books on photojournalism that from the late 1970s onward began to include

*Figure 5.5.* "Buchenwald, April 1945." (Margaret Bourke-White, *Life Magazine*
© Time Inc.)

photos from concentration camps as part of their repository of good
photojournalistic images. Numerous scholarly books likewise devoted pictorial space to the atrocity photos in their overviews of the profession, and
each reprinted Bourke-White's photograph (Goldberg 1991, 37).

The photograph has also appeared in other domains of visual representation. It was considered a candidate for inclusion into a Leonard Baskin
memorial to FDR in the late 1970s, and in 1989 *Time* selected it as one of the
ten great iconic images of photojournalism because it "informed the world
about the true nature of the Holocaust" (Carter 1978, 56). Baskin was thought
to have wanted to incorporate "the horror of concentration camps with a
scene like Margaret Bourke-White's memorable photograph through barbed
wire" ("Icons: The Ten Greatest Images of Photojournalism" 1989, 47).
Audrey Flack's "World War II (Vanitas)" of 1976 and 1977 reproduced the
photograph by positioning it inside an opulent still-life of butterflies, roses,
and carefully decorated pastries (fig. 5.6). The juxtaposition of the two sets
of images was peculiar in that it embedded the male survivors more deeply
within the photo. They peered out not only from behind the barbed wire but
also from behind the objects of the still-life. The object was to show "memory
receding in space: My idea was to tell a story, an allegory of war. . . . I wanted
to shock" (Flack 1981, 78–80).

*Figure 5.6.* "World War II (Vanitas)" by Audrey Flack, incorporating a portion of the Margaret Bourke-White photograph "Buchewald, April 1945." (Copyright Time Inc., courtesy Louis K. Meisel Gallery, New York)

The photograph's use as a commemorative tool, despite its not having been published at the time of the event, reveals critical features about memory work. An event's constitutive features can be blurred or rearranged in order to make memory effective. Images can work better in memory, where they are frequently positioned within alternative interpretive schema, than as tools of news relay.

## From the Image of Record to the Image of Memory

What does the transformation from the image of record to the image of memory reveal about the workings of visual memory? Photographs, both at the time of the liberation of the concentration camps of World War II and in the years since, have been instrumental in helping to interpret Nazi atrocities. That opening of narratives has challenged journalistic modes of representation that argue that the more horrific the image, the more detailed its anchoring needs to be. The press, however, has tended to provide fewer cues when information has been most unbelievable. At some point images seem to take over reporters' responsibility to document what they had seen.

This raises numerous questions about the role of photography as an aide-mémoire. One set of questions has to do with the shape of technological adaptation in newswork in which photographers became part of newswork despite the efforts of reporters. The photograph's emergence as the preferred tool of documentation in this particular news event was due primarily to circumstances that made its mode of documentation the more viable and illustrative mechanism of proof. But in retrospect those circumstances, coupled by photography's resulting triumph, helped consolidate the photographic image as a vessel of verisimilitude, particularly in events that require contested levels of evidentiary proof. The fact that this has not been adequately addressed in photojournalism itself, particularly the potentially enormous power attached to photographs as cultural documents, is an oversight that needs correction, particularly in an age where image-making technologies have increased in variety and sophistication.

The other set of questions has to do with the shape of memory. Journalism set up the photographic image to offer conclusive evidence of atrocities in the camps. For those who had not experienced the Holocaust firsthand, public belief hinged on the photograph. That offered certain limited representations of what had happened that were restricted in the nature, detail, scope, magnitude, and generalizeability of what they were able to document. The fact that people still repeatedly say that they remember the Holocaust through its images suggests a narrowing of memory over time that has come with the passage of years to favor a simplified tracking of the past. In conjunction with such a thrust it is no wonder that Holocaust photos are recycled in strategic and highly formulaic ways. Memory in such a view thrives on the impulses of simplicity and familiarity, which the visual domain represents so effectively.

Yet because the press at the time adopted uneven standards for processing images as news, and perhaps due to a more general need for universal markers and symbols of the atrocities, images of the camps were transformed from definitive indices of certain actions to generalized and symbolic markers. That raises important questions about why Holocaust representation continues to focus on the question of universalization. That pattern was already set in place at the time of the camps' liberation through circumstances that had more to do with the technicalities of processing images as news than with anything inherently connected to the atrocities themselves. That, in turn, raises other questions about the circumstances that create representation and shape the recollections of that representation. It is only when "literal memory ends [that] cultural memory can begin" (Alter 1993, 117). Yet often cultural memory begins when it is least expected. In the case of Holocaust photographs, it began in the establishment of the original record from which memory springs.

## Notes

This chapter is a revised version of material that appears in Zelizer (1998), © 1998 by The University of Chicago. All rights reserved.

1. Crudely paraphrased, Adorno lamented the inability to write poetry after Auschwitz, Lyotard asked how one measures an earthquake whose instruments of measurement have been destroyed, and Steiner declared that the world of Auschwitz resided beyond speech.

## References

Adler, Jonathan. 1983. "Hitler and the Holocaust." *Newsweek,* May 2, 62.
———. 1993. "After the Survivors." *Newsweek,* Dec. 20, 117.
Adorno, Theodor. 1973. *Negative Dialectics.* New York: Continuum.
"At Nordhausen." 1945. *London Times,* April 19, 6.
Beck, Melinda. 1981. "Footnote to the Holocaust." *Newsweek,* Oct. 19, 73.
Blanchard, Robert. 1935. "News and Pictures—Cameras and Reporters." In *Problems of Journalism* (proceedings of the 1935 convention of the American Society of Newspaper Editors, April 18–20), 54–58. Washington: ASNE.
"Bodies in Nordausen Gestapo Concentration Camp." 1945. *Boston Globe,* April 17, 16.
Brandenburg, George. 1938. "Huge Gains in Use of Pictures Shown in Survey of Dailies." *Editor and Publisher,* Feb. 19, 8.
Brown, J. L. 1938. "Picture Magazines and Morons." *American Mercury* (Dec.): 404–8.
"Buchenwald Remembered: They Were Not Alone." 1979. *MacLean's,* Sept. 24, 12.
Caiger-Smith, Martin. 1988. *The Face of the Enemy: British Photographers in Germany, 1944–1952.* Berlin: Nishen Publishing.
Carter, M. L. 1978. "The FDR Memorial: A Monument to Politics, Bureaucracy, and the Art of Accommodation." *Art News* (Oct.): 56.
Chicago, Judy. 1993. *Holocaust Project: From Darkness into Light.* New York: Penguin.
Codman, Charles R. 1945. "For the Record: Buchenwald." *Atlantic* (July): 54.
Denny, Harold. 1945. "'The World Must Not Forget.'" *New York Times Magazine,* May 6, 9.
Ditton, H. J. 1945. "Prison Camp Horrors Will Be Shown to Germans." *News of the World,* April 22, n.p.
"Europe's Problem: What M.P.s Say of the Nazi Horror Camps." 1945. *Picture Post,* May 12, 25.

Flack, Audrey. 1981. *On Painting.* New York: Harry N. Abrams.

"Gannett Reporters Will Carry Cameras." 1932. *Editor and Publisher,* June 11, 18.

"German Atrocities in Prison Camps." 1945. *Illustrated London News,* April 28, detachable supplement.

Gilbert, Martin. 1988. *Atlas of the Holocaust.* London: Pergamon Press.

Goldberg, Vicki. 1991. *The Power of Photography.* New York: Abbeville Publishing.

Goodman, Walter. 1982. "The Politics of the Holocaust." *Newsweek,* Sept. 27, 33.

Halbwachs, Maurice. 1980. *The Collective Memory.* New York: Harper and Row [originally published as *La memoire collective.* 1950. Paris: Presses Universitaires de France].

Hibbs, Benjamin. 1945. "Journey to a Shattered World." *Saturday Evening Post,* June 9, 22.

Higginbottom, F. J. 1935. "Work of News Photographers Is Not Journalism." *The Journal* (Aug.): 119.

"Hitler's Slaves." 1945. *Los Angeles Times,* April 24, 3A.

Hutton, Patrick. 1988. "Collective Memory and Collective Mentalities: The Halbwachs-Aries Connection." *Historical Reflections/Reflexions Historiques* 15(2): 314.

"Icons: The Ten Greatest Images of Photojournalism." 1989. *Time* (Fall): 47.

Kany, Howard L. 1947. "Experts Eye Pictures: Photographer as Reporter." *The Quill* (April): 10.

Knauth, Percival. 1945. "Buchenwald." *Time,* April 30, 42.

*Liberation 1945.* 1995. Washington: United States Holocaust Memorial Council.

Life *Celebrates 1945.* 1991. *Life* (Special Collector's Edition), June 5, 30–31.

Life: *Fifty Years.* 1986. *Life* (Special Anniversary Issue), Fall.

"Long Rows of German Victims at Belsen Await Burial." 1945. *Washington Post,* April 29, 8M.

Lyotard, Jean-François. 1988. *The Differend: Phrases in Dispute.* Minneapolis: University of Minnesota Press.

Marwick, Arthur. 1982. "Print, Pictures, and Sound: The Second World War and the British Experience." *Daedalus* (Fall).

Marzolf, Marion Tuttle. 1991. *Civilizing Voices: American Press Criticism, 1880–1950.* New York: Longman.

Mason, A. J. 1939. "With a Camera in Spain." *Photographic Journal* (March): 112–14.

"Moments Remembered." 1960. *Life,* Dec. 26, 100.

Nagorski, Andrew. 1995. "The Last Days of Auschwitz." *Newsweek,* Jan. 16, 46–59.

Newman, A. 1945. "Nordhausen: A Hell Factory Worked by the Living Dead." *Newsweek,* April 23, 52.

*1945: The Year of Liberation.* 1995. Washington: United States Holocaust Memorial Council.

"No Remorse, No Recourse" (advertisement). 1995. *New York Times,* Jan. 18, 17A.

"Official Report on Buchenwald Camp." 1945. *PM,* April 30, 9.

*150 Years of Photojournalism.* 1989. *Time* (Special Collector's Edition), Fall.

"The Pictures Don't Lie." 1945. *Stars and Stripes,* April 26, 2.

Price, Jack. 1944a. "Credit Line Asked for Photographers." *Editor and Publisher,* Oct. 28, 64.

———. 1944b. "Reporters Train to Be Photographers." *Editor and Publisher,* April 1, 52.

"Problem That Makes All Europe Wonder." 1945. *Picture Post,* May 5, 7–11, 26.

"Racks for Slave Workers . . . Buchenwald." 1945. In *Lest We Forget: The Horrors of Nazi Concentration Camps Revealed for All Time in the Most Terrible Photographs Ever Published.* London: Daily Mail with Associated Newspapers.

"Report on German Murder Mills." 1945. *Army Talks,* July 10, 8.

Sontag, Susan. 1977. *On Photography.* New York: Anchor Books.

Stanley, Edward. 1937. "This Pictorial Journalism." *The Quill* (Nov.): 5.

Steiner, George. 1969. *Language and Silence.* New York: Penguin.

Stott, William. 1973. *Documentary Expression and Thirties America.* New York: Oxford University Press.

Taylor, John. 1991. *War Photography: Realism in the British Press.* London: Routledge.

"The Problem That Makes All Europe Wonder." 1945. *Picture Post,* May 5, 7.

Voss, Frederick. 1994. *Reporting the War: The Journalistic Coverage of World War II.* Washington: Smithsonian Institution Press for the National Portrait Galley.

Walker, Patrick G. 1941. "The Terror in Europe." *Picture Post,* Oct. 11, overleaf.

"Why Join?" 1941. *The Camera* (advertisement).

Woodward, Kenneth L. 1975. "Facing Up to the Holocaust." *Newsweek,* May 26, 72.

———. 1977. "Hitler and the Holocaust." *Newsweek,* July 11, 77.

———. 1980. "Debate over the Holocaust." *Newsweek,* March 10, 97.

Zelizer, Barbie. 1995a. "Journalism's Last Stand: Wirephoto and the Discourse of Resistance." *Journal of Communication* 45(2): 78–92.

———. 1995b. "Words against Images: Positioning Newswork in the Age of Photography." In *Newsworkers: Toward a History of the Rank and File,* ed. Hanno Hardt and Bonnie Brennen, 135–59. Minneapolis: University of Minnesota Press.

———. 1998. *Remembering to Forget: Holocaust Memory through the Camera's Eye.* Chicago: University of Chicago Press.

*To ignore photojournalism
is to ignore history.*
*—Howard Chapnick, president,*
*Black Star Photo Agency*

## The Great War Photographs: Constructing Myths of History and Photojournalism

*Michael Griffin*

"Photojournalism" is a term and a concept that has been superimposed on the history of photography in hindsight. Coming into usage only after the rise of picture magazines in the 1920s and 1930s, the term has been applied freely in histories of photography to describe a wide range of photographic practice, often beginning with the first daguerreotype and calotype scenes of the 1830s.[1] The presentist tendency to apply current concepts and paradigms to the past is not unusual, but in this case it seems specifically linked to the belief that the stature of modern photojournalism will be enhanced by situating it in a time-honored tradition. Lacking the pedigree accorded to fine art, photojournalism seems always in search of a tradition. In any case, histories of photojournalism are often most telling not for what they reveal about the intentions and practices of photographers at the time pictures were made but for what they indicate about current views of history and the way people mark, condense, and symbolize the historical past in the present.

War photography is of particular importance in this regard, epitomizing as it does an ideal of photojournalism practice, providing a proving ground for photojournalistic reputation, and ultimately supplying national symbols of patriotism, solidarity, death, and sacrifice. Combat photojournalism has come to represent the height of photographic realism. Photo correspondents are described as wielding cameras like weapons, rushing with bravado into the midst of the action to "shoot" the valiant and grim events of human conflict. Yet the history of wartime pictures reveals a contradictory impulse; icons of warfare and national history prove less candid and realistic, less visually descriptive of specific events, than Chapnick's equation of photojournalism with history would suggest. The enduring images of war are not those that exhibit the most raw and genuine depictions of life and death on the battlefield, nor those that illustrate historically specific information about people, places, and things, but rather those that most readily present themselves as symbols of cultural and national myth.

## War Photography and the Rise of Photojournalism

During the course of the twentieth century, photography as a medium slowly and haltingly gained legitimacy as an art form, as professional practice, and as a serious subject of study. Concomitantly, photojournalism asserted itself as an increasingly legitimate, even indispensable, part of the popular press. Many characteristics of the later stages of industrialization—the evolution of secular, scientific worldviews, the waning of colonial empires, and the unprecedented national conflicts that rocked the century—were related to the growing importance of photography as a medium (Schiller 1982).

The advance of photographic practice beyond commercial portraiture and exotica was initially promoted through the activities of amateur photographers and photographic clubs, societies, salons, journals, and exhibitions in the decades before and after the turn of the century (Griffin 1987, 1995). By World War I, great numbers of amateur photographers carried cameras with them as they embarked on their service as soldiers and sailors, although the concept of photojournalism, or even the idea of a "war photo-reporter," was still largely unknown, and photographs of actual battlefield events, with rare exceptions, were routinely forbidden or censored. The number of camera operators in and out of uniform and the increasing use of the camera for military reconnaissance introduced the notion of photographic coverage on a scale beyond previous conceptions (Jussim 1988, 63–73; Lewinski 1978, 63–71; Tausk 1988, 62–74; Taylor 1991, 20–24, 42–51).

The Great War, with its "anonymous mass of cameramen" (Lewinski 1978, 67–68), was followed by the emergence and popular success of picture magazines in Europe and, subsequently, North America. It was a success intertwined with the growth of motion pictures, radio, advertising, and national political propaganda. Picture magazines and movie newsreels became so pervasive a part of everyday culture in so many parts of the world between the wars (and such an indispensable part of government propaganda) that the use of photographs in the press increasingly became routine and expected. Photojournalism emerged as an established practice, albeit one that loosely straddled conventional notions of documentary, news, information, opinion, publicity, and propaganda (Freund 1982; Fulton 1988; Hardt and Ohrn 1981; Osman and Phillips 1989).

As World War II erupted, it seemed taken for granted that the events of the war would be "recorded" photographically. In fact, many millions of photographs from the war, along with millions of feet of motion picture footage, still survive in museums, archives, and private collections. This time, the armed forces of nearly every nation trained and equipped thousands of photographers for military duty, and the number of formally trained military photographers increased throughout the war "until every unit of the armed forces—Army, Navy, and Air Force—had a basic team of one stills and one cine photographer" (Lewinski 1978, 95). Numerous cameramen accompanied the German armies that drove into Poland in September 1939. "The importance attached to the work was evident. In the advance on the Polish city of Gdynia, the attack is said to have been delayed so that cameramen could take positions ahead of the assault troops, so as to document their full impact. In the later conquest of Norway, which made unprecedented use of parachute troops in coordination with naval landings, three hundred German cameramen were said to be in action. Many German cameramen were killed during the war" (Barnouw 1983, 139).

The establishment of extensive documentary film and newsreel production in the Soviet Union during the decades following the revolution made it possible to mobilize a vast cadre of newsreel photographers at the outset of the German invasion on June 22, 1941. "The first wartime issue of the weekly *Kino* shows the Soviet film already on a war footing. . . . In the first week after invasion four crews were sent to four sectors of the long front, all headed by veteran newsmen. Newsreel cameramen covered every phase of the fight even to parachuting with paratroops and hiding with guerrilla fighters deep behind German lines" (Leyda 1960, 366–67). By the time Nazi armies were pushing into Russia,

> footage of some four hundred cameramen was converging on Moscow editing tables. . . . The film coverage of the war was the stuff of legends. More than one hundred Soviet cameramen died in action; their ranks were readily and eagerly

filled. The state film academy—founded in 1919 in the midst of revolution—added combat photography to its curriculum; diplomas were earned in part through front-line action. Combat cameramen won many awards. During an air battle a cameraman left his camera, took gun position and shot down a German pursuit plane. He won an award for valor, and a reprimand from his studio. (Barnouw 1983, 151, 154)

World War II served as the ultimate proving ground for photo-reporting on a massive scale, and photojournalism truly came of age. The gap between the millions of photographic images taken and the chosen few reproduced was staggering, however, and the relation of the famous images we still recognize to the larger universe of World War II photo-reporting is an open question.

At the conclusion of the war, thousands of militarily trained photographers reentered the civilian workforce, helping to fuel the expansion of commercial, industrial, and news photography that accompanied the postwar economic and advertising boom (Griffin, 1987). Photojournalism became fully established during the postwar era as circulation figures for picture magazines hit their peak in Europe and the United States; daily newspapers established photography departments that had full-time staff photographers; and press photographers themselves strove for greater respect and higher standards by establishing professional associations (the National Press Photographers Association [NPPA] was established in 1946), elite photo agencies (Magnum Photo Agency was established in Paris and New York in 1947), and international forums for the recognition of photojournalism (the World Press Photo Foundation in Holland was established in 1956).

Finally, the postwar boom in commercial photography was paralleled by the gradual establishment of photography departments in art museums, the increasing sale of photographs in galleries, and the sometimes reluctant acceptance of photography as a subject of academic study in university departments of art, art history, and journalism. By the time of U.S. involvement in Vietnam the professional practice of photojournalism was well established, and photographers and cinematographers of many nations and independent news organizations were routinely sent to "international hot spots" around the globe (Chapnick 1994). A photojournalistic ethos developed that greatly inflated expectations about access, independence, lack of constraints, and artless realism. That ethos encouraged mythical conceptions of photojournalism coverage: the ideas that photography could and should bring the world's dramatic events "into people's living rooms" and that by the 1990s there might even be a "live TV war."

## The Ontology of the Photograph:
## Photorealism and History

Ironically, scholarly attention to photojournalism really took off only in the late 1960s and 1970s, just when photography began to fade as a major mode of mass media.[2] As publication photography became overshadowed by television and popular picture magazines began to fold (*Look* in 1971, *Life* in 1972), serious writing on the history and theory of photography multiplied. In fact, the period immediately following the ascendancy of television (roughly 1965–85) saw a burst of critical and theoretical writing on photography and photoreporting, from Pierre Bourdieu's early work on *Photography as a Middlebrow Art* (1965); to Roland Barthes's essays on the nature of the photographic image ("Rhetoric of the Image" in *Image-Music-Text* [1977] and *Camera Lucida: Reflections on Photography* [1981]); to John Berger's series of books and critical writings on pictorial communication, some of them photo/text collaborations with photographer Jean Mohr: *A Fortunate Man* (1967), *Ways of Seeing* (1972), *A Seventh Man* (1975), *About Looking* (1980), and *Another Way of Telling* (1982). These years constitute what might be called a period of "high modernism" for photography scholarship.

Perhaps the most widely read and often cited work of this era is Susan Sontag's *On Photography* (1977), a collection of essays contemplating the ontology of photographic images. *On Photography* was symptomatic of the new scrutiny and analysis aimed at photography precisely when its centrality for the mass media was diminishing and arenas for the exhibition of high-quality photojournalism were shifting from magazines to art books and gallery walls. It joined several influential reflections on photography and photo history appearing during the late 1970s and early 1980s.[3] Sontag's book remains particularly emblematic, however, because it provides one of the most extended and far-ranging discussions of what has always been the central issue for writers on photography: the relationship between photographs and their subject matter.

Sontag doggedly revisits the question of photographic "reality." Echoing debates that raged in the photographic societies and journals of the nineteenth century, when the first generation of photographic connoisseurs argued over photography's rightful place as science or art, Sontag moves back and forth from reflections on the role of the camera as a documentary device to arguments for photography's shortcomings as a "record of reality" and its inescapable subjectivitiy in the hands of photographers. On the one hand, she writes, "To collect photographs is to collect the world. . . . Photographs really are experience captured, and the camera is the ideal arm of consciousness in its acquisitive mood" (Sontag 1977, 3–4). Yet, on the other hand, she also supports the contention that photography frames a photographer's perception: "The insistence that picture-taking is first of all the focusing of a temperament, only secondarily of a machine, has always been one of the main themes of the defense of photography" (118).

Sontag attempts to analyze the generic properties of photography in all its forms rather than treat different genres and styles of photography separately. Her "once startling, but now obvious-seeming assumption" that "all the different kinds of photography form one continuous and interdependent tradition" leads her to explore the recurrent tension in all photography between objective recording and subjective expression and the role that function and social use play in obscuring or foregrounding the fundamental ambivalence between "trace and transformation" (188).

Attempts by writers such as Sontag and Alan Sekula (1975) to establish a critical discourse that examines photography both as art and information fueled continuing reactions and debate. Berger's essay "The Uses of Photography" in *About Looking* (1980), for instance, is written as an explicit response to Sontag. This discourse was symptomatic of an increasing skepticism about distinctions between the use of the camera as a recording instrument and its use as a creative tool, a skepticism paralleled by an increasing tendency to exhibit documentary photography, and even photojournalism, on the walls of museums and galleries.[4]

The growing dissolution of boundaries between photographic genres and photographic criticism was also reflected in new histories of photography that attempted not only to go beyond chronicles of technical advance but also to break away from "great man" history and the creation of pantheons of "photo artists." The new histories gave greater attention to what Berger calls the "uses of photography" in public and private spheres of experience and explored issues of representation, imagination, memory, and institutional and social control.[5]

Still, such changes come slowly. Even toward the end of the twentieth century it remained rare for questions about the status of photographic representation to be brought to bear on the historical role of public media. Howard Chapnick, photojournalist, editor, photo educator, and long-time president of Black Star (one of the earliest and most influential photo agencies), may be correct when he says, "To ignore photojournalism is to ignore history," but perhaps not for the reasons that he suggests (Fulton 1988, xii; revised and reprinted in Chapnick 1994, 7). He refers to photojournalism as the "Eyewitness to History" (Chapnick 1994, ch. 1), writing with confidence that "the twentieth century belongs to the photojournalists" because "they have provided us with a visual history unduplicated by images from any comparable period of human existence." He explicitly accepts the "truth and reality" of photojournalistic records, calling them "the ultimate in anthropological and historical documents of our time" (7) and says of photojournalists, "As frontline witnesses, they have captured events to form a visual time capsule for our own generation and those to follow" (10).

Chapnick's use of the word *front-line* is telling, however, for the photojournalism-as-history to which he refers is largely a photographic portrayal of war and death. He concedes that although "photojournalists sometimes chronicle a world of simple pleasure and routine existence" and sometimes

> explore private worlds, revealing the complex personalities of the great, the powerful, the simple and the ordinary, . . . more often, the photojournalists' concerns are centered around war, poverty, famine, drought, and the natural and man-made disasters afflicting this complicated planet. . . . Still photographs have been characterized as "frozen moments in time." Frozen moments such as the mountain of discarded bodies in the charnel of Buchenwald, the My Lai massacre in Vietnam, and the Nick Ut photograph of the napalmed Vietnamese children running naked down the road reflect the circle of madness, death, destruction, and despair that too often afflicts mankind. The power of these images lies in their implausibility and inconceivability. (Fulton 1988, xiii, xiv)

Here, in a foreword to one of the few substantial histories of photojournalism in print, a fifty-year veteran of the craft assumes the documentary truth of photo records ("photojournalism as history") yet sums up the salient features of the most celebrated press photographs by noting not their candid depiction of the actualities of daily events and experiences or their detailed accuracy as "anthropological and historical documents" but rather their dramatic power as extraordinary "moments" of human struggle, catastrophe, destruction, and death. "The power of these images," Chapnick contends, "lies in their implausibility and inconceivability." And it is war that remains the primary source of "implausible" and compelling photographs of human drama and tragedy. Sontag goes so far as to say that "war and photography now seem inseparable, and plane crashes and other horrific accidents always attract people with cameras. A society which makes it normative to aspire never to experience privation, failure, misery, pain, dread disease, and in which death itself is regarded not as natural and inevitable but as a cruel, unmerited disaster, creates a tremendous curiosity about these events—a curiosity that is partly satisfied through picture-taking" (1977, 167).

## War Photography and Mythic Symbols

What are these photographic images that seem so influential in defining photojournalism and characterizing history? One is struck not by the specificity and details of the pictures reproduced in the most serious illustrated surveys of press and war photography as records of particular circumstances and historical events (Fralin 1985; Fulton 1988; Goldberg 1993; Heller, ed. 1990; Lewinski 1978; Tausk 1988; Taylor 1991) but rather by the high drama and emotional pull of symbolic moments of death, sacrifice, and patriotism. Such historical icons represent consensus narratives condensed in familiar, emotionally charged scenes. Chapnick praises them as products of a photographer's "storytelling vision" (Fulton 1988, xiii).

What is apparent when examining celebrated photographs, however, is that the discernible narrative allusions are tied not only to familiar literary themes of violence, courage, sacrifice, heroism, and sometimes tragedy but also to long-established conventions of visual depiction. The compelling realism of war photography—largely a product of a belief in the photographer's presence on the scene and his or her spontaneous recording of sensational, horrible, or "implausible" events—is presented for inspection by means of skillfully framed arrangements of tones and shapes, the articulation of scenes and compositions that resonate with a preexisting stock of familiar scenes and compositions. These photographs are encapsulating symbols, images that operate at the level of myth rather than description.

> The vicissitudes of our century have been summed up in a few exemplary photographs that have proved epoch-making: the unruly crowd pouring into the square during the "ten days that shook the world"; Robert Capa's dying *miliciano;* the marines planting the flag on Iwo Jima; the Vietnamese prisoner being executed with a shot in the temple; Che Guevara's tortured body on a plank in a barracks. Each of these images has become a myth and has condensed numerous speeches. It has surpassed the individual circumstance that produced it; it no longer speaks of that single character or of those characters, but expresses concepts. It is unique, but at the same time it refers to other images that preceded it or that, in imitation, have followed it. (Eco 1986, 216)

The general tension in photojournalism between a presumption of naturalism on the one hand and an emphasis on the craft of picture making on the other (Schwartz 1992) becomes heightened in war photography, a genre largely defined by an ultra-realistic sense of "capturing action," but its use and meaning is most often generated by a symbolic relationship to operative national mythologies (sports photography is similar in this regard).

Taylor (1991) provides substantial demonstrations of photography's link to national mythologies. Treating World War I, World War II, the Falklands conflict, and the civil strife in Northern Ireland, each in turn, he provides detailed analyses of the nature of photographic coverage in the British press and its relationship to official narratives of patriotic duty and national unity. Military and government censors tightly filtered photographs from the front in World War I and World War II, for instance, which were then used in the pages of the British press to establish and continually reaffirm the parallel heroic narratives of battlefield and home: "Men 'making their way out' and then returning 'their mission successfully accomplished'" (Taylor 1991, 24) on the one hand and, on the other, the continuity and endurance of British family life at home and (in the case of World War II) the stoicism of the home front in the face of the blitz. The photographs present images of willing and courageous sacrifice and resilience on the part of soldiers and civilians alike. The photographs of "disruption" printed in the British press during World War II, photos of "conscription, mobilization, evacuation, and the effects of bombardment," were faithfully countered, often on the same page, by those of undaunted family life (Taylor 1991, 84). The recurring themes of British wartime photography were the necessities of fulfilling one's duty without hesitation or complaint and maintaining a semblance of normality in the midst of destruction, disruption, and sacrifice.[6]

Similarly, during the 1982 Falklands campaign Taylor finds that family life and patriotism at home routinely reappeared as central themes of published photographs. Combat pictures from the South Atlantic were so tightly controlled and censored that few images of actual military confrontation were published. "The disturbing effects of shocking photographs remained a hypothetical question because there was none to be seen" (Taylor 1991, 112).

Taylor concludes that the preoccupation of the British press with family conserved a particular national history, a "heritage" that harkened back to "an older sense of community that in the folk memory had bound everyone together" (1991, 84). "These stereotypes enable a national history to be seen and learned. This history is not solely conserved as 'heritage': it is actively produced, turned into fiction and presented as the thing itself. It is simulated in replicas, or re-enactments, and massively represented in photographic realism" (165).

Taylor's analysis is specific to British press treatments of British conflicts. A fluid relationship between photographs as documentary records and photographs as mythic symbols seems endemic to war photography as a genre, however, inevitably implicated as it is in the propagation of national and cultural identity, political and ideological distinctions, and social differentiation and solidarity (Fussell 1989). Some of the most famous, and often reproduced, war photographs provide telling examples. The "great pictures," those customarily included in histories of war photography and photojournalism, are seldom analyzed as informational illustrations of specific events and locations. Rather, they are celebrated on a more abstract plane as broader symbols of national valor, human courage, inconceivable inhumanity, or senseless loss. It is precisely their nonspecificity that makes them timeless.

A key to their fame is often the very implausibility of such pictures being made at all; their value is at least partly due to the daring nerve exhibited by the photographers responsible for them. Together with the esteem attached to the astonishing or implausible photograph comes controversy over its authenticity. It is no coincidence that many of the most celebrated war photographs have at one time or another been denounced as fakes.

## Famous Pictures: Civil War Photography as a Foundation Myth

Histories of photography routinely recount the first attempts to photograph war as a critical development in the maturation of photography as a medium. Most general histories, as well as specialized histories of photojournalism or war photography, devote significant space to mid-nineteenth-century efforts to haul camera, tripod, glass plate negatives, and darkroom chemicals onto the battlefield. The nod is usually given to Roger Fenton, James Robertson, and Felice Beato as the first "war photographers" for their work photographing British military operations in the Crimea in 1854 and 1855 (Fenton, Robertson, and Beato); India from 1856 to 1858 (Robertson and Beato); and China in 1860 (Beato). But virtually every history identifies the American Civil War (1861–65) as the first conflict to be photographed widely from beginning to end. That was largely because Mathew Brady, an extremely successful studio portrait photographer at the start of the war, decided to make an ambitious attempt to create an extensive collection of photographic documents of the war and received permission from Abraham Lincoln himself to accompany Union troops on their campaigns.

Brady organized, financed, and equipped a team of professional photographers to follow the various detachments of the Federal army on their marches. During the course of a war that was longer, bloodier, and more devastating than anyone had imagined it would be, several of Brady's most skilled photographers split with him to launch their own war photography projects (most notable among these were Alexander Gardner, Timothy

O'Sullivan, and George Barnard). Between them, Brady and his operatives exposed at least seven thousand glass plate negatives in and around the encampments, fortifications, battlefields, and ruined towns of the war and produced grim photographic images of the carnage left on the great battlegrounds of Antietam, Fredericksburg, Gettysburg, Spotsylvania, Cold Harbor, Petersburg, and Richmond.[7]

What is most impressive about this photography is the sheer scale and magnitude of the images compiled. Following the war, when Brady, as well as Gardner, Barnard, and other photo entrepreneurs, found disappointingly little commercial interest in their collections, the War Department bought a set of six thousand plates that Brady was auctioning to cover unpaid warehouse fees. The department paid only $2,840 for the entire collection, which for many years was housed by the Army Pictorial Service, a branch of the U.S. Army Signal Corps (Taft 1964 [1938]). A duplicate set of plates was handed over to E. and H. T. Anthony Company of New York in lieu of unpaid bills for photographic supplies and equipment, and those eventually were handed down as the Ordway-Rand Collection and printed in the ten-volume *Photographic History of the Civil War* published in 1911 (Carlebach 1992; Taft 1964 [1938]).

Ultimately, public historical depositories such as the New York Public Library, the National Archives, and the Library of Congress became the beneficiaries of these bankruptcy sales. Although scores of photographers left records of their attempts to photograph aspects of the war and hundreds attempted to capitalize on the formation of massive armies by producing uncounted thousands of cartes-de-visite portraits of soldiers in uniform to send to families and friends, it was the existence of the Brady-inspired archives that eventually led to dozens of photo books documenting the war for posterity. These large collections of photo documents provide a vast amount of descriptive detail and visual information for scrutiny and evaluation. Outside the archives, however, only a very small selection of the photos have ever been published or exhibited, and when Civil War photographs are reproduced in photo histories it is inevitably the same handful of familiar pictures printed again and again.

The most frequently reproduced photos of all are two pictures taken by Timothy O'Sullivan and Alexander Gardner working together at Gettysburg following that decisive battle. Titled "Harvest of Death" and "Home of a Rebel Sharpshooter" (sometimes "Death of a Rebel Sniper"), they have been repeatedly praised by authors as the most noteworthy examples of Civil War work. Lewinski (1978), author of one of the few serious histories devoted exclusively to war photography, calls Gardner and O'Sullivan "the two most important photographers in Brady's team" and refers to "Harvest of Death" and "Home of a Rebel Sharpshooter" as "perhaps the finest pictures of the war" (1978, 44). William Stapp (1988) devotes a major portion of a discussion of Civil War photography to the authenticity, accuracy, realism, and impact of these two photographs and their reproduction. Carlebach (1992) also singles out "Home of a Rebel Sharpshooter" as one of the war's most noteworthy images, recounting historical evidence that suggests that Gardner and O'Sullivan likely collaborated in dragging the corpse from its original location and "setting up" the photograph.

"Harvest of Death" (fig. 6.1), known by the title that accompanied it in volume 1 of *Gardner's Photographic Sketch Book of the War* (Gardner 1959 [1866]), is conspicuously meant to symbolize the horrible scale of human sacrifice associated with the war. Attributed by Gardner to Timothy O'Sullivan, it shows corpses scattered over an open, treeless field, nearly all contorted with their backs arched and legs bent and stiffened. A group of five corpses sprawls across the frame in the foreground. The foremost figure's face is bent back toward the camera, his mouth gaping and his arms outstretched and stiff, almost as if he is regarding the viewer and crying out in agony. Numerous other figures are scattered away toward the background, blurring out of focus as they recede. Near the center of the frame on the distant horizon are two figures apparently moving among the carnage, one mounted on horseback and the other leading a horse on foot. Perhaps because of their movement and the receding photographic depth of field they appear as shadowy blurs in a hazy distance, almost ghostlike figures moving among the dead.

"Home of a Rebel Sharpshooter" (fig. 6.2) shows a single fallen soldier in a cleft among the rocks, his rifle leaning up against one of the boulders to form a triangular composition with the soldier's prone body and the rock wall. This picture, apparently taken by Gardner with O'Sullivan's assistance, is much less grim than "A Harvest of Death." Instead of evoking a ghostly atmosphere of death, it suggests repose. The fallen soldier's body is not contorted. He lies with his head resting on a knapsack (according to some reports placed there by Gardner); his head is tilted toward the viewer, with his eyes closed and his mouth only slightly open. One hand rests on his stomach, and the other lies bent at the elbow at his side. He looks as though he might be sleeping. The title suggests that the triangular niche in the rock where he lies is his "home." The triangular composition formed by his body, the leaning rifle, and the face of the rock fix him in that place as part of the structure of the landscape. It is a balanced and serene image that romanticizes death rather than suggests the macabre. The consensus of contempo-

*Figure 6.1.* "Harvest of Death, July 1863" by Timothy O'Sullivan/Alexander Gardner. (Courtesy George Eastman House)

*Figure 6.2.* "Home of a Rebel Sharpshooter, July 1863" by Timothy O'Sullivan/Alexander Gardner. (Courtesy George Eastman House)

rary historians is that "Home of a Rebel Sharpshooter," perhaps the single most famous image among all of the "Brady photographs" of the Civil War, was staged.[8]

This seeming contradiction, that the most elegantly composed, most purposefully mediated, and in some cases the most transparently staged photographs have become the most celebrated images, is a recurrent characteristic of war photography. The photography of Brady's generation was technically limited by the immobility of the heavy camera and tripod, the relatively long exposure times, cumbersome and fragile glass plates, and the need to have darkroom chemicals and developing apparatus immediately on hand to develop glass negatives soon after exposure. These limitations resulted in pictures that are static and depict settings rather than activities. The bulk of the Brady-era work shows either locations (long shots of battlefield sites, valleys, hills, towns, bridges, rail lines, farmsteads, mills, hospitals, encampments, batteries, and fortifications) or scenes of posed and unmoving figures (officers seated in front of their tents, groups of soldiers in camp, men standing guard at their batteries, formations of troops in ranks, and bodies scattered across the ground following battles).

Posed settings did not move or change quickly and the dead were always still, allowing the camera time to collect a sufficient amount of reflected light. As Sweet has argued, photographic scenes of battlefields in the Civil War cohere within a pastoral aesthetic. Photographers such as Brady, Gardner, and O'Sullivan used "regularized compositional forms" and accompanying captions and interpretive texts to create a "picturesque unity" of associations for viewers and readers. "In this way traces of war were mobilized as signs of Union" (Sweet 1990, 137).

Yet despite the obviously static and pastoral nature of Civil War photography, "The Civil War became a shockingly real encounter through the work of Mathew Brady's studio" (Fulton 1988, 107). At the time of Brady's first exhibition of photographs from Antietam in 1862, a reviewer for the October 20 *New York Times* wrote:

> Mr. Brady has done something to bring home to us the terrible reality and earnestness of war. If he has not brought bodies and laid them on our door-yards and along the streets he has done something very like it. . . . These pictures have a terrible distinctness. . . . Union soldier and Confederate, side by side, here they lie, the red light of battle faded from their eyes but their lips set as when they met in the last fierce charge which loosed their souls and sent them grappling with each other to the very gates of Heaven. (5)

This bit of *pictura poesis* provides an example of the way in which these photographs, like the history paintings they seek to emulate, possess the power of realism yet lend themselves to interpretation within a preexisting system of mythological themes, in this case nationalist myths of sacrifice for the higher cause and "truths dearer than life."[9] That helps explain why the static photographs of Brady, Gardner, O'Sullivan, and Barnard, along with those of Thomas C. Roche, Andrew J. Russell, and others, seemed to have provoked such a powerful response from some viewers.

Civil War photographers could not depict events of the war as they unfolded, but they realized that the next best thing was to photograph the aftermath of the unseen actions. As responses such as the *New York Times* show, at least some viewers were predisposed to view pictures of the war dead within a familiar moral narrative of noble sacrifice. Fulton has noted the rhetorical function of these early attempts at photo documentation and suggests a continuing influence of the "Brady tradition": "Photojournalists, in the photographic tradition of Brady, are more than spectators in an historical grandstand. Being there is important, being an eyewitness is significant, but the crux of the matter is *bearing witness*. To bear witness is to make known, to confirm, to give testimony to others. The distribution and publication of the pictures make visible the unseen, the unknown, and the forgotten" (1988, 107, emphasis in the original).

Of course, the public as a whole did not pay much attention to the Civil War photographs at the time. Whether that was because too much of the work was descriptive and without sufficient dramatic structure to prime viewers' mythic responses or whether Americans were simply weary of the catastrophic conflict and its moral lessons and wanted to put all reminders of it behind them is unknown. But now the descriptive body of the photographic collection remains buried in archives while a tiny selection of the photographs are reproduced over and over again. Some of the most celebrated among the limited selection routinely reproduced were created by adding or altering props, dragging bodies to new locations, or attaching different identifying captions to photographs taken of the same things. Knowledge of such manipulations does not seem to dampen enthusiasm for these photographs as mythic symbols of the war or as signs of the efforts of "pioneering photojournalists" to cover the war.

In fact, the Brady-era work is fascinating in the sense that it is more motivated by a concern for detailed visual description than is commonly the case in modern photojournalism. In many of the pictures the frame is replete with visual information concerning location and recent events—for example,

Confederate bodies strewn in the field near the easily identified old Dunker church at Antietam, dozens of wounded filling the frame at a field hospital at Savage Station following the battle of June 27, 1862, and Battery D, Second, U.S. Artillery stretching diagonally across the frame and into the distance in its deployment at Fredericksburg in 1863. Yet, ironically perhaps, such detailed visual records are not the photographs that draw the greatest attention a century later. Civil War photographers may have been motivated by the camera's potential for documenting the visible details of historically momentous events, but they achieved the most lasting fame with images that abstracted and symbolized transcendent cultural concepts.

Taylor tells a similar story regarding British war photography in World War I. Photographs that served as symbols of national myths were published and incorporated into press stories of patriotism, heroism, and national unity. Like "Home of a Rebel Sharpshooter," such pictures tend to be idealized. Yet, "Though unattainable, this idealization does not nullify the relation between history and experience. On the contrary, the only perfectible place for the relation is in the realm of myth: here contradictions are resolved by devices in the story, then made actual in tableaux and in the pervasive mode of realism" (Taylor 1991, 165). The millions of photographs made throughout the war that were not chosen for idealization in the press, for whatever reason, still languish in storage, an unseen and undoubtedly chaotic abundance of visual documentation.

## Robert Capa and Another Civil War: The Making of a Photographic Icon

The photographer who came to epitomize the war photojournalist in the twentieth century was Robert Capa. Beginning his career during the Spanish civil war, precisely when the European picture press had reached a highwater mark of influence, Capa immediately gained celebrity status when his photograph "The Death of a Loyalist Soldier" (fig. 6.3) was published in the October 1936 issue of the French picture magazine *VU*.

The picture shows an antifascist *miliciano* apparently stopped in his tracks by a bullet as he charges down a slope. His arms, head, and upper body are thrown back, and his rifle flies behind him out of his extended right hand. His legs are bent and his feet are forward as if they continued to slide forward down the slope as his upper body was driven back. There are no other figures in the frame nor any other identifying landmarks or scenery. It is simply this single soldier falling on a dry, grass-stubbled slope with some other hills visible on the distant horizon. Three-quarters of the background is gray-clouded sky.

*Figure 6.3.* "Near Cerro Muriano, Spain. Sept. 5, 1936. The Death of a Loyalist Militiaman" by Robert Capa. (Magnum Photos, Inc. © 1996. SPA 45CAR059+001)

Although other Capa photographs from Spain were published in the following months, it was largely on the strength of this single image that his reputation skyrocketed. In 1938 the London magazine *Picture Post* proclaimed that Capa was "The Greatest War Photographer in the World" (Fulton 1988, 144). Once again, however, this photograph has been challenged as a fake, and the controversy has never been settled. Some who knew Capa in Spain, such as *Daily Express* correspondent O. D. Gallagher, claim that the photo was staged. Gallagher contends that the picture was taken of a fascist soldier when Capa was allowed to photograph simulated battle maneuvers by Franco's troops. Others who also knew Capa in Spain contend that the photo is authentic.

A major reason that the controversy has continued, aside from the fact that the negative was not preserved and Capa never provided specific documentation concerning the circumstances of the picture, is that the photograph is nonspecific. Its fame, perhaps, rests on two factors: its implausibility (the capturing of split-second action by a photographer apparently putting himself at great risk on the front lines) and its treatment of the moment of death. Yet the stop-action quality of the photo lends it great realism and bolsters the notion that photojournalists with modern camera equipment can supply records of world events as they occur. The decontextualized soldier, his body flung and twisted at the instant of his death, provides an abstracted image of war and its costs. The photo confronts the moment of death symbolically, inviting "a strange and fearful interest" on the part of viewers.

Commenting on the popularity and continued reproduction of this photograph in the picture press of the time, Els Barents, director of photography at the Stedelijk Museum in Amsterdam, has written: "The visual war as it was waged in the magazines was probably somewhat overdone; Capa was well aware of the fact that this Civil War would determine the success of his career as a war correspondent. In the discussions following his famous photograph of the falling soldier (Cerro Muriano 1936) he was never able to dispel the suspicion that it might have been staged. But the media were mostly interested in the symbolic implications of the war, not in the heroic death of this one (anonymous) soldier" (1987, 135). Knightly, too, has observed:

> It is essentially an ambiguous image. However, as captioned in *Life*—"Robert Capa's camera captures a Spanish soldier the instant he is dropped by a bullet through the head in front of Cordoba"—it does tell us something, something beyond the face meaning of the words. It tells us that the picture was taken by someone who must have put himself at great risk, someone who was perhaps killed as well. With this caption the photograph thus becomes a famous and valuable property in both commercial and political terms. Yet—and there is nothing in the photograph to deny this—if we were to re-write the caption to read "A militiaman slips and falls while training for action" the photograph would become worthless in both senses. (Quoted in Lewinski 1978, 90)

What "The Death of a Loyalist Soldier" in particular, and Capa's work in general, suggests is that photography as a medium is characterized by two powerful and potentially contradictory qualities: its apparent ability to capture a particular moment and its tendency to transcend the moment. In one sense, transcending the moment is inevitable because a photograph often survives "long after its subject (and its maker) have passed on" (Rabinowitz 1994, 87). But transcendence also occurs at a more meaningful level and involves a connection to enduring cultural narratives, to memory, and to history. "Photographs are always doubled (at least) events—records of the camera's presence at the moment they were taken, and representations of that moment for another set of eyes. Here history and image rearrange themselves as the image produces historical meaning as much as history makes sense of the image" (Rabinowitz 1994, 87).

Yet the relationship of photographs to history becomes increasingly tenuous as photographs are published and republished in various contexts and begin to take on a widely recognizable form as cultural emblems. In these cases, history and image are rearranged to a point where history becomes irrelevant and the photograph's institutional use locks it into particular national, cultural, and professional myths. Moreover, certain types of photographs, especially those that emphasize dramatic aesthetic form but lack specific historical detail, most readily lend themselves to this abstraction process. Such metaphoric pictures are precisely the images that become most widely celebrated and are most likely to receive Pulitzer Prizes or World Press Photo awards and become the models that elite photojournalists strive to emulate.

The process of draining specific historical meaning from a photograph is not limited to the dramatic arena of war photography. Another photograph made in the same year as Capa's dying *milciano,* Dorothea Lange's "The Migrant Mother," provides a similar case study of evolution from photo document to cultural icon. Preston (1990, 1995) has detailed the circumstances surrounding the endurance of this picture as a cultural reference point and its elevation from one of a collection of 170,000 documentary photographs made between 1935 and 1943 for the New Deal's Farm Security Administration (FSA) to the leading emblem of America during the Great Depression and a work of art added to the photography collection of the Museum of Modern Art.

War photography ("international hot-spot photography" as Chapnick refers to it) represents, however, the most highly valued photojournalism genre and provides the most salient examples of the process of photographic symbolization and dehistoricization. Citing Preston, Rabinowitz provides a provocative description of the process:

> I do not need to remind my readers of the power of images—a power that includes their ability to exceed the original impulse of their creation. For instance, the troubling story of Lange's "Migrant Mother," told and retold, offers with acute poignancy an example of discourse as repository of meaning—the photograph as much as its checkered history includes a woman and her children, a photographer, a government bureau, popular magazines, museums, scholars, and a changing public—an image and tale composed, revised, circulated, and reissued in various venues until whatever reality its subject first possessed has been drained away and the image become icon. (1994, 87)

Capa's most famous photographs of World War II are "Normandy Invasion," a picture of blurred motion showing a soldier chest-deep in water and lunging forward (presumably toward the beaches), and "One of the Last Allied Soldiers to Die," a picture of a soldier crumpled in the doorway of a bedroom balcony where he has been shot. His body lays across the threshold in the foreground of the frame, his head bent against the open door, one arm extended into the bedroom, and a pool of now viscous-looking blood flowing from beneath his arm and shoulder into the room. Undoubtedly meant as a somber reminder at war's end, the photograph concentrates all attention on the painfully crumpled body and spilled blood of the soldier, who could be any slain soldier anywhere. The photo provides a tragic coda to the war, death until the very end. It is frequently reproduced in histories of photography and histories of the war as a poignant symbol of human cost, a metonym for the sacrifice that purchased victory for the Allied nations.

In "Normandy Invasion" Capa similarly focused on a single soldier in the foreground of the frame. The blur caused by Capa's moving camera is remindful of a cinematic swish pan. The movement not only gives the picture a sense of authentic action and "shooting on the run" but also effectively blurs the shapes of landing craft and other objects farther out in the water, creating a disquieting but indecipherable background against which the lone soldier lunges forward through the water. His jaw set and a seemingly determined look on his face, he desperately pushes forward to the danger or death that awaits him.

As with "The Death of a Loyalist Soldier," the implausibility of the shot generates much of its interest. It is a tribute to the bravado of the photographer as much as to the courage of the soldier. Capa became the yardstick by which later war photographers, and photojournalists in general, have been measured. The Overseas Press Club of America, in conjunction with *Life* magazine, established the Robert Capa Gold Medal, which it awards to photographers whose work demonstrates "exceptional courage and enterprise." Chapnick describes Capa as the archetypal "bang-bang" photographer: "In the photojournalistic vernacular, 'bang-bang' is synonymous with action, producing photographs approximating the archetypal Robert Capa photograph showing the instant of impact when a bullet struck a Spanish Civil War soldier. Editors revel in 'bang-bang' pictures, and readers are fascinated by them" (1994, 314).

## World War II, Vietnam, and Beyond

During World War II, the FSA gave way to the Office of War Information and the symbolic power of photography was embraced for the war effort. This involved some of the best known names in the history of photography, including Roy Stryker, director of the FSA documentary photo unit, and Edward Steichen.

Stryker had been instructed to shift the FSA work from its emphasis on disadvantaged working people to America's buildup for war. The new theme was to be America's growing strength as the nation prepared to defend itself—images of industrial power, the burgeoning defense factories, the scale and richness of agricultural production in the heartland, and the spirit and resolve of American men and women (Daniel et al. 1987; Stange 1989).

Steichen, who as a young man at the turn of the century collaborated with Alfred Steiglitz in launching the Photo-secession, a movement to ally photography with avant-garde art, volunteered at the age of thirty-eight for the American Expeditionary Force in World War I, helping to organize the first photographic reconnaissance division for the U.S. Signal Corps. In the years following the war he shocked friends in the photo art world by going to work for *Vogue* and *Vanity Fair* and the J. Walter Thompson advertising agency, establishing himself as the premier commercial photographer in New York. By 1938 he tired of commercial work, however, and announced his retirement. Now nearly sixty, Steichen was influenced by the poems of his brother-in-law Carl Sandburg to envision the possibility of a massive photo project, a "portrait of America" (Phillips 1981). About the same time, he encountered an exhibition of FSA photographs and, impressed with them, he arranged to reproduce several pictures in the *U.S. Camera Annual.*

A year later the world was again at war, and by the fall of 1940 Steichen, despite his age, was attempting to renew his World War I army commission. Rebuffed by the army, he accepted an offer from the Museum of Modern Art to curate a patriotic photo exhibition on the theme of national defense. Working with Stryker, he drew heavily from the FSA picture files to plan an exhibition entitled *Panorama of Defense.* But before preparations were completed, the Japanese attacked Pearl Harbor and the United States entered the war. *Panorama of Defense* was revised and recast as *Road to Victory.* The FSA and the Museum of Modern Art, like the Hollywood movie industry, mobilized behind the war effort (Phillips 1981, 1983; Stange 1989).

Before *Road to Victory* opened in May 1942, Steichen managed to convince the navy that his services would be valuable. High-ranking Naval Aviation officers became persuaded that the right kinds of pictures could help them win their rivalry with the Army Air Corps to recruit pilots. They hoped that photographs might even help to sell the new idea of "aircraft carrier power" to the navy itself. Steichen was commissioned as an officer in the U.S. Naval Reserve at the age of sixty-three. His first orders were to complete *Road to Victory.* In the meantime he began to recruit photographers for a special Naval Aviation Photo Unit, a unit that in the following three years filled the pages of *Life, Look,* the *New York Times,* and other newspapers with photographs of the naval air war. In 1945 Steichen's military work culminated in another exhibit at the Museum of Modern Art—*Power in the Pacific* (Phillips 1981, 1983; Stange 1989).

The unquestioned ease with which these MOMA exhibitions used photojournalism to symbolize unifying themes of American patriotism, strength, and spirit makes clear that World War II photographers and curators alike understood that it was the symbolic aspects of photographs more than their descriptive potential that gave them power. In that context, it is not surprising that Joe Rosenthal's "Old Glory Goes Up on Mt. Suribachi, Iwo Jima" (fig. 6.4) should emerge as the most famous picture, in the United States, of the war. What would have been less easy to predict is that the Pulitzer Prize-winning shot has continued to be hailed as one of the greatest news photographs of all time.[10]

Of course, the huge reputation of the famous image is also marred by controversy over staging. Several of the soldiers present on the day that American Marines fought for control of the heights of Mt. Suribachi have

*Figure 6.4.* "Old Glory Goes Up on Mt. Suribachi, Iwo Jima" by Joe Rosenthal.

protested over the years that the Rosenthal picture was staged some time after the first flag had been hastily raised at the summit. According to these reports, bullets were still whistling by when the first flag was raised, and no one in his right mind, not even a photojournalist, would have stood in the open to provide a clear target. Rosenthal agrees that the photograph was taken when a second, larger flag was later raised to replace the first. But he insists that the picture is a candid shot of soldiers raising the second flag. Still, some witnesses maintain that Rosenthal provided a larger flag himself and asked the soldiers to repeat the second flag-raising as he made photographs. Some of these accounts seem to come from soldiers involved in one of the earlier flag-raisings (it is unclear how many there may have been in all) who were miffed at not appearing in the more famous depiction of the event (Evans 1978, 145–47).

The point is not whether the photograph was actually restaged but whether its classically posed composition and metaphoric allusions (characteristics consistent with staging) were largely responsible for its immediate popularity and rapid elevation to icon status. Fulton recounts how readily the picture was embraced for its symbolic value: "'Old Glory goes up on Mt. Suribachi, Iwo Jima,' arguably the most famous photograph to come out of World War II, is an excellent example of the photograph as icon. People believed in the spirit it conveyed and were cheered by its sense of victory over adversity. It had an immediate, overwhelming impact on the nation. The powerful message of the men surging forward with the wind-whipped flag to raise in the sands of Iwo Jima as the fighting continued was communicated instantly" (1988, 160).[11] Goldberg (1993) notes, "The photograph was already a symbol of American history; and *Life* paired it with 'Washington Crossing the Delaware.'"

Yevgeny Khaldei saw Rosenthal's photograph and recognized its power to shape the way the war would be remembered, a mythic image that codified the victor's sense of triumph and moral superiority. Khaldei, a veteran Soviet war photographer, had spent most of the war traversing the battlefields and ruined cities of the Eastern Front. When the Soviet army closed in on Berlin, he searched for a Soviet flag he could use as a prop. Finding none, he persuaded his uncle to sew a yellow hammer and sickle on a red tablecloth. He took that makeshift flag with him to Berlin, where, after the fall of the city, he went to the Reichstag and directed three soldiers to take the flag to the roof and wave it above the entrance, setting the stage for his most famous photograph "Raising the Flag over the Reichstag, May 2, 1945."[12]

Despite the scale of World War II and the presence of photographers in every theater of the war, a small handful of images, including Rosenthal's and Khaldei's, have been installed as the major symbols for this grim conflict, symbols that shape the way we store this chapter of history in memory. Similarly, in later conflicts public perceptions coalesced around small numbers of often reproduced images. In Korea there were David Douglas Duncan's heroic images of advancing and weary U.S. marines. The Vietnam war became symbolized by a small collection of photographs that included Larry Burrows's photograph of wounded and desperate U.S. soldiers in a muddy quagmire, one soldier with a bloody bandage tied around his face moving in the center of the frame to help a fallen, and possibly dead, comrade (1966); Phillip Jones Griffith's gruesome portrait of a horribly burned napalm victim, his head completely covered in bandages and a shriveled and blackened hand held over his face (1967); Eddie Adams's "Rough Justice on a Saigon Street" (which won a Pulitzer Prize in 1969), showing national police chief Gen. Hguyen Ngoc Loan executing a Viet Cong suspect with a pistol at point-blank range in the middle of a city street; Nick Ut's often reproduced "Terror of War" (which won a Pulitzer Prize in 1973) in which nine-year-old Kim Phuc Phan Thi runs naked down a road after tearing off her napalm-burned clothing; and army photographer Ron Haeberle's photographs from the My Lai massacre, especially the frequently reproduced "And Babies?" first published in the *Cleveland Plain-Dealer* more than twenty months after he photographed it.

The inadequacy of these photographs as representative of war coverage becomes apparent when paging through larger collections of Vietnam photographs or the more complete work of a single photographer (e.g., Griffith 1970; Jury 1971; McCullin 1981). At these times, confronted by the great diversity of pictorial records available treating U.S. involvement in Southeast Asia, one is hard-pressed to understand how collective memory can be so tightly circumscribed by so few visual images. Of course, these images have not been singled out because they are representative of the way that Vietnam was covered. Rather, they symbolize generalized impressions of war, especially in retrospect: the needless violence and brutality inflicted on the civilian populace, the wasteful sacrifice of American "boys" in a far-away and hostile land, the atrocity of war itself, and the capacity of humans for inhumanity.

The same images continue to reappear as symbols of Vietnam. In a forty-year anniversary catalog compiled by World Press Photo (Mayes, ed. 1996), for instance, a total of six different Vietnam war photographs are reproduced among the 234 photographs illustrating the catalog's nine essays, which have titles such as "Newsmakers," "Lessons of History," "Photo History," and "Icons of an Age." Not surprisingly they include Larry Burrows's photo of wounded American soldiers, Eddie Adams's "Rough Justice on a Saigon Street" (reproduced three times in three different essays), and Nick Ut's "Terror of War" (reproduced three times in three essays). In a section of the book entitled "Photo History," "experts in press photography" are asked to select photographs of the previous forty years that they consider significant. Vincent Alabiso, executive photo editor for the Associated Press in New York, observes:

> Selecting the single most significant image in the past forty years was more than a daunting challenge. For me it's not one photograph, but two which remain inseparable in my memory; Eddie Adams' Vietcong execution and Nick Ut's South Vietnamese napalm victims. Each of these clearly withstood the test of time, and is powerful in its own right. Together, however, they define more than the conflict in Southeast Asia. From different perspectives, they illustrate the nature of all war. As a photo editor, my discipline, that which I have been taught and now try to teach others, is to be decisive in choosing the moment. For me, the work of Adams and Ut clearly stands out as a composite moment in time. (Mayes, ed. 1996, 172)

In the same volume, the Ut photo also appears across one page of "The Newsmakers" by Kathy Ryan, photo editor of the *New York Times Magazine.* On the facing page is a portrait of Kim Phuc Phan Thi, the nine-year-old girl in Ut's shot shown as an adult twenty-three years later. She is holding a baby, and her back, shoulder and arm are bare. The shoulder is turned toward the camera to reveal napalm scars that still cover her body and arm. Like many others who comment on the history of press photography, Ryan sees metaphoric images of conflict and human misery as quintessential photojournalism and conflates war photography with the development of photojournalism. "War and photojournalism merged shortly after the discovery of photography. Since then, the collaboration has flourished" (Ryan 1996, 26).

## Photography and Memory

James Nachtway, a three-time winner of the Robert Capa Gold Medal, repeat winner of the NPPA Magazine Photographer of the Year Award, and winner of the World Press Photo Photographer of the Year Award for 1995, has made his career covering war and conflict. He appeared on public television in June of 1996 with Peter Galassi, a curator at the Museum of Modern Art, to discuss the opening of an exhibit of photojournalism at the museum.[13] One of the things they discussed was the idea that the most famous photographs were also the most emblematic. Galassi commented that the best pictures were usually "pictures that come to stand, as icons, for a time period or a class of events"; a picture, that is, transformed into an emblem or abstraction. Nachtway added that he prefers using black-and-white film to color because black and white is better than color for "distilling the essence of a subject." The discussion recapitulated the notion that people remember pictures stereotypically, memory being based on organizing schema that filter experience according to the most essential and familiar concepts. In reviewing the state of research on memory, Daniel Schacter, a Harvard psychologist, has written, "It is now clear that we do not store judgment-free snapshots of our past experiences but rather hold onto the meaning, sense, and emotions these experiences provided us" (1996, 5).

As markers of collective memory, photographs are most useful when they symbolize socially shared concepts or beliefs rather than present new or unfamiliar information. Annette Kuhn contemplates the role of photographs for memory and concludes that although they do constitute a kind of evidence they cannot be taken at face value, nor as a "mirror of the real," nor even as offering "any self-evident relationship between itself and what it shows" (1995, 11). Rather, she argues, they are simply "material for interpretation, evidence in that sense: to be solved, like a riddle; read and decoded, like clues left behind at the scene of a crime. Evidence of this sort, though, can conceal, even as it purports to reveal, what it is evidence of. A photograph can certainly throw you off the scent" (11–12). For Kuhn, photographs serve as "memory texts" linking private and public life, personal and collective memory.

In public memory ("history"), such decontextualized photographic moments become enveloped in aesthetic genres, historical narratives, and cultural mythology (Kammen 1995). They similarly offer evidence of a sort to be decoded "like clues left behind at the scene of a crime." Photographs are also tied to the evocation of familiar and meaningful themes. As Schacter (1996) and Schudson (1995) note, photographs act as primes and metaphors for mental images that draw from social expectations and schema outside of and beyond the photograph. Photographs and media images are mnemonic symbols, "road signs," both prompting memory and encapsulating and condensing it. They are, in Eco's terms (1986, 216), "already seen images" that no longer represent single characters or events but express concepts. "Each of these photographs seems a film we have seen and refers to other films that had seen it."

Collective memory is highly complex and not fully understood. Yet it seems clear that we mark memories with relatively simple, predictable images. The connection to myths is what makes this possible. Photojournalism is a place of contestation between photorealism and visual evidence on the one hand and ceremony and glorification on the other. War photography represents the most dramatic and mythologically charged arena for this contest. Press photographs become largely narrative emblems, symbolic more than descriptive, and war photography becomes the symbolizing of national and mythic narratives. Photographs, as facts, begin to be questioned when the narratives to which they are linked lose authority.

Throughout the nineteenth and much of the twentieth centuries, commentators on photography were preoccupied with its status as a new recording technology. Photographers were often referred to as "camera operators," and a certain presumption of realism dominated the mechanical process of making "light impressions." In this context photojournalism and history were not explicit (or even implicit) concerns. New photo technologies were important primarily because they offered new means of livelihood. Appearances could be manufactured for commercial distribution and profit: studio portraiture, cartes-de-visite, stereographic views, and commercial sketchbooks of exotic faraway lands, wilderness, or war. The photographs made by Brady, Gardner, O'Sullivan, Barnard, and others fit this entrepreneurial frame insofar as they provided photographic portraits and views meant to be sold to the curious. The photographs were published as scenes and views of the war in various series of large and small prints, stereo cards, cartes-de-visite for assembling in albums, and sketchbooks. Photographs of battlefield locations were often referred to as "battle landscapes." Brady's catalog, published in 1869, was entitled the *National Photographic Collection of War Views, and Portraits of Representative Men* (Barnard 1977 [1866]; Brady 1869; Gardner 1959 [1866]).

Stapp (1988) and Carlebach (1992) both survey these developments in search of the early roots of photojournalistic practice. They see in nineteenth-century photo work raw documents, albeit of mostly posed and static subjects, and examine the use of these recorded views and scenes as templates for the printed engravings and lithographs of press pictures. A major issue and problem for Carlebach is the degree to which the transformations from photographic record to book or press illustration involved altering the original in one way or another to better fit a desired narrative or stereotype. A portrait of Seminole leader Och-Lochta Micco, for example, was "enhanced" in a lithographic print copied from the photo by adding a rifle across his lap, reinforcing a stereotype of natives as hostile. Stapp discusses the publication of wood engravings based on Civil War photographs and notes examples not only of alterations but also of composites (engravings created by combining the content or attributes of more than one photograph). He describes

(1988, 18) how alterations and captions were used in the many engravings published by *Harper's Weekly* "to ensure their maximum effect upon the imaginations of *Harper's* readers." That sometimes involved concocting "fictitious scenarios" for the images to reference.

The transfer of images from photograph to printed page is a process full of intriguing issues, and Carlebach examines numerous examples and case studies. Like many photo historians, however, he never escapes the implication that photo reports remain faithful records until compromised by the vagaries of reproduction. He seems to assume, like most contemporary critics of digital photo manipulation, that the integrity of photographs as mirrors of reality will be preserved so long as no retouching or alteration follows developing and printing.

Of course, the nineteenth-century absorption of photo images into the narratives of books and press accounts presaged the photojournalism of the twentieth century in which the reproduction of pictures is inextricably bound with the structure, formats, and rhetoric of picture magazines, motion picture newsreels, illustrated newspapers, and, eventually, television. The imperfect process of printing copies of photographs in the nineteenth century was not an impediment to some purer form of photojournalism; it was precisely what photojournalism is—the incorporation of pictures into the narrativization process. The development of the cinema, the magazine photo story or essay, and television news reporting have exiled the single image as a descriptive record to the bowels of archives and museum collections.

Taylor, in his analysis of the use of war photographs in the twentieth-century British press, begins with the realization that photographs offer meaning and memory only in the forms in which they are used and in terms of the news narrative in which they are embedded: "Photographic realism infiltrates stories of terror and stamps them with the authority of verified fact, but is bound to fit the conventions of storytelling" (1991, 159). In the same way that those studying the mysteries of human memory have found memories to be selective and motivated by emotional and cognitive engagement with the world, Taylor notes that encapsulating historical memory in photographs involves the pleasures and rituals of engagement with the news media.

> Photographic realism delivers interwoven pleasures: "history itself" in the currency of the document, the fascination of human interest, and the dream of unity. No single photograph could carry this weight of potential meaning, nor needs to, because the pleasures are always related in a context that is practiced every day and has been commonplace for as long as anyone can remember. It is the utterly limpid and normal look of realism and its enchantments that

support the content of news value, gathering around the spectacular and the stereotypical. (161)

## Conclusion: Photojournalism and History

This "history itself" to which Taylor alludes (and Chapnick subscribes) has been described by Sekula as a "faith in history as representation. The viewer is confronted, not by *historical-writing,* but by the appearance of *history itself*" (1983, 198, emphasis in the original). But Sekula goes on to analyze how the "appearance of history itself" is constructed as popular narrative and aesthetic form:

> The widespread use of photographs as historical illustrations suggests that significant events are those which can be pictured, and thus history takes on the character of *spectacle.* But this pictorial spectacle is a kind of rerun, since it depends on prior spectacles for its supposedly "raw" material.
>
> The viewer of standard pictorial histories loses any ground in the present from which to make critical evaluations. In retrieving a loose succession of fragmentary glimpses of the past, the spectator is flung into a condition of imaginary and temporal geographical mobility.[14] In this dislocated and disoriented state, the only coherence offered is that provided by the constantly shifting position of the camera, which provides the spectator with a kind of power-less omniscience. Hence the spectator comes to identify with the technical apparatus, with the authoritative institution of photography. In the face of this authority, all other forms of telling and remembering begin to fade. But the machine establishes its truth, not by logical argument, but by providing an *experience.* This experience characteristically veers between nostalgia, horror, and an overriding sense of the exoticism of the past, its irretrievable otherness for the viewer in the present. Ultimately then, when photographs are uncritically presented as historical documents, they are transformed into esthetic objects. Accordingly, the pretense to historical understanding remains, although that understanding has been replaced by esthetic experience. (1983, 199, emphasis in the original)

The place and treatment of war photographs in histories of photography and the writings of photojournalists suggest that the shifting conflict between photographs as documents (photographic realism) and photographs as aesthetic forms (photographic artifice) becomes subsumed by the acceptance of photographs as ritualized symbols. As particular pictures become established as routine symbols of places, events, cultures, and eras they tend to shed whatever specificity of historical content they may have contained, or to which they may have been linked in their previous context, and tend to lose importance as aesthetic forms. Instead, they take on a relatively simple emblematic function as marker of cultural belief.

Perlmutter (1992) found that school textbook publishers chose historical photographs for reproduction on the basis of particular aesthetic features, color, clarity, action, and, perhaps even more important, on the basis of thematic topicality and conformance to expected genres of representation. In other words, pictures were chosen that fit traditional patterns of representation for conventional themes. A photographic portrait of George Armstrong Custer, for example, illustrates a textbook section on the "Indian wars" because it is conventional practice to picture military leaders as emblems of armies and wartime events. Seldom did Perlmutter find that photographs or other illustrations contributed specific visual information supportive of or pertinent to accompanying historical accounts.

In a similar vein, Griffin and Lee (1995) found that the photographs reproduced in U.S. news magazines during the Gulf War failed to provide images of ongoing events in the Gulf despite media promotions of a "live TV war." Instead, more generic symbols (often file photographs) were substituted to symbolize American military prowess and high technology, the "showdown" between George Bush and Saddam Hussein, or the "knockout punch" delivered to the Iraqis in a purging American victory. The level of specific information in published Gulf War photographs was so low that photos of military exercises and pictures from defense industry arms catalogs often appeared in place of images of actual combat or troops on location in the Gulf without noticeable alarm or complaint from the reading public.

Like press coverage of previous wars, Gulf War photographs were highly routinized and almost entirely symbolic. But the way this war was pictured diverged significantly from previous wars in the sense that the human consequences of warfare remained almost completely invisible. Few glimpses of the impact of Allied firepower on Iraqi troops and civilians were allowed to make their way through the maze of military censorship, media self-regulation, and media wariness to reach television screens and the pages of newspapers and magazines. Virtually no photographs of American casualties were shown or published until several months after the war. In this war there were no ritual images of sacrifice to consecrate the valor of "our boys," the sacred nature of their mission, or the nation's triumph. Instead, the preponderance of published photographs celebrated the American arsenal. The icons of this war consisted of images of high-tech weaponry, effective advertisements to the rest of the world for American arms manufacturers.[15] The victory was more commercial than moral.

In the end, is it possible that "to ignore photojournalism is to ignore history"? Should Chapnick's claim be dismissed as the natural hyperbole of a photojournalist's unbridled enthusiasm? Perhaps there is something more to it than that. It is true that the celebrated photographs examined in this chapter bear little resemblance to the kind of careful, detailed documentation that undergirds serious historical inquiry and representation. For most, history is not the meticulous, analytical, and sometimes esoteric work of historians but rather popular beliefs about people's origins and cultural explanations for their circuitous trajectory as a society. Photojournalism provides a growing body of images that sometimes describe particular aspects of the world but more often dramatize and aestheticize the most sensational of world events.

> The importance in news-value of the spectacular event and its representation in pictures is connected to the hope of everlasting movement and to its impossibility.
>    The stereotypical world is both dangerous and exciting, and so is the world in the newspapers. Side by side, and often overlapping, are the agencies of life and death. (Taylor 1991, 161)

The stereotypes of photojournalism seduce with the authority of witness as they pander to craving for icons of death and life, symbols of sacrifice, and triumph. The published photographs of war have a ritual quality, like the monuments and commemorative displays constructed as markers of collective memory. Do they offer a picture of history? Yes, but only when history is understood as national mythology.

## Notes

I wish to acknowledge support provided by an Annenberg Scholars Program Fellowship for research on "The Future of Fact" during the 1995–96 academic year. Thanks are also due to Elihu Katz at the University of Pennsylvania for his support and encouragement and to Carolyn Marvin at the University of Pennsylvania for her interest in this project and her assistance in obtaining information related to photographer Yevgeny Khaldei.

1. See, for example, some of the most widely cited histories of photography and photojournalism: Carlebach (1992); Fulton (1988); Jeffrey (1981); Newhall (1982); and Rosenblum (1984).

2. Perhaps increased academic attention is inevitably spurred by signs of antiquation.

3. Other important new theoretical statements on the nature of photography in this period included Burgin, ed. (1982); Eco (1976, 1986); Sekula (1975); and Tagg (1988).

4. By the mid-1980s, exhibitions such as *On the Line: The New Color Photojour-*

*nalism,* organized by the Walker Art Center in Minneapolis, provoked no controversy whatsoever for displaying framed press photographs on white museum walls. On the absorption of photojournalism by the art world, see Schwartz (1990).

5. See, for example, several essays in Bolton, ed. (1989); Gross, ed. (1995); and Tagg (1988).

6. An example reproduced by Taylor (1991, 84) is a page from the *Daily Mirror* carrying a photograph of a couple and their three children seated around the dinner table for a family meal, a bombed-out building prominently visible through the window. Across the page is a photo of an air raid warden posing with a woman and her baby in the bedroom where he assisted "as midwife" in the child's birth. Below that are photos of a boy carrying home a pail of water, others fetching water, and the Union Jack "still flying and still overlooking" the rubble of a ruined building. Alongside these photographs is an advertisement for women's shampoo and a homemaker's testimonial headlined "I Look after My Children Husband and Home and Also Go to Work." The subheading reads, "Never Feel Ill or Tired."

7. Dozens of books contain histories of Brady's Civil War photography enterprise. Perhaps the best concise accounts are in Carlebach (1992, ch. 3) and Stapp (1988).

8. Several writers have discussed the fact that the "Rebel sharpshooter's" body appears in more than one photograph and that it was almost certainly moved and rearranged (with the rifle added) for the famous image "Home of a Rebel Sharpshooter." See Carlebach (1992); Frassanito (1975); and Stapp (1988).

9. *Pictura poesis* refers to the association of narrative and literary themes with pictures. It is related to the Greek rhetorical exercise of *Ekphrasis:* a tradition of describing pictures through narrative and thematic extrapolation (Griffin 1990; Mitchell 1994).

10. In a poll of National Press Photographers Association (NPPA) members around 1990, Rosenthal's flag-raising photograph was voted "the greatest news photograph" of all time.

11. Editors at *Life* magazine questioned the authenticity of the photograph immediately, reckoning that the composition was too idealized and "perfect." But after the photograph was published by *Time* and hundreds of other magazines and newspapers, *Life* relented and printed the photo as well. It was soon being used as the model for 3,500,000 War Drive posters and commemorative postage stamps, and at the end of 1945 Rosenthal was awarded a Pulitzer Prize for his photojournalism.

12. For a review of a New York exhibition of Khaldei's work featuring "Raising the Flag over the Reichstag," see Goldberg (1997).

13. They appeared on a "Charlie Rose Show" that aired on PBS on June 7, 1996.

14. Kuhn (1995, 5) describes memory similarly: "Memory, it turns out, has its own modes of expression: these are characterized by the fragmentary, non-linear quality of moments recalled out of time. Visual flashes, vignettes, a certain anecdotal quality, mark memory texts."

15. Numerous newspaper reports in the summer months following the war drew attention to a steep rise in U.S. arms sales abroad.

## References

Barents, Els. 1987. "The Snowball Effect of Documentary Photography." In *The Photographic Memory: Press Photography—Twelve Insights,* ed. Emile Meijer and Joop Swart, 127–45. London: World Press Photo Foundation.

Barnard, George N. 1977 (1866). *Photographic Views of Sherman's Campaign.* New York: Dover.

Barnhurst, Kevin. 1994. *Seeing the Newspaper.* New York: St. Martin's Press.

Barnouw, Erik. 1983. *Documentary: A History of the Non-Fiction Film.* New York: Oxford University Press.

Barthes, Roland. 1977. *Image, Music, Text,* trans. Stephen Heath. New York: Noonday Press.

———. 1981. *Camera Lucida: Reflections on Photography,* trans. Richard Howard. New York: Hill and Wang.

Basinger, Jeanine. 1986. *The World War II Combat Film: Anatomy of a Genre.* New York: Columbia University Press.

Baughman, James L. 1992. *The Republic of Mass Culture: Journalism, Filmmaking and Broadcasting in America since 1941.* Baltimore: Johns Hopkins University Press.

Berger, John. 1972. *Ways of Seeing.* New York: Penguin.

———. 1980. *About Looking.* New York: Pantheon.

Berger, John, and Jean Mohr. 1967. *A Fortunate Man.* New York: Pantheon.

———. *A Seventh Man.* 1975. London: Writers and Readers Cooperative.

———. 1982. *Another Way of Telling.* New York: Pantheon.

Bolton, Richard, ed. 1989. *The Contest of Meaning: Critical Histories of Photography,* Cambridge: MIT Press.

Bourdieu, Pierre. 1990 (1965). *Photography as a Middle-brow Art.* Translated by Shaun Whiteside. Stanford: Stanford University Press.

Brady, Mathew B. 1869. *National Photographic Collection of War Views, and Portraits of Representative Men.* New York: C. A. Alvord.

Burgin, Victor, ed. 1982. *Thinking Photography.* New York: Macmillan.

Carlebach, Michael L. 1992. *The Origins of Photojournalism in America.* Washington: Smithsonian Institution Press.

Chapnick, Howard. 1994. *Truth Needs No Ally: Inside Photojournalism.* Columbia: University of Missouri Press.

Daniel, Pete, Merry A. Foresta, Maren Stange, and Sally Stein. 1987. *Official Images: New Deal Photography.* Washington, D.C.: Smithsonian Institution Press.

Doherty, Thomas. 1993. *Projections of War: Hollywood and American Culture, 1941–1945.* New York: Columbia University Press.

Eco, Umberto. 1976. *A Theory of Semiotics.* Bloomington: Indiana University Press.

———. 1986. "A Photograph." In *Travels in Hyperreality.* Translated by William Weaver. New York: Harcourt Brace Jovanovitch.

Evans, Harold. 1978. *Pictures on a Page.* New York: Holt.

Fralin, Frances, ed. 1985. *The Indelible Image: Photographs of War, 1846 to the Present,* with an essay by Jane Livingston. New York: Abrams.

Frassanito, William A. 1975. *Gettysburg: A Journey in Time.* New York: Scribner.

Freund, Gisele. 1980 (1974). *Photography and Society.* Translated by Richard Dunn, Yong-Hee Last, Megan Marshall, and Andrea Perera. Boston: David R. Godine.

Fulton, Marianne. 1988. *Eyes of Time: Photojournalism in America.* Boston: Little, Brown.

Fussell, Paul. 1989. *Wartime: Understanding and Behavior in the Second World War.* New York: Oxford University Press.

Gardner, Alexander. 1959 (1866). *Gardner's Photographic Sketch Book of the War.* 2 vols. New York: Dover.

Goldberg, Vicki. 1993. *The Power of Photography: How Photographs Changed Our Lives.* New York: Abbeville.

———. 1997. "Beyond Battle: A Soviet Photographer's Portrait." *New York Times,* Jan. 31, C1, C29.

Griffin, Michael. 1987. "Amateur Photography and Pictorial Aesthetics: Influences of Organization and Industry on Cultural Production." Ph.D. diss., University of Pennsylvania.

———. 1990. "Pictures and Storytelling: The Role of Narrative in Pictorial Interpretation." Paper presented to the Conference on Narrative in the Human Sciences, The University of Iowa.

———. 1992. "Looking at TV News: Strategies for Research." *Communication* 13(2): 121–41.

———. 1995. "Between Art and Industry: Amateur Photography and Middle-Brow Culture." In *On the Margins of Art Worlds,* ed. Larry Gross, 183–205. Boulder: Westview Press.

Griffin, Michael, and Jongsoo Lee. 1995. "Picturing the Gulf War: Constructing Images of War in *Time, Newsweek,* and *U.S. News and World Report.*" *Journalism and Mass Communication Quarterly* 72(4): 813–25.

Griffin, Michael, and Simon Kagan. 1999. "National Autonomy and Global News Flows: CNN in Israel during the Gulf War." In *International Media Monitoring,* ed. Kaarle Nordenstreng and Michael Griffin, 73–93. Creskill, N.J.: Hampton Press.

Griffiths, Phillip Jones. 1970. *Vietnam, Inc.* New York: Macmillan.

Gross, Larry, ed. 1995. *On the Margins of Art Worlds.* Boulder: Westview Press.

Hardt, Hanno, and Karin B. Ohrn. 1981. "The Eyes of the Proletariat: The Worker-Photography Movement in Weimar Germany." *Studies in Visual Communication* 7(4): 72–83.

Heller, Jonathan, ed. 1990. *War and Conflict: Selected Images from the National Archives, 1765–1970.* Washington: National Archives and Records Administration.

Jeffrey, Ian. 1991. *Photography: A Concise History.* New York: Oxford University Press.

Jury, Mark. 1971. *The Vietnam Photo Book.* New York: Vintage Books.

Jussim, Estelle. 1988. "'The Tyranny of the Pictorial': American Photojournalism from

1880–1920." In *Eyes of Time: Photojournalism in America,* ed. Marianne Fulton, 36–73. Boston: Little, Brown.

———. 1989. *The Eternal Moment.* New York: Aperture.

Kammen, Michael. 1995. "Some Patterns and Meanings of Memory Distortion in American History." In *Memory Distortion: How Minds, Brains, and Societies Reconstruct the Past,* ed. Danial L. Schacter, 329–45. Cambridge: Harvard University Press.

Koppes, Clayton, and Gregory Black. 1987. *Hollywood Goes to War: How Politics, Profits, and Propaganda Shaped World War II Movies.* New York: Free Press.

Kuhn, Annette. 1995. *Family Secrets: Acts of Memory and Imagination.* London: Verso.

Lewinski, Jorge. 1978. *The Camera at War: A History of War Photography from 1848 to the Present Day.* New York: Simon and Schuster.

Leydo, Jay. 1960. *Kino: A History of the Russian and Soviet Film.* London: Allen and Unwin.

Mayes, Stephen, ed. 1996. *This Critical Mirror: Photojournalism since the 1950s.* New York: Thames and Hudson.

McCullin, Don. 1981. *Hearts of Darkness.* New York: Knopf.

Meijer, Emile, and Joop Swart, eds. 1987. *The Photographic Memory: Press Photography—Twelve Insights.* London: Quiller Press.

Mitchell, William J. 1994. *The Reconfigured Eye: Visual Truth in the Post-Photographic Era.* Cambridge: MIT Press.

Mitchell, W. J. T. 1994. *Picture Theory.* Chicago: University of Chicago Press.

Newhall, Beaumont. 1982. *The History of Photography: From 1839 to the Present.* Boston: Little, Brown.

Osman, Colin, and Sandra S. Phillips. 1988. "European Visions: Magazine Photography in Europe Between the Wars." In *Eyes of Time: Photojournalism in America,* ed. Marianne Fulton, 75–103. Boston: Little, Brown.

Perlmutter, David. 1992. "The Vision of War in High School Social Science Textbooks." *Communication* 13(2): 143–60.

Phillips, Christopher. 1981. *Steichen at War.* New York: Harry N. Abrams.

———. 1982. "The Judgement Seat of Photography." *October* 22 (Fall): 27–63.

Preston, Catherine. 1990. "'Migrant Mother' and the Historical Endurance of Cultural Representations." Presented at the annual convention of social science historians, Minneapolis, October.

———. 1995. "Trading Places in the Art World: The Reputations of Dorothea Lange and Walker Evans." In *On the Margins of Art Worlds,* ed. Larry Gross, 207–29. Boulder: Westview Press.

Rabinowitz, Paula. 1994. *They Must Be Represented: The Politics of Documentary.* London: Verso Press.

Rosenblum, Naomi. 1984. *A World History of Photography.* New York: Abbeville.

Ryan, Kathy. 1996. "The Newsmakers." In *This Critical Mirror: Photojournalism since the 1950s,* ed. Stephen Mayes, 22–53. New York: Thames and Hudson.

Schacter, Daniel L. 1996. *Searching for Memory.* New York: Basic Books.

Schiller, Dan. 1982. *Objectivity and the News*. Philadelphia: University of Pennsylvania Press.

Schudson, Michael. 1995. "Dynamics of Distortion in Collective Memory." In *Memory Distortion: How Minds, Brains, and Societies Reconstruct the Past*, ed. Daniel L. Schacter, 346–64. Cambridge: Harvard University Press.

Schwartz, Dona. 1990. "On the Line: Crossing Institutional Boundaries between Photojournalism and Photographic Art." *Visual Sociology Review* 5(2): 22–29.

———. 1992. "To Tell the Truth: Codes of Objectivity in Photojournalism." *Communication* 13(2): 95–109.

Sekula, Alan. 1975. "On the Invention of Photographic Meaning." *Art Forum* 13 (Jan.): 36–45.

———. 1983. "Photography between Labor and Capital." In *Mining Photographs and Other Pictures: A Selection from the Negative Archives of Shedden Studios, Glace Bay, Cape Breton, 1948–1968*, ed. Benjamin Buchloh and Robert Wilkie, 193–268. Halifax: Press of Nova Scotia College of Art and Design and the University College of Cape Breton Press.

Sontag, Susan. 1977. *On Photography*. New York: Farrar, Strauss and Giroux.

Stange, Maren. 1989. *Symbols of Ideal Life: Social Documentary Photography, 1890–1950*. New York: Cambridge University Press.

Stapp, William. 1988. "Subjects of Strange . . . and of Fearful Interest: Photojournalism from Its Beginnings in 1839." In Marianne Fulton, *Eyes of Time: Photojournalism in America*, 1–33. Boston: Little, Brown.

Sweet, Timothy. 1990. *Traces of War: Poetry, Photography, and the Crisis of the Union*. Baltimore: Johns Hopkins University Press.

Taft, Robert. 1964 (1938). *Photography and the American Scene: A Social History, 1839–1889*. New York: Dover.

Tagg, John. 1988. *The Burden of Representation: Essays on Photographies and Histories*. Amherst: University of Massachusetts Press.

Tausk, Petr. 1988. *A Short History of Press Photography*. Prague: International Organization of Journalists.

Taylor, John. 1991. *War Photography: Realism in the British Press*. New York: Routledge.

# ■ 7

## Objective Representation: Photographs as Facts

*Dona Schwartz*

On December 31, 1996, the *Minneapolis Star Tribune* published a photograph on its front page that had been shot by one of the staff's most respected photographers, Stormi Greener. The photograph showed the snow-covered St. Croix River and the bridge that spans it and connects Wisconsin to Minnesota. The photograph accompanied a story about the U.S. Department of the Interior's veto of a proposal to build a new bridge. Rather than the usual kudos recognizing her efforts, the newspaper awarded Greener a two-day suspension without pay. She had committed an egregious offense: Unbeknown to her editors, she had digitally eliminated power lines from the photograph before it went to press. The *Star Tribune*'s "visual content editor," Bill Dunn, explained that Greener had violated the newspaper's policy governing digital manipulation of photographs: "We do not manipulate or alter any photography, with the exception of dust spots or imperfections on the negative. . . . we make every effort to publish what the camera saw" (Gilyard 1997, 7).

The incident unearths some deeply embedded assumptions and raises important issues regarding the use of photographs in the press. While the suspension of a respected photographer foregrounds the controversies surrounding digital-imaging technology, it is the underlying beliefs regarding news photographs that warrant scrutiny. The *Star Tribune* stance implies that photographs, left unmolested by overzealous photo technicians, offer an unmediated view of the world. Dunn's response expressed the view most succinctly when he said, "We make every effort to publish what the camera saw."

Of course it is the photographer who sees, not the camera; nor do cameras themselves make pictures. Nevertheless, Dunn perpetuated the point of view that the photographs appearing in the *Star Tribune* offer readers a factual representation of the world, unbiased by the intervention of the photographer, the photo technician, or any other employee of the newspaper. Although the credibility of other kinds of photographs may be compromised by their makers, news photographs remain sacrosanct according to the view espoused by photojournalists and their editors. The newspaper has adopted a formal policy regarding the use of digital technology, along with sanctions for rule violations. Publicly excoriating Greener demonstrated to readers that the *Star Tribune* makes good on its claim to present only unmanipulated photographs.

Newspapers nationwide have enacted policies on photo ethics that govern the practices of photojournalists on their staffs. The *Milwaukee Sentinel*, for example, endorsed the following statement:

> Photographers and picture editors are responsible for the truthfulness and objectivity of their photographs.
>
> To maintain the newspaper's credibility, documentary photographs should not be manipulated in any way that alters the reality of the photographs. Documentary photos encompass all spot news, general news, documentary, sports and feature pictures. The same ethical standards that apply to written stories are applied to documentary photography.
>
> Retouching of documentary photographs beyond conventional techniques is prohibited. Conventional techniques include color and tonal balancing through dodging and burning, electronic sharpening and spotting to eliminate dust, line hits and technical flaws. Careful consideration is always given to color/tone balancing and image-sharpening to ensure faithful reproduction.
>
> To keep the integrity of documentary photographs, we do not alter backgrounds, use color screens or colorize photos, create photomontages, or flop or mortise them. We do not reverse or overprint type on documentary photographs. (Quoted in Gessert 1991)

Ethical standards like these are intended to assure readers of the continued integrity of news photographs despite the digital revolution in contemporary photojournalism. Adherence to these principles addresses what news professionals consider the potential for abuse introduced by computer-imaging technology. The ethical debates spawned by the widespread adoption of digital imaging have rarely encompassed what takes place before the process of photo-editing—decisions made by photographers in the act of making news pictures. If, as Dunn's response suggests, photojournalists simply record what the camera sees, then only willful acts of intervention subvert their work. But photographs are not simple records of the real world in front of the camera, and ethical codes enacted to allay readers' fears of overt manipulation cannot assure a photograph's objective status.

Photojournalism is distinctive for its dual rhetoric, which simultaneously asserts the objectivity of news photographs while praising the skill and artistry of its best practitioners. It is a field of endeavor in which competing, contradictory claims coexist in apparent harmony. Why are individual photographers singled out for special recognition if their cameras do the work? Photojournalists perform their task with conspicuous skill under difficult conditions and facing tight deadlines. They tacitly make choices among lenses, decide how to respond to lighting conditions, choose what will be included in and left out of the frame, and select the appropriate moment to make an exposure. These choices, among others made in the moment of shooting, contribute to the way in which objects and events in front of the camera appear in the image. Institutionally sponsored competitions reward photojournalists for creativity, enhancing photographers' reputations among colleagues. But the recognition earned in monthly "clips contests" occupies the backstage while photographers and editors alike spotlight the objectivity of the image for public appreciation, linking photography with truth rather than artistic self-expression.

Like newsmakers working in other media, photojournalists have developed their own set of strategic rituals that allow them to lay claim to objectivity (Schwartz 1992). Codes of professional conduct guide decisions regarding both photographic form and content. Photographers working within other professional arenas make different claims for the images they produce. The history of photography narrates the ascension of the photographic image to the status of art, linking art photography with painting, sculpture, printmaking, and the like. Although art photographers may claim that their work offers truth of some kind, they make no claims to objective fact. Advertising photography has a tenuous relationship with truth and is most often linked with the desired rather than the real, with emotions instead of facts.

Comparing the characteristics attributed to photographs produced in differing institutional contexts suggests the important role the institutions themselves play in fixing public perceptions of photographic representations. All photographs are made by photographers and, through the battery of decisions those photographers make, all photographs encode a photographer's point of view and the institutional requirements constraining his or her activities. The questions probed here concern how journalism has framed news photographs to appear to have excised the photographer's viewpoint—yielding an objective, machine-made reflection of the world—and toward what end that view has been constructed and perpetuated. An examination of this kind necessarily follows some of the same paths cut by journalism historians tracing the emergence of objectivity in the press (Schiller 1981; Schudson 1978), but studying the specific role of illustrations in newsmaking maps a slightly different course. The inclusion of pictures in the press has generated a distinctive set of issues concerning the role of images as vehicles of information, and attitudes toward images themselves require examination. Rather than review the history of photojournalism from the vantage point of exceptional images or valiant attempts at reportage (following the paradigm of art histories and most recent histories of photojournalism), this chapter shifts the frame to investigate the role played by publishers in the establishment of photojournalism as an objective reportorial strategy.

## The Illustrated Press

Many histories tracing the origins of photojournalism start their narratives with the emergence of the *Illustrated London News* on May 14, 1842. The number of wood-engraved illustrations appearing on its pages, and the regularity with which they were published, has earned the newspaper its designated ancestral status. In his social history of photography, Robert Taft (1964 [1938]) indicated a line of succession of illustrated newspapers that moves from England to Europe and then across the Atlantic to the United States: *L'Illustration*, published in Paris in 1843; the *Illustrirte Zeitung*, published in Leipzig, also in 1843; and, in the United States, *Frank Leslie's Illustrated Newspaper*, which began on December 15, 1855, and was followed by *Harper's Weekly* in 1857, the New York *Daily Graphic* in 1873, and the *World* in 1883.

Although Taft's account may be selective, it suggests the rapid diffusion of illustrated periodicals to Western urban centers. Although most historical accounts begin with the *Illustrated London News*, its approach was built upon other popular periodicals, the illustrated weeklies preceding it. The *Illustrated News* attempted to stake out its own territory in contradistinction to its predecessors while simultaneously incorporating the commercially successful strategies they employed. Understanding the attitudes and values encoded in earlier illustrated publications, whether devoted to information or entertainment, helps situate the approach the *News* subsequently adopted.

Two histories aid attempts to understand the cultural milieu shaping illustrated periodicals of the mid-nineteenth century: Celina Fox's *Graphic Journalism in England during the 1830s and 1840s* (1988) and Patricia Anderson's *The Printed Image and the Transformation of Popular Culture, 1790–1860* (1991). As they trace the history of the English periodical the *Penny Magazine,* both authors illuminate the purposes initially conceived for massreproduced visual images. In Britain during the early nineteenth century, Anderson argues, elite art images were virtually inaccessible to working people, and visual images of all kinds remained marginal to the daily experience of the working class. A limited range of published materials included wood engravings, which were generally considered quite crude. Popular religious tracts and self-help chapbooks, literary entertainment published in chapbooks or on broadsides, and political materials appearing in pamphlet or broadsheet format might all be accompanied by illustrations.

The Society for the Diffusion of Useful Knowledge (SDUK), a British organization devoted to social reform, published a monthly series of self-help tracts known as the "Library of Useful Knowledge." The society hoped its periodical publications would compete with and counteract the disruptive influence of the radical political press. Increased urbanization during the nineteenth century had created both new prospects and problems for elites. Urban population growth provided a conveniently accessed labor force as well as a centralized cache of consumers for manufactured goods and popular periodicals, but the perceived potential for labor unrest and social upheaval caused elites concern. Partisan periodicals were construed as threats to the established social order insofar as they disseminated revolutionary ideas among the working class and could conceivably incite oppositional political action. Despite government efforts to eliminate or at least to control dissident publications, an illegal radical press emerged and flourished. Publications such as the *Penny Magazine* (sponsored by the society) and its successors the *Art-Union,* the *Pictorial Times,* and, later, the *Illustrated London News* offered alternatives to the partisan press and attempted to present transcendent, universal values that would unite rather than split the populace. Many believed the civilizing influence of art could be used to quell political unrest. Exemplifying this sentiment, the following passage appeared in the pages of the *Penny Magazine:* "By diffusing a love of nature and of art amongst the people, the higher faculties of the mind will be awakened, and the impulses under which men seek for excitement in vicious indulgences, will be more easily overcome" (quoted in Fox 1988, 9).

Charles Knight, the *Penny Magazine* publisher, considered delivering high-quality, wood-engraved images to the working class a "mission into the field of popular education" (Anderson 1991, 53) as well as a potentially profitable business venture. Knight believed that "intellectual culture" did not only depend on books and lectures. Pictures provided "eye-knowledge" that was "sometimes more instructive than words." Not just any kind of picture would do; Knight particularly advocated using illustrations that reproduced fine art works. Anderson quotes Knight, who wrote, "Faithful and spirited copies of the greatest productions of painting and sculpture" were among the most "valuable accessories of knowledge [and] instruments of education" (1991, 70).

Anderson also argues that the introduction of such illustrated periodicals fundamentally altered working people's day-to-day experience by opening up access to art images once viewed almost exclusively by elites. The *Penny Magazine* quickly achieved an unprecedented circulation. By December 1832, nine months after the appearance of its first issue, the magazine's circulation reached two hundred thousand; its actual readership numbered one million (Anderson 1991, 52).

According to Anderson, the *Penny Magazine* was the earliest inexpensive serial publication to realize the commercial possibilities of mass-reproduced imagery. Entrepreneurs noted its success, and it spawned a succession of imitators that eventually cut into the magazine's circulation and endangered its existence. In 1845 the *Penny Magazine* ceased publication.

Second-generation illustrated periodicals built upon the popularity of the *Penny Magazine,* initially invoking some of the same rhetoric found in its pages, yet Anderson notes an important distinction. The reformer's emphasis on art gave way to light entertainment. Moral instruction and intellectual enlightenment of whatever kind would be delivered through an amalgam of illustrated literary fiction (tales of romance, crime, and intrigue), fashion news, recipes, and more overtly educational material such as articles on art, science, or current events. The new periodicals' shift in focus and the demise of the *Penny Magazine* shifted art back to the elite domain from which Knight had wrested it. But even though reproductions of artwork decreased, art was still invoked in order to enhance the new periodicals' reputations as worthy reading fare suitable for a broad-based audience that included elites.

## From Art to Fact

Like many other second-generation periodicals, the *Illustrated London News* followed the lead set by the *Penny Magazine.* But the *Illustrated London News* distinguished itself from popular publications ("penny dreadfuls") that pandered to the basest instincts of contemporary readers by providing a steady diet of indelicate stories detailing crimes, scandals, acts of debauchery, and the like, complete with vivid illustrations. The *Illustrated London News* claimed the moral high ground, positioning itself as a periodical suitable for the drawing-room table. It pledged to observe proper decorum, concentrating on domestic matters and providing "homely illustration." It would eschew the partisan politics of the radical press and remain neutral on the matters it reported. And, like its predecessor the *Penny Magazine,* the *Illustrated London News* aspired to elevate and educate its intended readership, both the audience for "trashy" periodicals and readers of the "quality" press, through art.

For the *Illustrated London News,* the meaning of "art" diverged importantly from Charles Knight's use of the term. To him, art was represented by painting, sculpture, and architecture; wood-engraved reproductions served as the artistic vehicle through which legitimized works of art could be reproduced and therefore accessed by a general readership. In the service of presenting news, the *Illustrated London News* understood that "art" referred to the engravings themselves, the product of a collaborative effort among sketch artists and the draftsmen who translated them into engraved plates for the press. Its illustrations invested "the realities of life with a superior interest, by the aid of the exhaustless and ennobling graces of art" (Fox 1988, 312). Rather than representing art through wood engravings, the illustrations were themselves presented as works of art.

The characteristics attributed to art warrant further scrutiny. Nineteenth-century educational reformers advocated widespread access to art based on the belief that it ennobled all who view it, elevating both the intellectual and the moral level of its audience. That belief, in turn, built upon the view that visual art is directly perceived and universally comprehensible and can therefore transform anyone exposed to its influence. Made accessible to the public, art could contribute to the common good, rally its audience behind transcendent social values, and thereby diminish class conflict. Belief in the universality of the visual image was tied to its fidelity: Artists' representations provided objective transcriptions of the external world. Consonant with this view, on May 14, 1842, the *Illustrated London News* asserted the factuality of its wood engravings: "The public will have henceforth under their glance and within their grasp, the very form and presence of events as they transpire, in all their substantial reality, and with evidence visible as well as circumstantial" (quoted in Fox 1988, 12).

When a new chancellor was installed at Cambridge University, the *Illustrated London News* announced its ability to represent the affair without political bias "uncontaminated by party spirit—in a word, with truth, and without bias—to present to its readers pictorial records of all the high festivals of the nation" (quoted in Fox 1988, 12).

Once these claims had been asserted, it was logically consistent to proffer the grander notion that illustrations in the press advanced the tradition of history painting. The *Illustrated London News* referred to its illustrations as the "pictured register of the world's history," suggesting that the engravings offered not only a record of contemporary events but also a treasure trove for future generations.

As with the *Penny Magazine,* imitators emerged competing for the audience claimed by the *Illustrated London News.* Fox (1988) identifies the *Pictorial Times,* founded in March 1843, as the "nearest rival." In an 1844 preface, the *Pictorial Times* characterized illustrated newspapers for its readers in terms that must have seemed familiar. They were:

> children of the fancy as well as of the actual world; they are not only papers of *news,* but pictures of nature and art; they are intended to instruct and refine the feelings and the taste, as well as to convey information . . . and we venture to think that the amount of intelligence and good feeling which may be acquired through the medium of the eye alone, from works of art, in truthfulness, entireness, and in its immediate effect upon the sensibilities and the mind, has never yet been sufficiently estimated. (Quoted in Fox 1988, 285–86)

The ideas of universality and factuality associated with art proved useful to second-generation pictorial magazine publishers. The contention that art could unite the nation was certainly an overly optimistic conceit nurtured by elites. But asserting the transcendence of art performed a different, more pragmatic function: bridging the gap separating diverse social groups in order to build a mass readership. By proclaiming that they were unallied with any one group's interests, professing to uphold common-sense family values, and liberally using "factual" illustrations to present stories, second-generation publishers hoped to market their products to elites as well as the working class. They intended to bridge the cultural boundaries created and maintained through social class affiliation in order to increase circulation.

Both Fox (1988) and Anderson (1991) locate the emergence and popular acceptance of the illustrated press during the 1830s and 1840s. Fox argues that despite the meteoric growth of these publications they were regarded by 1850 "in the main as synonymous with bland respectability and universal comprehensibility" (1988, 319). Worse yet, public confidence in their claims to factuality appeared to be waning. Critics questioned the ability of sketch artists to render complex subjects with accurate detail, and some suggested that representations were compromised by the practice of integrating previously drawn figures, settings, and objects into new tableaux as need arose. Although publications such as the *Illustrated London News* and the *Pictorial Times* claimed the "photographic fidelity" of their illustrations, the wood engravings they published fell short of the real thing—photographs themselves.

## Photography's Art

Photography eventually eclipsed wood engraving as the preferred vehicle for factual visual representation, but for several reasons the shift came about slowly. Introduced in 1839 while the illustrated press was gaining popularity, photographic images could not provide what sketch artists could: representations of events "as they happen" (in motion). Early light-sensitive emulsions required long exposure times, a limitation that made portraiture, landscapes, and the still life the most appropriate subjects for photographic depiction. A succession of refinements at the end of the nineteenth century led to photography's conquest of motion, but until that time the fidelity of sketch artists' renditions of transpiring events surpassed what photography could offer.

Technology posed another problem obstructing the initial adoption of photography by mass-circulation periodicals. No practical process existed before the 1870s that would allow the direct reproduction of photographs with type. Photographs could only be used as source material to be translated into wood engravings for reproduction. There were additional points of resistance. Professionally entrenched sketch artists and engravers had no intention of ceding their posts to accommodate the upstart medium (Schuneman 1969). Too, "machine-made" photographic images could not immediately invoke the same legitimizing claim to art maintained by wood engravings. Nevertheless, the technological nature of photographic image-making would eventually become a selling point and provide a public rationale for what would prove to be a more efficient process for mass-reproducing illustrations. But until these various hurdles could be overcome, photographs functioned primarily as grist for the draftsman's mill.

Photography offered an antidote to the problem of declining public faith in sketch artists' credibility, and the prospect of bolstering both faith and circulation made jumping technological and professional hurdles appear worthwhile. Nineteenth-century writers widely proclaimed photography unsurpassed in veracity. Representing the contemporary view, in 1857 Lady Elizabeth Eastlake, writing in the *London Quarterly Review,* described photography as follows: "She is the sworn witness of everything presented to her view. What are her unerring records in the service of mechanics, engineering, geology, and natural history, but facts of the most sterling and stubborn kind?" (quoted in Newhall 1982, 85).

The universality and factuality of art were the cornerstones upon which the illustrated press had built its claim to a mass audience, and photography appeared the logical heir to wood engraving. Heralded as a medium of fact, photography took up the mantle of realistic representation while art, at the turn of the century, veered off its traditional path. The rise of formalism in modern art shifted claims of universality and factuality away from handmade images to images perceived to be machine-made. By 1920 linking the visual arts with fact may have proven a difficult notion to sell. In 1884 the introduction of the halftone process opened the door to efficient massreproduction of photographs in the press, and by the 1920s photographs had displaced wood engravings almost entirely.

Simon Michael Bessie (1938) makes clear the parallels between the rise of mass-market periodicals in Britain and the United States. In each case, publishers endeavored to create and maintain a public for their wares. As in Britain, advocating public education could benefit publishers by increasing literacy and thereby expanding potential markets. In order to attract the largest possible readership, American publishers imitated successful British miscellanies by combining information with entertainment and making liberal use of illustrations. Indeed, illustrations played a key role: "Most successful of the technical advances was the increased use of illustrations and photographs. Pulitzer used this attraction to the limit and it was to the *World*'s unprecedented exploitation of pictures that the *Journalist* attributed its unparalleled circulation. By September of 1886 the *World* was selling 250,000 copies daily, 'the largest circulation ever attained by any American newspaper' up to that time" (Bessie 1938, 45–46).

Far from being a novel phenomenon, the sensational yellow journalism of the late nineteenth century continued previously established traditions that emerged and persevered due to market pressures. "Mass newspapers must advocate popular causes but, first of all, they must attract mass attention and this the *World* did by ceaseless manipulations of the ancient curiosities in Love, Death, Sin, Violence and Money" (Bessie 1938, 43–44).

Bessie's account of the emergence of tabloids in the United States offers a useful contemporary perspective. Tabloid newspapers have been neglected by most scholars, many of whom consider them to be a debased form of journalism and therefore unworthy of attention (see Becker 1992 for a noteworthy exception). Yet their tremendous popularity and heavy reliance on photography make tabloids worth at least some scrutiny because all newspapers, whether they target a class or mass readership, exist within a commercial environment and compete to attract the largest possible audience. The primary reason for tabloids' popularity concerned the use of photography. Before World War I, photographs had accompanied an "occasional story," a practice altered by the proven success of tabloid newspapers.

> When the tabloid taught its readers to expect a picture with every story, the large papers were forced to imitate this popular practice. They did not attempt to produce an illustration for each account but the sports, entertainment and society pages were always decorated with pictures and the rotogravure section became a weekly feature of every newspaper in the country. When anything really important occurred—a big athletic event, a major political happening, a great tragedy or a stirring crime—the big papers learned to carry as many, if not more pictures than the tabloid. (Bessie 1938, 233)

During the 1920s, newspaper readers viewed the press cynically, giving rise to a commonplace: "You can't believe all you read in the newspapers." Yet Bessie (1938, 69) suggests that photographs had maintained their credibility, and readers were more apt to trust what they saw than what they read: "To a generation which had yet to learn that the camera can be the author of as many lies as truths, seeing was still believing and a newspaper picture taken (allegedly) on the spot was accepted as proof of a story's accuracy."

In addition to enlivening a page with vivid illustrations, photographs may have restored some measure of credibility to newspapers. The contention may seem tenuous, especially given the practice among some tabloids of constructing fake photographs ("composographs"), but even these may have been received with too little skepticism due to the veracity widely attributed to photographic images.

An early textbook devoted to graphic journalism supports several of Bessie's contentions and demonstrates the persistence of early nineteenth century conceptualizations of illustrated periodicals. *Pictorial Journalism* was written in 1939 by a group of journalism professionals, all of whom had at one time worked at the *Washington Post*. Laura Vitray and John Mills, Jr., had gone on to other jobs by the time of the book's publication, and Roscoe Ellard was a professor of journalism at the University of Missouri. The book anticipated changes in the style of the modern newspaper that were necessitated by the impact of radio and motion pictures on newspaper journalism, or so the authors implied. Other new technologies also motivated change: the introduction of wirephotos, improvements in printing, color photography, and color engraving. The book resulted from "experimental work . . . seeking better methods of presenting and coordinating reading matter, newsphotos, and advertising" (Vitray, Mills, and Ellard 1939, xi).

The authors offered a justification for the increased use of news photographs that builds on the idea advanced by early publishers of illustrated periodicals—pictures are universally communicative. They reworked universality by applying a modernist frame of reference that yielded a newly valued attribute: "instantaneousness." Asserting news photographs' value in this way also responds to the competitive threat introduced by radio, newsreel, and television reporting:

> Newspaper executives, many of whom still regard journalism as uniquely a writing profession and photography as an unwelcome interloper in the field, are apt to believe they have been forced to a more pictorial presentation of the news by the competition of radio reporting, with television in the offing, and of the newsreels.
>
> The truth goes much deeper. The development of modern photographic and engraving processes might not have been so rapid and so amazing if what they had to offer had not so well answered the demand of the modern mind for a quality best described as "instantaneousness."
>
> As living has become more complex, as the boundaries of communication have been pushed farther and farther out, until every man's thoughts and interests encompassed the entire earth, the mental and emotional reaction has been one of stripping away all that was superfluous and cumbersome, in order to arrive at essential things as rapidly as possible.
>
> In the arts, in architecture, and in the applied arts, this speed or "purism" of the modern mind has resulted in forms which the artist is apt to call "elemental" and which the everyday man dubs "streamlining." The word is a graphic one and has come to be applied to everything from a skyscraper or an automobile to the latest forms of layout for the newspaper front page. Perhaps the most streamlined of all is modern thought itself. It has cast off all the curlicues of olden days and insists at arriving at beauty, at fact, and at knowledge by the shortest route.
>
> That is the surest reason why picture reporting, the "instantaneous" route to realization of the world's events, has succeeded in pushing column after column of mere words out of the daily paper. So inevitably has the transition taken place that it may be said to have happened in spite of the reluctance and opposition of men of the old newspaper school, rather than with their cooperation. (Vitray, Mills, and Ellard 1939, 4)

Thus Vitray, Mills, and Ellard asserted the factuality (and the modernity) of photographs while maintaining the link between picture reporting and the arts. Although painting had moved from realism to formalism, by the 1920s photography's most vocal claim to status as a fine art revolved around what were deemed the essential characteristics of the medium. *Straight photography* and *pure photography* were the terms used to describe the work of art photographers who eschewed their painterly, pictorialist predilections and advocated sharp-focus pictures that exploited the medium's technical capacities. Charles Sheeler's comparison of his own painting and photography illustrates the attitude of artists during the 1920s: "I have come to value photography more and more for those things which it alone can accomplish, rather than to discredit it for the things which can only be achieved through another medium. In painting I have had a continued interest in natural forms and have sought the best use of them for the enhancement of design. In photography I have strived to enhance my technical equipment for the best statement of the immediate facts" (quoted in Newhall 1982, 178).

Art photography of the period reflected other perspectives as well, and photographers made various kinds of abstractions, composites, and montages that paralleled the formalism predominating painting. But among the differing approaches to art photography, the purist "straight photography" movement offered the most opportune way to maintain news photography's link with art.

Beaumont Newhall's history of photography (1982) makes clear that formal aesthetic criteria are used to judge art photographs, whether or not they adhere to the tenets of the "straight" approach. Newhall praises Sheeler's work for its "sensitive interpretation of form and texture" (1982, 178). A news photograph, conversely, is judged first "for its essential value, or *content*" (Vitray, Mills, and Ellard 1939, 30) and then for its reproducibility. Vitray, Mills, and Ellard proposed a rating scale that divides the content attributes of a photograph into equal thirds: 33⅓ percent for the importance of the personality involved, 33⅓ percent for the news it reports, and 33⅓ percent for the amount of action portrayed. Photographs must earn an overall rating of 60 percent in order to merit publication.

Photographers were advised to keep up to date on important people in the community and in the world at large in order to fulfill the first criterion. The second criterion, the definition of newsworthiness, suggests the importance of presenting news in an entertaining package and invokes the same values guiding publishers of nineteenth-century illustrated miscellanies, values subsequently adopted by publishers of tabloids.

All news, near or far, concerns four great elemental human themes: *Survival, sex, ambition, and escape.* These are the four great *motives* or instincts, which

form the patterns of man's existence on this earth. Of the four, survival is perhaps the most elemental. . . . *Survival*—or anything that threatens it—is *news*.
Next to survival, sex is probably the second great human interest. . . . *Sex*—
romance, love, and hate—is *news*. Third of these great pillars of the news is the
ambition theme—the appeal to man's urge to surpass his fellows, to gain power,
to be an important person in wealth or in influence over the lives of others. . . .
*Ambition*—getting to the top—is *news*. Fourth of the forms of news appeal in
pictures is *escape*. . . . *Escape*—adventure, prowess, and daring—is *news*. (Vitray,
Mills, and Ellard 1939, 34–35, emphasis in the original)

Such news values bear out Bessie's contention that the tabloid press influenced more conservative, mainstream newspapers such as the *Washington
Post*. The criteria for newsworthiness represented here parallel attributes often
associated with popular fiction, suggesting that competition with other mass
media may have tipped the balance toward entertainment value.

The third criterion for successful news photography is action, which Vitray,
Mills, and Ellard equated with motion, either the physical activity of a person or the movement of an object through space. Their definition also encom-
passes "action in the human face" or the display of emotion. Portrayals of
stationary objects shot from an angle, the authors pointed out, can introduce
a greater sense of action and warn editors to be wary of such shots, which offer
only "pseudo-action": "The ideal toward which all sections of the newspaper
should strive is that of more interest through more action" (38).

Formal criteria used to assess the quality of news photographs emphasize
their reproducibility. "Judging for copy" ensures the instantaneousness of
published news photographs. Vitray, Mills, and Ellard recommended a rating
scale evaluating degree of sharp focus, detail, and tonal contrast. "Art department" employees retouch "imperfect" prints with water-soluble paint, making them more suitable for halftone reproduction. Retouching, however, is not
done in order to "pretty up" halftones: "The things we do to them are done to
*increase their emotional pull*" (Vitray, Mills, and Ellard 1939, 178, emphasis in
the original). As the text details strategies for page layout, the authors reveal
an important factor determining the role performed by news photographs:
advertising. Vitray, Mills, and Ellard's recommendations make clear that news
photographs serve a publicity function, drawing readers to page one and then
to the inside pages where advertisements await. The front page can be conceived
as an advertisement that sells the advertising inside the newspaper.

Given this conception of the dynamics of newspaper reading, emphasizing photographs' instantaneousness and emotional pull seems a logical
stance.

Pictures can lead the reader into the paper as surely as stories can—perhaps more surely, because of the emotional appeal of good news photographs. When a single dramatic shot of a big news story is played boldly on the front page, and the reader is referred to the daily picture page or to an inside page for more, he is practically certain to turn to them. Picture appetite can be depended upon as a means of getting the paper read, much more than appetite for reading matter. The same man or woman who never reads the jumps probably always looks at the pictures. (Vitray, Mills, and Ellard 1939, 260)

Economic considerations drive such recommendations. Throughout the text the authors cautioned against using layout strategies that undermine the visibility of advertising. "Unless a newspaper can produce page layouts which *get the advertising read,* it may find itself without revenue," and:

> we must not seek the bizarre in layout on news pages, for exaggerated effects would detract from the appeal of the advertising and would not work into the general page plan.
>
> Layouts for inside pages on the daily must usually consist of very simple asymmetric arrangements of two or three pictures so placed as to balance advertising. Where the advertising runs strong, any layout may be too much, yet a single newsphoto may be effectively placed. (Vitray, Mills, and Ellard 1939, 203, 215, emphasis in the original)

That pragmatic view suggests the evolutionary course traveled by mass-marketed illustrated publications. The need to cultivate audiences and build circulation was a consistent factor influencing periodicals published between 1830 and 1930. The periodicals discussed here all performed a similar hegemonic function, implicitly maintaining social class distinctions and preserving elite leadership. But, as Fox (1988) and especially Anderson (1991) argue persuasively, the first generation of publications conscientiously worked toward quelling social unrest by attempting to inculcate an appreciation for elite cultural values, thereby maintaining the status quo. For Charles Knight and publishers of his era, art became a mainstreaming apparatus employed to coalesce divergent values. Through their publishing efforts they hoped to elevate the intellectual level of the working class and instill in the populace a sense of shared commitments.

In the second generation, art became a different kind of tool. Despite the fact that the illustrations found in the new periodicals seldom reproduced fine artwork, these illustrations were considered art that bestowed upon wood engravings a common-sense legitimacy that their subject matter might otherwise have discouraged. Invocations of art's universality and factuality—its objectivity—helped set illustrations beyond the reach of political controversy, and it could therefore be argued that they were accessible and valuable to all. Following the lead of popular illustrated miscellanies, mass-circulation periodicals catered to an imagined public taste, and, in accordance with the debased view of their audience held by commercial publishers, they heightened entertainment values above the educational ideals held by the previous generation. Art retreated to elite confines while dramas revolving around crime, romance, catastrophe, and intrigue became standard fare. The proven success of illustrations as a means of building circulation led to their routine use, and their asserted fidelity rather than their expressiveness became the source of their value.

Given this evolutionary trend, the invention of photography occurred at an opportune moment. Photography emerged as the visual medium best suited to take up the mantle of objectivity, based on the popularly held view that a mechanical device, a camera, makes photographs. The deficiencies attributed to images produced by sketch artists' hands were eradicated by the modern, technological picture-making medium. Over time, as the use of photographs became more routine and institutionalized, strategic invocations of art diminished. In Vitray, Mills, and Ellard's text the vestiges of art remain in such expressions as "art desk" and "art department": "Most large papers have a picture desk or art desk located in the city room, where pictures for each edition of the paper are delivered from the photo studio and from the services" (1939, 13). According to the authors' usage, all editorial images used in the various sections of a newspaper were referred to in general terms as the publication's "art." The "art department" housed those technicians responsible for retouching photographs to improve them for halftone reproduction. In this usage, "art" is a term used to describe handwork done by the art department staff, recalling the craft process of wood engraving. Although nineteenth-century writers called picture reporters "sketch artists," by the 1930s authors such as Vitray, Mills, and Ellard did not employ the term when referring to the photographers producing illustrations for the press. The end of the first hundred years of illustrated periodicals was marked by a conceptual shift from art to fact, from hand-made images to pictures conceived as emerging from a machine.

Photographers have been conceptualized as camera operators rather than artists or authors, technicians who initially received no credit or byline for the work they produced. It comes as no surprise that photographers have often been considered "second-class citizens" in the newsroom. As their ranks increased, newspaper photographers began organizing associations to bolster their professional profile, and by 1945 a national organization emerged: the National Press Photographers Association (NPPA). The explicit rationales for starting the NPPA were to improve working conditions and assure the rights of press photographers and to improve their public image by raising standards and professional norms of behavior.

Establishing the organization performed other implicit functions as well, and chief among them was standardizing professional practice. The NPPA engaged in a variety of educational outreach activities, both to improve the work of current press photographers and to recruit and train the next generation by composing photojournalism curricula for colleges and universities. With funding from the *Encyclopedia Britannica,* the NPPA initiated the "Flying Short Course," a professional training program that travels the United States each year. The NPPA began publishing its own magazine in 1946. In addition to its educational outreach activities, the organization sought open access to news events, worked toward formalizing relationships with gatekeepers such as police and fire departments, drafted anti-assault legislation, and offered job placement and insurance to its members. By the 1950s photojournalism had settled into a period of stability, with institutionally ensconced staffs and a national organization inculcating shared professional norms. Aesthetic standards became fixed through regular clips contests that exemplified successful reproduction of photojournalism's visual codes.

## The Credible Image

The 1980s ushered in revolutionary changes in photographic technology that opened a Pandora's box of issues concerning the medium's credibility and the future of photojournalism. Digital-imaging technology has compromised the perceived factuality of the photographic image—the quality upon which its use in the press now depends. Current scrutiny of press illustrations recalls the disrepute that sketch artists suffered toward the end of the nineteenth century. Ironically, the technological nature of photography, which once seemed to assure its truthfulness, now raises suspicion. In a published statement of values published in 1997 the Minneapolis *Star Tribune* made clear the importance its publishers attribute to credibility. After testifying that the newspaper acknowledges a distinction between journalistic values and corporate values and that the *Star Tribune* endeavors to keep them from intermingling in the process of producing news, the statement concluded: "[The] *Star Tribune* strives to provide information that is accurate, fair and unaffected by the special interests of advertisers or top company executives. Credibility is the most important 'product' *Star Tribune* has."

Considering the special effort made by the newspaper to address readers regarding the issue of credibility, it seems logically consistent that the *Star Tribune* would take such a strong public stand against Stormi Greener when she digitally removed the power lines visible in her photograph. Newspapers nationwide have publicly stated their intention to preserve the integrity of news photographs by instituting formal guidelines governing the use of the digital-imaging technology that has become a professional norm.

Controversy surrounding the initial adoption of digital-imaging technology set the stage for self-scrutiny, reassessment, and potential innovation in the conception and practice of photojournalism. Although self-scrutiny and reassessment are much in evidence in trade journals such as the NPPA's *News Photographer,* innovation seems an unlikely outcome of discussions among industry professionals and academics. Photojournalists' past attitudes regarding appropriate professional practice provide a foundation for examining these more recent debates and the continuities and shifts they represent. Discussions of photojournalism ethics and articles reporting ethical breaches suggest photojournalists' approaches to upholding the credibility and the viability of their profession. Discussions fall into two broad categories: infractions perpetrated in the act of shooting and violations introduced in the darkroom or in production.

The single most cited violation of photojournalism norms involves what photojournalists refer to as "set-ups," the addition of elements or directorial interference that allows photographers to "liven up the shot," making for a more interesting visual image. That can be accomplished in a variety of ways, among them using props, posing subjects, directing reenactments, constructing fabrications, and using models. The literature abounds with references to photographers (usually of a former generation) who along with their photo equipment carried props such as teddy bears or other objects that could be strategically positioned within the frame in order to humanize and add poignancy to photographs. When subjects' activities or positions fail to meet photographers' aesthetic requirements, they may be asked to pose or subtly motivated to strike a more photogenic pose. That practice is most obvious and least controversial in portraits. When photographers arrive too late to catch an action as it occurred, or if an act was not performed in a manner considered appropriately aesthetic, photographers have been known to ask subjects to walk through their activities a second or third time. Photographers may invent visually appealing scenarios and enlist the support of subjects to enact a supplied script. When people actually involved in hard-to-find, often illegal practices cannot be photographed, models can be used to save time, money, and alleviate deadline pressures.

All of these kinds of set-ups receive serious treatment by professionals who

claim that public knowledge of such photographer manipulations undermines the profession, casting doubt on the images produced by all photojournalists, guilty and innocent alike. The prohibition against enhancing
photographs parallels nineteenth-century criticisms of sketch artists' elabo-
ration of their illustrations with stock figures, objects, and settings.

Another threat to credibility discussed in trade journals results from a
photographer's own presence on the scene. They may intentionally or un-
intentionally act as catalysts, provoking behavior among subjects that would
not otherwise have occurred. The most extreme example of such reactivity
is the photo-opportunity, an event staged solely for the purpose of provoking news coverage.

News organizations worry about their public image, as the *Star Tribune*'s
actions demonstrate, and the behavior of employees in the act of news-gathering may promote either goodwill or scorn. One of the NPPA's inaugural
agenda items concerned improving and standardizing the behavioral norms
considered appropriate among photojournalists nationwide. These issues
were revisited during the mid-1970s when codes governing ethical behavior
proliferated, reportedly in response to Watergate-era media circuses that
shined an unflattering spotlight on representatives of the press. Areas singled
out for improvement included sensitivity to individuals' privacy, adhering
to professional codes of dress, aggressiveness in the act of accessing subjects,
and overall courtesy. Much like the film industry's self-initiated Motion Picture Code, industry self-censorship often represents an attempt to craft good
public relations and ward off the potential for external intervention.

According to the trade magazines, once a photographer enters the darkroom other procedures compromising the integrity of an image must be
avoided. Basic photographic procedures are widely accepted—burning,
dodging, and cropping pose no threat to credibility—unless their use dramatically changes the meaning evoked by a straight print. These tools enhance images and do not remake them, as Vitray, Mills, and Ellard claimed
in 1939. More controversial procedures elicit a mixed response. Most photographers agree that flipping a negative is inappropriate, and toning down
or eliminating backgrounds, airbrushing, and cutting and pasting all provoke
disapproval. That attitude represents a departure from the elaborate practices of art department staff. Judgments regarding acceptable retouching have
become more stringent since the 1980s and may be responsive to improvements in printing technology that have reduced the need to clean up prints
for halftone reproduction. Photographers who advocate minimal enhancement are considered purists, although most recognize the occasional need

for some special technique. Adopting stringent restrictions on photographic manipulation offers an antidote to suspicion similar to the cure that photography once provided for the dubiety of sketch artists' illustrations.

The full force of these restrictions applies to news and sports sections of newspapers, although most consider manipulating features, food, and fashion photographs relatively noncontroversial. The fact that photojournalists debated the appropriateness of different kinds of manipulation throughout the pre-digital era indicates that no uniform set of standards was applied across publications. Because the veracity of news photographs was underscrutinized there was no urgent need for consistent guidelines. Photographers and their editors both resisted the imposition of rules and regulations governing professional activities.

When the Associated Press began transmitting photographs electronically it helped its major newspaper clients make the transition to digital imaging by giving them the hardware necessary to receive the dispatches. The AP effectively set in motion the transformation of major metropolitan dailies to digital imaging. Most urban newspapers no longer maintain so-called chemical darkrooms. Photographers continue to shoot and process film and will do so until digital cameras can produce the necessary image quality for newspaper reproduction, but all subsequent picture preparation takes place on computer screens, often foregoing paper prints altogether. The new technology ushered photographers out of the isolated confines of the darkroom and into the newsroom. As their work was transformed, a maelstrom of commentary issued forth from photojournalists and picture editors nationwide. Fear and anxiety filled much of the response to digital technology.

What could technology do that traditional methods of photographic image-making could not do? The two most significant changes are that manipulations once done in the darkroom can be accomplished more easily and quickly by computer, and computer manipulation is much more difficult to detect than conventional printing techniques, airbrushing, or cutting and pasting. Computer-based digital imaging heightens the potential for deception in the print preparation process. One editor's view encapsulates the fervent attitude espoused by many: "All photographers change reality somewhat by using different types of lenses or dodging and burning . . . electronic manipulation is more insidious because it takes those tools and multiplies them by ten thousand" (Rogers 1989, 17).

As digital-imaging technology spread, so did the debate. The wave of change compelled newspapers to compose guidelines for the technology's use in an effort to protect the integrity of the journalists' enterprise—to main-

tain credibility. Assuming that photographers still conformed to ethical standards governing shooting that were already in place, the onus for protecting
credibility shifted to members of the newspaper staff responsible for oper-
ating computer systems and preparing photographs for publication. Some
questioned whether these people had sufficient journalistic training to but-
tress the decisions that would face them, casting aspersion on technicians who
might be eager to exploit the capabilities digital-imaging offers. Others distinguished the more fully developed ethical sensibilities and experience base
of staffs working on major metropolitan dailies from staffs at smaller papers,
worrying that the latter group might jeopardize the reputations of all photojournalists.

   As with attitudes regarding the unimpeachable honesty of the camera,
many photojournalists argue that technology is neutral even though its users may not be. Therefore, the technology already in place in newsrooms
across the country could also be construed as nonproblematic; all that might
need fixing was the ethical standards of those who use it. National Press
Photographers Association president John Long took a more pessimistic view
in 1989, although the point of his position was consistent with conclusions
drawn by advocates of the new technology: "The only hope lies in you and
me. We must be honest in all our professional dealings. We ourselves, the
photojournalists, must be trusted because the images themselves will no
longer be proof positive. Reporters have a long and honored tradition of
honesty. It is a tenet of their profession, it is their Hippocratic oath. We need
to develop the same internal standards, the same deep beliefs in the right-
ness of what we are doing. Our future depends on us and no one else" (Long
1989, 14).

   Prodded by the technological revolution in their midst, photojournalists
began discussing the basic tenets of professional practice in the digital age.
After several years of argument at conferences and in the trade journals, a
consensus began to emerge. Motivated by a series of celebrated cases—
National Geographic's decision to move pyramids to better fit the magazine's
cover, a cola can digitally eliminated from a portrait, the digital manipulation of the cover photos on "A Day in the Life of _____" books, and the
heads of famous people showing up on others' bodies—most photojournalists and editors agreed that manipulating the content of news photographs
must be prohibited. That restriction parallels the taboo on photographers
adding elements or moving objects before shooting pictures.

   Manipulating the form of an image receives less stringent treatment. As
in the past, computer equivalents of burning, dodging, cropping, color cor-

rection, and eliminating dust spots or scratches are deemed acceptable. But using computers to airbrush, a common technique formerly employed to improve news photographs, has been widely rejected. A case in point illustrates the fine line photojournalists draw in the pursuit of credibility. An extraneous cola can detracting from the composition of a photograph should not be eliminated by computer, but cropping the frame to eliminate the can is acceptable. The motivation for this fine distinction in acceptable practices is clear—eliminating one picture element using digital technology implies that the practice is acceptable and may have been employed on any given image.

Photojournalists have taken a conservative position toward digital imaging. The guiding philosophy adopted in an effort to maintain credibility can be summarized as "don't do anything that can't be done in the darkroom." Ironically, for decades photographers have altered images significantly by using chemical processes. The current catch-phrase ignores that well-known fact, invoking a purism few photojournalists ever emulated. In order to clarify this position, both the NPPA and the AP have issued statements regarding manipulation. The NPPA released a "statement of principle" on digital manipulation of photographs that was adopted on November 12, 1990:

> As journalists we believe the guiding principle of our profession is accuracy; therefore, we believe it is wrong to alter the content of a photograph in any way that deceives the public.
>
> As photojournalists, we have the responsibility to document society and to preserve its images as a matter of historical record. It is clear that the emerging electronic technologies provide new challenges to the integrity of photographic images. This technology enables the manipulation of the content of an image in such a way that the change is virtually undetectable. In light of this, we, the National Press Photographers Association, reaffirm the basis of our ethics: Accurate representation is the benchmark of our profession.
>
> We believe photojournalistic guidelines for accuracy currently in use should be the criteria for judging what may be done electronically to a photograph. Altering the editorial content of a photograph, in any degree, is a breach of the ethical standards recognized by the NPPA. ("A Statement" 1990, 6)

In order to avoid these problems altogether, photographers now shoulder an additional burden: the expectation that they will shoot in such a way that alteration is unnecessary. Although newspapers have adopted guidelines governing the use of digital-imaging technology, the conundrums the technology introduces can be avoided by clever photographers who successfully compose pictures so invasive editing is not required. But what do photographers do when they use their brains? Debates have failed to embrace larger issues regarding the authorship of photographic images or the artistry involved in making a successful image. Although passing reference has been made to the manipulations inherent in the image-making process, that avenue remains mostly unexplored. Photojournalists note the significance of a range of choices that photographers make—angle of view, the capacities and aesthetic qualities of film stocks, the use or non-use of artificial lighting and other exposure controls, lenses and their differing representations of space and spatial relationships, and the limitations imposed by the frame. And there are more, all of which indicate that photographers interpret reality rather than record it. The inherently expressive aspects of the medium are obscured by the dichotomy constructed between overtly manipulated and pure photographs.

The proliferation of discussion and debate sparked by the digital revolution in photography might have embraced these fundamental issues, seizing the moment of change as an opportunity for innovation. But the positions taken by the rank and file represent a retreat to a moral high ground from which to fend off assaults on credibility. In 1990 NPPA leaders began to reinvoke objectivity and truth, canons that had often been reined in and replaced with fairness and accuracy. Statements of principle fail to work out the inconsistencies that regularly appear in print. Photographers still must take prohibitions against manipulation into account when shooting a picture.

The history of photojournalism helps explain the rhetorical stance that contemporary photojournalists and editors are adopting. The strategic elevation of recording above expression, of fact above art, that emerged along with the commercial press has encouraged denial of the constructed, authored nature of photographic representations. Over time, as photojournalism has become institutionalized as a field of endeavor distinct from other kinds of photographic imaging, the camera's role in representing events has been framed in such a way as to eclipse the activity of the news photographer who uses it. There is seldom talk about "illustrations" in the press; people are encouraged to believe that they witness events firsthand through the technological capacities of the medium of photography. It is therefore incumbent upon editors and publishers to safeguard what photography offers and protect the public from abuses introduced by those practitioners who subvert the neutrality of camera-made images when they act as though they are making pictures. The newspaper business, particularly in an era of shrinking readership, can hardly afford to let go of its claims to objectivity, a historically proven marketing tool. The rhetoric of photojournalism still abounds in contradictions that result from the collision of firsthand experience with the picture-making process and the economic imperative to build and preserve credibility. The tenor of ongoing debates suggests that the controversy digital technology has introduced will be short-lived, whereas the contradictions inherent in photojournalism will endure.

## References

Anderson, Patricia. 1991. *The Printed Image and the Transformation of Popular Culture, 1790–1860.* New York: Oxford University Press.

Becker, Karen. 1992. "Photojournalism and the Tabloid Press." In *Journalism and Popular Culture,* ed. Peter Dahlgren and Colin Sparks, 130–53. London: Sage.

Bessie, Simon Michael. 1938. *Jazz Journalism: The Story of the Tabloid Newspapers.* New York: E. P. Dutton.

Fox, Celina. 1988. *Graphic Journalism in England during the 1830s and 40s.* New York: Garland, 1988.

Gessert, Sherman. 1991. "The Protocol Story at the *Milwaukee Sentinel.*" In *Protocol,* ed. Chris Harris. Washington, D.C.: NPPA.

Gilyard, Burl. 1997. "Stormi Weather at the STRIB." *Twin Cities Reader,* Jan. 30, 7.

Long, John. 1989. "Fakes, Frauds and Phonies." *News Photographer* 44(11): 14.

Newhall, Beaumont. 1982. *The History of Photography from 1839 to the Present.* New York: Museum of Modern Art.

Rogers, Elizabeth. 1989. "Now You See It, Now You Don't.: Coke Can's Disappearance Spotlights Potential for Editing Abuse." *News Photographer* 44(8): 17.

Schiller, Dan. 1981. *Objectivity and the News: The Public and the Rise of Commercial Journalism.* Philadelphia: University of Pennsylvania Press.

Schudson, Michael. 1978. *Discovering the News: A Social History of American Newspapers.* New York: Basic Books.

Schuneman, R. Smith. 1969. "Art of Photography: A Question for Newspaper Editors of the 1890s." *Journalism Quarterly* 46(3): 43–52.

Schwartz, Dona. 1992. "To Tell the Truth: Codes of Objectivity in Photojournalism." *Communication* 13(2): 95–109.

"A Statement of Principle on Digital Manipulation of Photographs." 1990. *News Photographer* 45(10): 6.

Taft, Robert. 1964 (1938). *Photography and the American Scene: A Social History, 1839–1889.* New York: Dover.

Vitray, Laura, John Mills, Jr., and Roscoe Ellard. 1939. *Pictorial Journalism.* New York: McGraw-Hill.

# 8

## Fact, Fiction, or Fantasy:
## Canada and the War to End All Wars

*David R. Spencer*

It is not always true that a word or series of words can create a thousand pictures in the mind of any one given human being. For example, radio may have well been the "theater of the mind," but the pictures it created were as wide and varied as the number of people who visualized them during the medium's so-called golden age.

Historians who deal with words exclusively, especially those transcribed on paper, confront many of the same difficulties that scholars attempting to incorporate the visual into historical analysis experience. It can be argued that documents, minute books, letters, memoirs, and other similar sources should not have any more historical value than pictures. As John E. Carter has cautioned, however, "Calling a photograph a document implies that the information it contains is intrinsically truthful, an argument that contains its own refutation" (Carter 1993, 56).

Surely the same concerns can be directed toward the printed word. It is critical that historians explore the circumstances under which a document, minute book, letter, or memoir have been created. A photograph may be no less truthful than any other source of historical evidence once these influences have been examined rigorously.

Had a scholar been present at an event deemed of historical importance, that person's unique cultural biases would certainly come to play in the transcription of the event, even at the subconscious level. Walt Whitman's recollections of his role in the Civil War and his subsequent literary career are peculiarly Whitman's and no one else's. His memoirs stand in stark contrast to the experiences of Mary Chestnut. In the same vein, it is difficult to rationalize that John Stuart Mill and Karl Marx lived and worked in the same city in Victorian Britain and arrived at very different and contrasting views of the society around them.

It is fair to claim that all human activity is subject to editorial filtering, conscious or otherwise. Although somewhat of an extreme example, it is not beyond the boundaries of reason to assert that Richard Nixon's interpretation of his fall from grace conflicted with views held by those responsible for the end of his presidency. And, thanks to television, Nixon's demise was a very visual event.

From the time that the first lasting image was captured on a metal plate by Joseph Nicéphore Niepce in 1827, world events have become increasingly captured by visual record keeping. It is not a phenomenon restricted to the twentieth century and to the rise of the motion pictures and television. America recorded its anguish in the Civil War in various photographic modes that are still being used. As digital technology forges more and more links around the globe with the consequence that visual information, and thus visual history, becomes more readily available, historians will be increasingly forced to use such sources. As Christopher Lasch has observed, "The curious thing about all this is that our collective understanding of the past seems to be faltering at the very moment when our technical ability to recreate the past has reached an unprecedented level of development. Photographs and motion pictures and recordings, new techniques of historical research, the computer's total recall provide a rich documentary record of the past" (1989, 60).

Because motion video technology and its use as a documentary format is relatively young, having matured only since the introduction of television in the late 1940s, the most plentiful source for historical analysis remains still photographs. As Andrew Rodger and Brian Carey, curators of the National Photography Collection at Canada's National Archives in Ottawa, have noted, "Though by the mid-1970s more and more publishers, television producers, authors and researchers were making use of historical photographs in their work, much of the general public was not aware of the growing importance of photography" (1985, 10).

In many respects, photographic images are the one source of historical record that comes the closest to a sense of "being there." Filmmaker Ken Burns gave photography a "realism" seal of approval when he reconstructed the Civil War for yet another visual medium, television. As Burns and his audience undoubtedly observed, pictures can explore many images that documents cannot, such as detailed street scenes, facial expressions, glimpses of architectural designs and their uses at a given period that may no longer exist, graphic demonstrations of clothing styles, and a literal treasure of past family activities (Jensen 1988, 41). Oliver Wendell Holmes wrote that photography ensures that family remains with us forever. "Those whom we love no longer leave us in dying, as they did of old. They remain with us just as they appeared in life; they look down upon us from our walls; they lie upon our tables, they rest upon our bosoms" (Humphreys 1993, 686).

The purpose of this research is to examine the photographic record of a conflict between French and English Canadians over military service in the midst of 1917. The true power and impact, not to mention technical facility, of the art of the camera was still in its infancy when Canadian photographers began to record the World War I under very difficult circumstances.

Until the latter half of the Victorian period photography was predominantly, but not exclusively, one of the favored fetishes of the wealthy. That can be explained in part by the fact that photographic equipment was far from a portable medium. As a consequence, most late-Victorian photography has a rigid, staged quality, whether taken outdoors or indoors. To produce reliable results photographers were required to employ large, bulky cameras that hungrily consumed copious quantities of either natural or artificial light. The spontaneity of recording events as they occurred, taken for granted by modern photographers, did not exist. In fact, this lack of spontaneity complicated the lives of war photographers as well. As Alan Noon, a Canadian historical photographer, discovered in his study of working-class life in the east end of London, Ontario, documentary photography did not exist in the province before 1905 (Noon 1989, 7). In the United States, it remained for Jacob Riis and Lewis W. Hine to use the camera as an instrument of social analysis in the late nineteenth and early twentieth centuries and give legitimacy to the place of photography in documenting not only people but also events (Freund 1980, 108).

As much as photography may play a valid role in the telling of a collective past, it must, like all other forms of historical evidence, be treated with its own set of reflections. Debra Harmon Parson has cautioned that "historic photographs have the potential to deceive the viewer. Historians and curators must be constantly aware that photos may have been taken for a reason known only to the photographer. Recording moments of experience which were deemed important, photographs are a valuable but tiny piece of the story" (1990, 125).

Parson's wise words should be heeded. As Timothy Brookes discovered in his analysis of Jacob Shenkel's 1863 *Gettysburg Diary,* the famous "action" photos of the battle captured by local photographer Peter S. Weaver had been staged. Shenkel's admission that he posed as a corpse in one photograph confirmed William A. Frassanito's suspicions (1975) that the pictures did not portray authentic battle scenes. Frassanito had observed that the bodies in the photographs had unusually healthy appearances (Brookes 1987, 49, 52, 54).

Nonetheless, Weaver's deception should not be cited as an excuse for dismissing photography as a legitimate tool in historical research, within reason. Such incidents, however, should lead researchers to question the validity of all source materials, photography included. John Tagg has raised the problem of the use of photography as a vehicle for propaganda. In his analysis, Franklin Delano Roosevelt marshaled forces sympathetic to the New Deal to produce a series of documentary photographs to legitimize its cause. "It deployed a rhetoric with larger claims than this: with claims to retrieve the status of truth in discourse, a status threatened by crisis but whose renegotiation was essential if social relations of meaning were to be sustained and national and social identities resecured, while demand for reform was contained within the limits of monopoly capitalist relations" (Tagg 1988, 9).

In fairness to Roosevelt, Tagg reveals an intellectual admiration for Michel Foucault and Louis Althusser, neither of whom could be accused of harboring much sympathy for capitalist objectives, moral or otherwise. An observation on the opposite side of the political divide on the value of photography as historical evidence comes from Edward Steichen, creator of *The Family of Man.* Steichen, although recognizing the inherent biases in the work he displayed through 503 images in New York City, observed, "It is essential to keep in mind the universal elements and aspects of human relations and the experiences common to all mankind rather than the situations that represented conditions exclusively related or peculiar to a race, an event, a time or a place" (Sandeen 1986, 373).

In the words of Susan Sontag (1973, 22–23), photography has made the world "more available than it really is." That observation suggests that photography, specifically in its role as the recorder of history, is somehow artificial. Richard Whelan does not agree. He argues (1981, 17) that photographs are taken "to fragment experience into manageable pieces, . . . to

analyze episodes of life, to exercise a form of voyeuristic aggression, to transform experience into objects, that can be possessed and hoarded like money,
to learn about the structure and meaning of the world, or simply to make
aesthetically and intellectually provocative images."

By the turn of the century, photography took its first cautious steps from
the studio to the street and began to document human behavior in two for-
midable and complementary media: newspapers and postcards. The explosion in the numbers of late nineteenth and early twentieth century daily
newspapers in Canada, the United States, and Great Britain has been well
documented.[1] The short-lived history of the postcard and its role in image
creation, however, is less well known. By the time World War I broke out in
1914 Britain alone had three hundred post card manufacturers, some of them
serving Canadian clients.

In many respects postcards provide a more detailed pictorial record of
events between 1914 and 1918, although postcard purchasers were spared the
gore of the war. In the years just before World War I, "postcard collecting
ranked among the greatest fads of the era" (Brock 1992, vi). At the turn of
the century, Canada's 5.4 million residents posted twenty-seven thousand
cards, and by the outbreak of World War I, the nation's 7.2 million people
posted an incredible sixty million (Brock 1992, vi). These cards were commissioned by local Canadian distributors such as the Red Star News Company and S. H. Knox and Company in London, Ontario, and Steadman
Brothers in Brantford, Ontario. Many were actually produced outside the
country by Raphael Tuck and Sons in London, England, and by Valentine and
Sons in Dundee, Scotland (Brock 1992, viii).

When war broke out in Europe in 1914, Canada entered the conflict as part
of its imperial commitment. Pictures, in many cases for the first time on a
large scale, joined words to document the country's effort in the theater of
war. But the pictures differed as much as the words, depending upon where
one lived in Canada. While documenting the progress of the conflict, photography, both in the press and on the postcard, became as much an instrument of propaganda and persuasion in both English and French Canada as
it became an agent of history. In many respects, the pictorial record of the
First Great War reveals as much by what it excluded as by what it included.

Photography came early to the Canadian newspaper industry. In 1869
Georges Edouard Desbarats, a Montréal journalist, launched the *Canadian
Illustrated News.* Two years later the newspaper became the first to publish a
photograph, a shot of the newly constructed Montréal Customs House.
Desbarats and his partner William Leggo launched the *New York Daily*

*Graphic* in 1873, the first daily tabloid in the United States. They firmly be-lieved that photography could eventually become the medium through which much if not all news would be disseminated. On December 2, 1873, the *Daily Graphic* carried a halftone photoengraving picture of New York's Steinway Hall. Although Emery and Emery claim that the first halftone to appear was of a hobo encampment and appeared on March 4, 1880, Fetherling (1990, 66) notes, "The facts [of the 1873 halftone] seem beyond dispute, though most sources contend that the feat was first achieved in 1880 with a halftone of a hobo shantytown."

Although the technology developed by Desbarats and Leggo was readily available to newspapers across the United States and Canada, it was slow to catch on, largely because of the expense of reproducing photographs on newsprint. Newspapers were also hesitant to assume the cost of hiring pho-tographers and installing darkrooms. It was not until March 28, 1891, that a photograph appeared in a Canadian daily. The Saturday edition of the *Toronto Globe* carried a picture of Wilfrid Laurier, the leader of the federal opposition, just three weeks before his Liberal Party faced the Canadian elec-torate. It should be noted that the *Globe* was a Liberal Party supporter. A short time later when Canada's first prime minister, Sir John A. Macdonald, died, the *Toronto Globe* carried a photograph of the late minister's empty parlia-mentary office. As Gisele Freund explains:

> The introduction of newspaper photography was a phenomenon of immense importance, one that changed the outlook of the masses. Before the first press pictures, the ordinary man could visualize only those events that took place near him, on his street or in his village. Photography opened a window as it were. The faces of public personalities became familiar and things that happened all over the globe were his to share. As the reader's outlook expanded, the world began to shrink. . . . Photography became a powerful means of propaganda and the manipulation of opinion. Industry, finance, government, [and] the own-ers of the press were able to fashion the world in images after their own inter-ests. (1980, 103)

At the turn of the century, however, only a handful of Canadian newspa-pers possessed the technology to reproduce photographs. Like any revolu-tionary innovation, it was initially treated with suspicion, and most editors refused to allow photographs to intrude on a good news story. Although Montréal's English-language *Daily Star* strongly supported Canadian in-volvement in the Boer War, it published no photographs of the conflict even though the war was the subject of numerous conversations in most Canadian homes. When Alberta joined the Canadian Confederation on September 2, 1905, the province's leading newspaper, the *Edmonton Journal*, published no photographs of the ceremonies marking the event. It was not until 1906 that the first action shot appeared in a Canadian newspaper. Arthur Blackburn, proprietor of the *London Free Press*, photographed horses competing in Canada's most prestigious equestrian event, the King's Plate.

In spite of a slow start, telling tales by a combination of words and pictures could not be stopped. By World War I, photography had become an accepted method by which to capture or at least enhance local news. Covering events beyond one's border was a more difficult undertaking. Telegraphic transmission of images was still in its infancy when the war broke out. Only those periodicals willing to take the risk and pay the freight were able to capture the horrors of the European theater in their pages (Fetherling 1990, 66–69). But, as Canadian historian Douglas Fetherling concludes, "For their news content alone, photographs grew almost as important as stories, and by the 1920s, it was possible to transmit them by wire" (108).

With the occasional exception, virtually no major Canadian English-language newspaper carried action photos from the theater of war between 1914 and 1918 for reasons that will be discussed in this chapter. Photographs became part of a determined propaganda program designed specifically to create hate and repulsion for an enemy who needed to be visualized as something less than human (fig. 8.1).

The photograph shows passengers jumping from the torpedoed French passenger liner *Sontay* into the Mediterranean Sea. This picture could be counted among those which could raise emotions to a fever pitch, because attacking passenger ships was considered to be the work of a special kind of inhuman devil. The Germans had set the precedent on May 8, 1915, when they torpedoed the *Lusitania*, which they believed was carrying ammunition, which in fact it was (Keshen 1996, 15). When the ship went down, 1,198 people drowned, more than 170 of them from Ontario (Wilson, ed. 1977, xxx). Photographs such as that of the *Sontay* incident would certainly rekindle nightmarish memories of the *Lusitania* disaster for the *Star*'s readers. This act, combined with the shooting of British nurse Edith Cavell in October 1915, transformed the "German" into the "Hun." In the *Sontay* tragedy, on June 6, 1917, the *Star* reinforced the impact of the disaster by reporting that the captain had made his way to the stern of the ship as water rose over the bow. There, shouting "Vive la France!" he was last seen slipping below the waves.

Unlike their British counterparts who openly fought press censorship, Canadian journalists were reigned in by an ominous piece of legislation called

Figure 8.1. *Toronto Daily Star,* June 6, 1917

the War Measures Act that passed through the Canadian Parliament on August 22, 1914. Included in its clauses were measures that "provided for censorship and control and suppression of publications, writings, maps, plans, photographs, communication and means of communication" (Keshen 1996, 65).

And censorship there was, practiced particularly by William Maxwell Aitken, head of the Canadian War Records Office and an imperial jingoist who was philosophically more British than the British themselves. Aitken recognized the power of the pictorial in maintaining morale at home when he mused that pictures would create "enthusiasm and eager interest in our army in France" (Keshen 1996, 36). It was some years later before Canadian school children discovered that a famous photograph in their history texts depicting Canadian soldiers jumping over parapets during the battle of the Somme had in fact been taken at a French army training facility under Aitken's orders. Aitken later became a major icon in British social circles as the press baron Lord Beaverbrook.

Thanks to the efforts of Aitken and others of like mind, war photography was restricted primarily to events on the home front. A postcard from London, Ontario, published in 1914 when enlistments filled the ranks of the armed forces (fig. 8.2), could just as easily be a picture of a Boy Scout camporee. There is little, with the exception of the cannon on the lower right,

*Figure 8.2.* Carling Heights Military Camp, London, Ontario, 1914. (Courtesy
J. J. Talman Regional Collection, University of Western Ontario)

to indicate that the purpose of the camp was to house men who would eventually participate in a life-threatening conflict. Aitken would have been proud
of this pictorial rendering.

The inhumanity for which World War I became known—horrors such as
gas attacks, vermin-ridden trenches, maiming and mutilation, rampant disease, and unexplainable increases in casualties—did not make it to the front
pages of most Canadian newspapers, either in photography or in script.
Photographs such as figure 8.2 were intended to counter any suggestion that
the war was nothing more than one great escapade for adventurous lads at
home. Written accounts of the numerous bloody confrontations that made
up the action seldom revealed the depth of the carnage on the battlefield.

Both written and pictorial accounts of the war effort, designed to maintain support and morale at home, were almost as bloodless as the weekly
death toll in the television series "Murder, She Wrote." Yet ten thousand
Canadians became casualties when they assaulted Vimy Ridge in late April
1917. The losses were so heavy that the depletion of the ranks directly contributed to the federal government's decision in the summer of 1917 to aban-
don its policy of voluntary enlistment and move to compulsory service. But
there was no suggestion of a crisis in an article in Montréal's *La Presse* on May
3, 1917, less than a week after the Vimy assault concluded. The text, too, was
bloodless. Datelined London, England, the article stated: "English troops have
begun a new offensive movement. The following communiqué was published
today. 'A violent battle is underway along the entire front, proceeding along
the Hindenburg line south of the river Sensee near the Acheville-Vimy road.

Our troops are making progress and they are already anticipating taking possession of several fortified positions.'"[2]

Photography complimented text. It became a vital propaganda vehicle, especially in English Canada, to muster support for the war. In French Canada, the visual record of the conflict was contained in one daily newspaper, Québec City's *Le Soleil*. Although far from being the province's largest French-language daily, *Le Soleil* was critically placed in the provincial capital, where it acted as the conscience of the nearly one-third of all Canadians whose mother tongue was French. It would be a simplification to suggest that the conflict between English and French Canadians could be reduced to the matters of language and religion alone. It was more than that. It was a conflict with deep roots that extended back to the defeat of the French general Montcalm on the Plains of Abraham outside of Québec City. And it had much to do with prevailing attitudes in Canada's two largest cities: English-speaking Toronto and French-speaking Montréal.

Toronto was the cultural center of English Canada in 1914 when the war broke out. It had a distinctly British character, and many Canadians believed it to be more British than any major center in Britain itself. William Maxwell Aitken would have prospered in that community, at least culturally. Toronto, the seat of government for Canada's largest province, had a population of 440,000. The city's three highest-circulation newspapers were chosen for this study. The *Toronto Daily Star* was a politically independent journal although it often expressed strong small *l* liberal tendencies. It had a daily circulation of 82,764. The *Evening Telegram,* a Conservative Party newspaper, had a daily run of 67,483, and the daily circulation of the *Globe*, a Liberal Party newspaper, was 61,851. In addition, the *London Free Press*, a Conservative Party newspaper in the heart of the Liberal Party fiefdom of southwestern Ontario, was studied, particularly in those months leading up to the implementation of conscription. The newspaper had a stranglehold on the city—33,143 subscribers in a population of 46,300.

Montréal, Québec's metropolis, had 470,480 residents, making it slightly larger than Toronto. However, the city did not have the linguistic singularity of its Ontario counterpart. Approximately one in three Montréalers spoke English. Isolated in population pockets within the city such as the Town of Mount Royal and Westmount, many Canadians outside Québec considered them extensions of an English-speaking Ontario culture. Many English-speaking Québeckers were the descendants of United Empire Loyalists who settled in Canada after leaving the United States following the American Revolution.

As a consequence, only the two leading French-language dailies were examined, *La Presse,* Canada's largest daily with a circulation of 126,155, and *Le Devoir,* an independent newspaper with a circulation of twenty thousand that became the voice of Québec nationalism during the conscription crisis. Because Montréal was not the provincial capital, as noted previously Québec City's *Le Soleil* was also reviewed. Located in the administrative center of a province with a population of 78,190 persons, the newspaper had a daily circulation of twenty thousand, most of whom were provincial politicians and civil servants. The newspaper was directed specifically to the opinion-makers in the province (Ayer 1914, 1120, 1122, 1131, 1132).

Of these newspapers, *Le Soleil* published the most extensive collection of action photography during the four-year conflict. During the summer of 1917 it published, on an almost daily basis, scenes of the conflict in Europe although there was no one specific page that was chosen consistently. Nevertheless, war photography received a prominent place centered directly above the fold on whatever page was chosen for the picture.

Although no sources were cited, it appears that of the journals examined for this study only *Le Soleil* had access to wire photography. Montréal's *Le Devoir,* in spite of its opposition to Canadian involvement in foreign wars, published no photographs, restricting its anti-war message to editorial columns. The journal's editors never advocated anything but passive resistance to conscription, but pro-conscription advocates in English Canada blamed it for anti-draft riots that broke out in Québec on Easter weekend in 1918.

The city's largest newspaper, *La Presse,* carried a limited number of photographs that were nearly always restricted to activities of a military nature within Montréal itself. They featured much of the same approach as the postcard depicting the camp at London's Carling Heights. A photograph in the Thursday, May 3, 1917, edition, for example, shows a brewery truck parked in front of a school and a soldier pointing to thirty-eight sacks of potatoes. Students at the Mont-Royale elementary school had collected the potatoes to donate to returning wounded servicemen who wanted to use them to start gardens elsewhere in the city. A caption at the bottom of the photograph noted that the newspaper was responsible for taking the picture.

A second photograph, taken at a Canadian hospital at Saint-Cloud in France, captures the image of an auditorium filled with wounded soldiers, many of whom were receiving decorations for bravery from a number of assembled dignitaries from France, Canada, and the United States. The photograph, which appeared on May 19, 1917, was not received by wire transmission. The caption noted that it had been taken by one M. E. Crépault, who had returned to Montréal from Europe just after the event. Most of the pictorial record of the war in *La Presse* was contained in a series of line drawings that were freely extracted from English-language newspapers, including some from the United States. Most were value-laden, constantly depicting the German empire and its leader Kaiser Wilhelm as the singular expression of evil in a world consumed in turmoil. Universal Studios further aggravated feelings in Canada by distributing *The Kaiser: Beast of Berlin* to studios in Toronto and Montréal, complete with a eighteen-by-fifteen frame cutout of the German emperor pointing his sword downward toward a woman who seems to be terrified and in fear for her life (Keshen 1996, 20).

In Toronto, the majority of war photography was published in the *Globe.* The *Evening Telegram* carried no photography at all during the conscription crisis of 1917, with the exception of head and shoulder shots of soldiers either killed or missing in action. As the conscription crisis was coming to a head during the summer of 1917, a June 1, 1917, front-page headline exhorted readers to "Stand by the Old Flag!" The article that followed encouraged subscribers to attend a mass pro-conscription rally that Saturday in the city's central Queen's Park. The *London Free Press* carried a few well-chosen photographs in aid of the war effort.

Canadian reaction to the war, specifically during the conscription debate, shook the very foundations of the state, producing consequences that remain to this day. The war that Robert Borden and William Maxwell Aitken felt would pull the country together and lay the groundwork for a new Canadian pan-nationalism created just the opposite impact (Vance 1997, 259–60). Yet the photographic record of events that took place from the declaration of war between Britain and the Central Powers in August 1914 remains fragmented, divided by race, language, religion, and class. As much as Mill and Marx saw two different Britains, Canadians were treated to two different wars, one symbolized by a patriotic call to duty and the other marked by death, mutilation, misery, and endless despair.

With only a few exceptions, war photographs, both in the newspaper and on postcards, sheltered Canadians from the reality of the battlefront. As much as the photographs contained in this study are representative of what took place at specific times and places, their value as a historical record must be placed within a well-defined framework. Consciously or not, the tone and temper of the majority of the photographs do nothing to question the validity of the action in Europe. In fact, many provide precisely the opposite view. Soldiers sent overseas were automatically granted a week's leave to inspect historic sites. Postcards arriving in Canada contained shots of the Tower of London, Westminster Abbey, St. Paul's Cathedral, and Buckingham Palace (Keshen 1996, 161–62). Yet as a propaganda vehicle they failed to achieve a consensus in the country for the war agenda.

The war effort had to live with the fact that Canada had never been a military power and the military has never been a major part of Canadian life. It was not until 1855 that the country's first militia was organized, ostensibly to fight on Britain's behalf in the Crimean War. But no Canadian soldiers were sent overseas in support of their British comrades. Following Canadian Confederation in 1867, Canadian military personnel fought in only two theaters, one in the prairies in 1885 when the newly formed North-West Mounted Police put down a Métis rebellion led by dissident parliamentarian Louis Riel (fig. 8.3), a military action that cost him his life, and the other in South Africa when a contingent of Canadian troops volunteered to assist the British in the Boer War.

English Canada's chief spokesperson was Sir Robert Borden, leader of the Conservative Party and prime minister since 1911. Borden (fig. 8.4) represented a point of view that dominated political thinking in English Canada at the time. For Borden and his supporters, Canada was obliged to be a partner in the effort against Germany because the country was a member of a family of nations first colonized and then governed by Britain. Nation-building in Canada was, in Borden's view, intrinsically tied to the fortunes of the Empire. But as the war dragged on seemingly without end and fewer and fewer volunteers returned home in one piece or at all, support for the war effort became taxed. And as rumblings of discontent began to spread across the country, the military's demand grew for more and more healthy, physically fit young Canadian men.

Every one of the men in figure 8.4 would have been volunteers. It is remarkable that Borden saw fit to visit military installations. It gave the image of solidarity in the ranks, that at least the war effort was one of community if nothing else. For many a young Canadian male of military age, joining the army meant adventure, excitement, and travel, not to mention escape from poverty. Fighting and potential maiming and possibly death were seldom if ever mentioned.

Henri Bourassa, a member of Parliament and founder of *Le Devoir*, did not share Borden's enthusiasm for the British connection. Like many of his fellow French-speaking minority, Bourassa was wary of the objectives of English-speakers. For him, World War I was not a war to end all wars as the rhetoric in English-Canada loudly proclaimed but rather one more example of British imperial arrogance. To go along with Canadian participation meant

*Figure 8.3.* Louis Riel addressing his trial in Regina, 1885. (Courtesy Archivist Canada)

*Figure 8.4.* "Premier Borden Reviewing Over-seas Forces at Niagara Camp," early 1915. (Courtesy J. J. Talman Regional Collection, University of Western Ontario)

justifying the imperial connection and thus the dominance of the English language and British values in Canada.

Bourassa wanted to create a climate for a pan-Canadian nationalism built on the Confederation partnership between the French and English communities, which, in theory at least, treated the two as equal in nation-building. For Bourassa, that meant disentangling the Canadian state from imperial obligations. At this point in history it also meant physical disengagement from British wars. Bourassa felt that Canada's contribution to the war should be limited to supplying food, clothing, and medicine for the starving populations of Europe who had been caught up in the tragedy (Heick 1980, 67). His fellow editors in English Canada did not agree. John W. Dafoe, one of the country's most influential journalists, the editor of the *Winnipeg Free Press,* and a strong Borden supporter, referred to the editor from Montréal as a "cowardly, selfish viper" (Donnelly 1968, 77).

When the Canadian National Service League, a pro-registration lobby founded in April 1916, argued for the compulsory registration of all Canadian men, the increasing divide between English and French Canada was foremost on the mind of Sir Robert Borden. He would have much preferred the inherent enthusiasm apparent in figure 8.5.

Rectory Street is in the heart of working-class, industrial London, not far from the Wolseley Barracks where the Royal Canadian Regiment was sta-

*Figure 8.5.* Troops marching on Rectory Street, East London, Ontario, 1914. (Courtesy J. J. Talman Regional Collection, University of Western Ontario)

tioned as early as 1832 to ward off a potential American invasion. The photograph clearly depicts both interest and support by the residents of the area and indicates that significant support for the war effort existed in typically English-Canadian cities such as London. As now, Rectory Street was a fairly narrow pathway, and in the photograph sidewalks are jammed with people viewing the parade and wishing their "boys" well as they journey to take on the terrible "Hun."

In a letter to the secretary of the Canadian National Service League Dr. A. H. Abott, Borden argued that in his mind "registration means in the end conscription and that might mean civil war in Québec" (Bray 1980–81, 19). Borden and his government, however, were constructing the foundations for an infrastructure to implement conscription should the prime minister deem it necessary. In August 1916 Borden's government issued an order-in-council, a legislative procedure that does not require parliamentary approval, to found the National Service Board. Its director-general R. B. Bennett argued that registration was necessary, if only to collect information on the availability of manpower by location and occupational distribution.

Canadian unionists did not agree. They were furious with the government for ignoring them when the board was constituted. They felt that registration would threaten their unions and eventually result in compulsory military service for their members (Robin 1966, 103). Organized labor had been suspicious of the Borden government when it recruited its first overseas contingent from an army of unemployed workers cast aside in a deep economic recession that began in 1912 (Morton 1990, 101). When Borden opted for conscription, he unwittingly created a pan-Canadian meeting of the minds of French Canadians, organized labor, European immigrants of Germanic extraction, and Canadian farmers that would eventually result in the permanent rise of third party politics in the country.

A cursory examination of the photography would certainly lead an uninitiated observer to conclude that there was harmony regarding the war effort in English Canada and dissension in French Canada. In the weeks before the enactment of the conscription legislation, the *London Free Press* secured a photograph of Canadian prisoners of war from the son of a local resident (fig. 8.6).

Although charges of the mistreatment of prisoners took a back seat to the revelations that the German army was using gas on the battlefield, the photograph clearly suggests that the worst possible outcome of a failure in battle would be indeterminate residence somewhere in Germany. The photograph, not surprisingly, shows no wounded, no maimed, and certainly gives no

*Figure 8.6.* Prisoners of war in Germany. (Courtesy *London Free Press,* May 30, 1917)

impression that the soldiers in the picture were suffering any hardships. There is a clear indication that joining the service was a risk-free ticket to excitement and adventure with very few life-threatening consequences. But neither does the picture contain images of smiling prisoners. Even when scenes of casualties were taken and later published, Canadian dead were covered and German dead were left exposed (Keshen 1996, 36).

A second photograph in the *London Free Press,* published on July 4, 1917, shows a contingent of soldiers who have returned home from the front. Although they are referred to as "battle-scarred heroes," not one of the combatants shows any sign of physical injury or disability.

Other photographs, one of which appeared in the *Toronto Globe* on June 6, 1917, show the queen discussing the war with what the caption refers to as a "Naval Hero." He is fully dressed in a military uniform and sitting in a wheelchair. There are no clues in the text as to how he came to be in such a condition. Readers are not invited to share his most private feelings. In all fairness to the editorial direction of these newspapers, a photograph in the *Toronto Star* on May 31, 1917, did show the destruction inflicted on the Cathedral of Arras in France by fleeing German troops. The picture is notable by its absence of any form of human existence, living or dead. The war, a clinical, patriotic exercise, continued on amid growing concern and growing frustration.

In Toronto, Ontario, two prominent members of the Liberal Party who had previously supported Sir Wilfrid Laurier decided to do something to encourage enthusiasm for the war effort in French Canada. Among other factors, the almost plastic scenes emerging from Europe were being countered by stories of extensive losses in places such as Vimy Ridge. Clearly, photography when combined with censorship could not meet the demands of creating unity in an increasingly divided state.

Under the leadership of Toronto lawyer John Godfrey and Arthur Hawkes, an Ottawa-based journalist for the *Toronto Star,* members of *Bonne Entente* (good understanding) visited schools, manufacturing plants, hospitals, and national monuments in Québec. The movement concluded its public activities by sponsoring a conference in Montréal from May 23 to 25, 1917: "The Win the War and National Unity Convention." The title is revealing because it placed the main focus of the organization on the war effort. In contrast, French-speaking participants translated the title with precisely the opposite emphasis as "Le Congrès de l'Unité National et pour gagner la guerre" (the Congress of National Unity and to Win the War).

Although both parties had a vested interest in healing the schisms that divided the English and French communities, it is clear that although English Canadians felt that winning the war would lead to a better definition of national unity, the French-speaking contingent felt that nation would have to be healed before any commitment to the war effort could be made.

While the 660 delegates met in Montréal, Sir Robert Borden was on a ship bound for Canada from a meeting in London hosted by the British prime minister, Lloyd George. The conscription issue was heating up as he returned. *La Presse* made its first reference to the debate to come in a series of four headlines that appeared in the Thursday, May 18, 1917, edition. The newspaper noted that parliament had been extended to review the situation but predicted that the federal Conservative Party was far from united on the issue.

In Québec City, *Le Soleil* alarmed readers on May 19 by predicting that the government would need to draft anywhere from fifty to a hundred thousand soldiers, a direct consequence of the extensive losses at Vimy Ridge. The newspaper had been reinforcing its anti-war position in 1917 by publishing a series of gory photographs. While the three major Toronto dailies carried stories on the valor of the Canadian fighting contingent in the battle, along with a noticeable lack of photography, *Le Soleil* chose to publish a scene of dead and wounded Canadian soldiers shortly after the battle concluded (fig. 8.7).

While French-speaking Québeckers were being exposed to the less desirable sides of a military career Toronto's English-language press was coming to side with the Borden government, with varying degrees of support. On June 4, 1917, the jingoistic, pro-war *Toronto Evening Telegram* published a story

*Figure 8.7.* "Soldats Canadiens sur la crete de Vimy" (Canadian Soldiers at the
Crest of Vimy). (Courtesy *Le Soleil*, Ville Quebec, P.C.)

about a group of "enraged" returned soldiers who had broken up a meeting
of anti-conscriptionist socialists in the city's Labor Temple.

Having introduced the compulsory service legislation in parliament,
Borden felt he needed to legitimize his government's position and called a
national election for December 1917. Borden was oblivious to mounting
opposition to the war effort within both the agricultural community and
organized labor. When his minister of militia and defense, Gen. S. C. Mewburn, appeared before a hostile farming audience in Dundas, Ontario, in
November 1917, he retreated from confrontation and announced that he
would exempt any laborer who could prove he was working on a farm to
produce food for the war effort. The government responded to Mewburn's
promise by acting on his guarantee on December 6 (Young 1972, 305–6).

With farm support guaranteed, Borden won the election handily. Laurier
and Bourassa were forced back to Québec, and the Liberal Party ceased to
be a national force. In Ontario, the country's most populous province, the
party took only eight ridings compared to seventy-four for the Unionist government. In spite of its overwhelming majority in the legislative chamber,
anti-conscriptionists running on Laurier's Liberal Party ticket in Ontario
managed to muster 263,000 votes compared to the Unionists' 509,307. It was
a warning bell that Borden and his colleagues ignored, an act that would have
devastating consequences for his party and the national political culture
(Young 1972, 307).

On the surface at least, Borden appeared to have achieved his objectives.
French Canada had been reduced to a virtual colony, and the war effort con-

tinued unabated. The photography of the period changed little in English Canada. There is virtually no anxiety on the faces of soldiers pictured as they were being shipped off to the front from the Canadian Pacific railway station in London, Ontario (fig. 8.8). Many of the recruits would have been farm boys. Like nearly all of the photography that appeared in English Canada during the period, the emphasis is on activity on the home front.

Whether the soldiers were drafted or had enlisted, their faces show no sign of resignation to their fate as cannon fodder on the European battlefield. In fact, just the opposite impression is created. Once again, the image of the soldier as tourist emerges, of course in a total lack of recognition that most were on the train to replace comrades and relatives slain at the battle of Vimy Ridge.

One of the ridings that voted for an anti-conscriptionist Liberal in 1917 was North Waterloo, a mixed urban and rural electoral district. Had Borden and his fellow Conservative Ontario premier Sir William Hearst been able to peer into a crystal ball and foresee the future, the events in North Waterloo would prove prophetic. While the two politicians were concentrating on the "treason" of Québec they had missed important signposts of political disturbance that would end their respective careers. In spite of the determined efforts at control by the likes of Aitken, the War Measures Act, and the Canadian War Records Office, the events of 1917 and later of 1919 would clearly demonstrate that the manipulation of words and images had failed.

The district was represented by William G. Weichel, a Conservative mem-

*Figure 8.8.* Postcard. "Canadian Troops leaving for the Front. c1917." (Courtesy J. J. Talman Regional Collection, University of Western Ontario)

ber of Borden's coalition. When the election was called, three-quarters of the local Conservative riding association committee deserted Weichel when he publicly announced his support for conscription. Along with two members of the Liberal association committee and several members of the Kitchener city council, they approached William D. Euler to run on the anti-conscriptionist Laurier ticket. The local Social Democratic Party had already announced its intention to field an anti-conscription candidate in the person of local trades unionist Mervyn Smith.

Class and ethnicity became two of the major cleavages that both Smith and Euler faced in the upcoming election. The local press pointed out that pro-conscription forces were being led and funded by members of the local business hierarchy. That made union opposition a foregone conclusion. Because Kitchener had a strong industrial base, the union vote, although nowhere near a majority, had to be recognized as influential. Borden's supporters appealed to Samuel Gompers, president of the American Federation of Labor, for support. They felt that a pro-war, pro-conscription endorsement from the high-profile labor leader could bring local labor figures on side. Gompers rushed into the fray, declaring his allegiance to the war cause. In the process, he pushed local unionists in the opposite direction— the anti-conscriptionist camp. Gompers chose to ignore the position of the Canadian Trades and Labor Council, which had many U.S.-based unions when it declared in the *Industrial Banner* on May 25, 1917, that conscription could only be justified when Borden and his cohorts were prepared to conscript wealth as well, a position that appeared with increasing frequency in the trades union press.

When the smoke cleared in December, Euler went to Ottawa as the member for North Waterloo, having taken 63 percent of the vote. Weichel trailed badly with 34 percent, and Smith succeeded in garnering only 3 percent (Heick 1980, 70, 82, 86). Although it was only one of eight non-Unionist ridings in Ontario, the seeds had been sown for a farmer-labor rebellion in 1919 that would take power in Ontario, become the official opposition in Ottawa, and trigger third-party movements in Nova Scotia, New Brunswick, Manitoba, Saskatchewan, and Alberta.

Sir Robert Borden had no way of knowing when he addressed the Canadian parliament on April 19, 1918, that within eight months an armistice would be signed in a railway car in France that would end the war intended to end all wars. In his speech on that spring day in the nation's capital, Borden announced that all exemptions to conscription would henceforth be cancelled (Young 1972, 307).

With the end of hostilities, war photography disappeared from the front

pages of the country's newspapers. In every respect, however, the few photographs the newspapers did choose to publish marked the beginning of
international pictorial journalism. Shortly after World War I ended a new
technology appeared: wire transmission of photographs. Postcards returned
to portraying idyllic scenes of the country's rural and urban communities.
In fact, the postcard "craze" had reached a zenith during the war, and the end
of hostilities marked the beginning of its steady decline.

If one can make at least one positive assessment of the photography that
appeared during World War I in Canada, it can be concluded that only the
French-language media portrayed the carnage in Europe with any sense of
accuracy. The cleavages between a pro-imperial stance that emerged in the
political establishment in English Canada and the antipathy toward the war
in French Canada are apparent in the pictures that emerged in the press and
on post cards. They represent a division between two cultures that tells of
the differences among languages, ethnicity, and, to some degree, religion. Yet
none of the photographs captures with any sense of intensity and reality the
dissension that arose in the farm and labor communities of English Canada.

Canadian history has generally depicted the debate over involvement in
World War I as a national split between English Canadian Protestants and
French-speaking Catholics. To a significant degree that existed, and its importance should not be underestimated. Yet little historical attention has
been paid, especially within the framework of a class and ethnic analysis,
of the tensions in the country outside Québec that pro-war photography and
censorship could not address. As much as there was a divide between English and French Canada, a second cleavage arose that pitted farm against
city, producer against manufacturer, and old blood against fairly new arriv-
als. If scholars were to rely exclusively on images that appeared on film in
English Canada they could only conclude that the war effort, and eventually conscription, enjoyed almost universal support. Nothing could be further from the truth.

As visual images take a more important place in the relating of historical
events it is critical that their impact be placed squarely within the context of
events as they occurred. To do otherwise would be to ignore events that emerge
from all segments of society. The cynicism with which photographers sought
to capture the war effort in English Canada provides reasons to be exacting
when examining such events. Photography can play an increasing important
role in understanding the past. Nonetheless, it is not, and must not be, an exclusive source of vision of the events that took place before long ago.

The war is over. Only the memories remain. Canada returned to peace, and

*Figure 8.9.* "Best wishes from London Ontario." (Courtesy Dan Brock)

pastoral scenes such as that of Victoria Park in the center of London, Ontario (fig. 8.9) do little to remind people of the tragic loss of life and limb that took place. Only the valor and the victories recycle themselves in legends, helped of course by mementoes such as the row of stilled cannon imported from Sevastapol by local brewer John Carling as a monument to the dead of the Crimean War.

## Notes

1. The number of studies is far too long to list. Canadian sources are primarily Fetherling (1990) and Rutherford (1982).

2. The original text was published in French. The translation is the responsibility of the author.

## References

Ayer, N. W. and Son. 1914. *American Newspaper Annual and Directory.* Philadelphia: N. W. Ayer.

Bray, R. Matthew. 1980–81. "A Conflict of Nationalism: The Win the War and the National Unity Convention, 1917." *Journal of Canadian Studies* 15(4): 18–30.

Brock, Daniel J. 1992. *Best Wishes from London, Canada: Our Golden Age of Postcards: 1903–1914.* London, Ont.: Gatherick Press.

Brookes, Timothy R. 1987. "The Last Shot? Jacob Shenkel's Gettysburg Diary." *Timeline* 4(3): 46–54.

Carter, John E. 1993. "The Trained Eye: Photographs and Historical Context." *The Public Historian* 15(1): 55–66.

Donnelly, Murray. 1968. *Dafoe of the Free Press*. Toronto: Macmillan of Canada.

Fetherling, Douglas. 1990. *The Rise of the Canadian Newspaper*. New York: Oxford University Press.

Frassanito, William A. 1975. *Gettysburg: A Journey in Time*. New York: Scribner's.

Freund, Gisele. 1980. *Photography and Society*. Boston: David R. Godine.

Heick, W. H. 1980. "If We Lose the War, Nothing Else Matters: The 1917 Federal Election in North Waterloo." *Ontario History* 72(2): 67–92.

Humphreys, Kathryn. 1993. "Looking Backward: History, Nostalgia, and American Photography." *American Literary History* 5(4): 686–99.

Jensen, Oliver. 1988. "Windows on Another Time." *American Heritage* 39(2): 38–52.

Keshen, Jeffrey. 1996. *Propaganda and Censorship during Canada's Great War*. Edmonton: University of Alberta Press.

Lasch, Christopher. 1989. "Politics and Culture." *Salmagundi* 81: 51–60.

Morton, Desmond. 1990. *Working People*. Toronto: Summerhill Press.

Noon, Alan. 1989. *East of Adelaide*. London, Ont.: London Regional Art and Historical Museums.

Parson, Debra Harmon. 1990. "West Virginia Women at Work: A Pictorial Sampler." *West Virginia History* 49: 125–38.

Robin, Martin. 1966. "Registration, Conscription, and Independent Labour Politics, 1916–1917." *Canadian Historical Review* 47(2): 101–18.

Rodger, Andrew, and Brian Carey. 1985. "The National Photography Collection: The First Ten Years." *Archivist (Canada)* 12(4): 16–19.

Rutherford, Paul. 1982. *A Victorian Authority*. Toronto: University of Toronto Press.

Sandeen, Eric J. 1986. *"The Family of Man* at the Museum of Modern Art: The Power of the Image in 1950s America." *Prospects* 11: 367–91.

Sontag, Susan. 1973. *On Photography*. New York: Farrar, Straus, Giroux.

Tagg, John. 1988. *The Burden of Representation*. Amherst: University of Massachusetts Press.

Vance, Jonathan F. 1997. *Death so Noble: Memory, Meaning, and the First World War*. Vancouver: University of British Columbia Press.

Whelan, Richard. 1981. *Double Take: A Comparative Look at Photographs*. New York: Clarkson N. Potter.

Wilson, Barbara M., ed. 1977. *Ontario and the First World War, 1914–1918*. Toronto: University of Toronto Press.

Young, W. R. 1972. "Conscription, Rural Depopulation and the Farmers of Ontario, 1917–1919." *Canadian Historical Review* 53(3): 289–320.

# 9

## The Family of Man:
## Readings of an Exhibition

*Monique Berlier*


Historians sometimes go to great lengths to avoid unbecoming contact with photographic imagery and other "disreputable" visual artifacts, and despite occasional nudging from visually oriented scholars they lag behind anthropologists, sociologists, ethnologists, and other social scientists in their use of photographs as documents or sources of information in their research (Borchert 1981; Haskell 1993).[1] Undoubtedly, historians' reluctance to bestow documentary value on photographic data lies in their firmly anchored belief in the sacrosanct authority of the written record.[2] To many historians, photographs and other visual sources cannot be used as sources of evidence because of their inherent ambiguity, which can at best be confusing and at worst can "pervert" history (Haskell 1993). The ambiguity of an image itself, coupled with the difficulty of determining authorship, place and date of production, and purpose, makes photographic documents undependable sources of evidence for historians.[3]

The idea that the written word should not be taken at face value has nevertheless been advanced on numerous occasions by a variety of scholars. Historians, including Bloch (1953), Fisher (1970), Gottschalk (1969), Nevins (1963), Shafer, ed. (1980), and Smith (1989), as well as communication scholars such as Berlo (1960), Fiske (1987, 1989), and Hall (1993), offer caveats. Because "meanings are in people, not in words" (Berlo 1960, 175), Berlo suggests that the meaning of a message depends on how receivers interpret its words rather than on the intended message itself. To Fiske (1987), the meaning-making of a message is a conscious or unconscious process of negotiation between the text and its socially or culturally situated readers. In the context of history and historiography, cultural and intellectual differences create varying inter- pretations of the written record, which leads to different perspectives and understandings of history.

In contrast to scholars who consider the polysemy of photographic im- ages a major drawback to their scholarly use, there are those who suggest that although photographs do not contain any meaning themselves they may still be used as sources in historical or cultural studies. Malmsheimer, for instance, argues that the propensity of photographs to "deconstruct *themselves* so eas- ily" makes them "ideal documents with which to begin and end any cultural inquiry for which they are relevant" (1987, 34, emphasis in the original). The open nature and flexibility of the imagery are seen as the very reasons why photographs should be widely used rather than automatically rejected in scholarly inquiry. Following that perspective, it is the varied interpretations of, or reactions to, a photograph (or a corpus of images) rather than the image itself that becomes the focus of analysis.[4]

This chapter presents a photographic exhibition as a historical source of varying, if not contradictory, readings of a collection of photographs. It ad- dresses the original conceptualization of *The Family of Man* along with con- temporary reactions and current responses to a revival of the exhibition and the continued publication of a book by the same title. It is based on an un- derstanding of history as a negotiated, intellectual construction of an event and its place in a specific social, political, or cultural context. By concentrat- ing on readings of the exhibition, this chapter explores the use of such an event as a historical document, not unlike a photo album or picture maga- zine, to reconstruct notions of intent, questions of effects, and the potential of photographic truths as historical evidence in contemporary thought.

An exhibition, like a composite of ideas from different authors, is the prod- uct of a creative mind and a reflection of specific social or even political con- siderations. In this case it is a statement based on photographic evidence produced for different purposes that has been de- and recontextualized in a collection whose goal is the celebration of the genius of photography and its potential as a topic of documentation itself, the commonality of human life. The multiple readings of *The Family of Man* produce a number of meanings and demonstrate how a photographic event (or historical evidence in the photographs themselves) is generalized, categorized, and stigmatized to serve specific purposes.

Photographs are a record of their times. Just as they reflect topics and perspectives related to the cultural and social conditions of specific historical periods and to the particular interests of their authors, their readings and interpretations reflect the experiences and particular interests of their viewers. The late 1940s and early 1950s were a time of reconstruction. Lessons of World War II became the guiding principle of a politics of reconciliation, and the end of colonial rule and liberation from military and economic domination elsewhere in the world preoccupied the imagination of a new generation of reformers and politicians. The United States became a leader of the "free" world, whose economic aid to postwar Western Europe and political support of the United Nations were indications of a commitment to peace and freedom.

Within this atmosphere of hope, imagery that reinforced the commonality of life and photographs as products of a contemporary technology of mass communication may be seen as a perfect means of airing shared experiences. In addition, photographs meet the expectations of observers who believe in the perfection of the camera's eye, the authenticity of the image, and its ability to represent "a slice of life." Together, the familiarity of shared experiences and the credibility of the photographic image form a strong and appealing message that is ideologically as well as commercially successful.

More specifically, this chapter is concerned with the creation and reception of *The Family of Man,* both in the past and in the present. Several commentators (Barrett 1990; Beloff 1985; Gee 1989; Green 1984; Sandeen 1987, 1995) argue that over the years the perception of the exhibition has shifted from critical acclaim to extensive, harsh criticism. This chapter offers an understanding of what Ritchin describes as "the most successful photography exhibition of all time" (1990, 104). It begins with the man who created the show, Edward Steichen, and his motivations and intentions for the photographic exhibition. After briefly describing *The Family of Man,* both in terms of content and presentation, the analysis turns to a review of the reactions it roused and the meanings it acquired. In addition to retracing various reactions to *The Family of Man,* including those of professional photographers, it focuses on the exhibit and the role it played in the larger context of the political, cultural, economic, and social history of the United States. The chapter also examines how the meaning of the exhibit has fluctuated throughout the years before 1994, when it found a permanent resting place in Luxembourg's Clervaux Castle museum.

## The Most Successful Photography Exhibition

On Sunday, May 8, 1955, *New York Times* camera editor Jacob Deschin wrote, "When 'The Family of Man' photographic exhibition closes at 7 P.M. today . . . it will have run up the greatest attendance record at the Museum of Modern Art since the 1940 'Italian Masters' show. The total will be in excess of 270,000 visitors for the 103-day period since the opening on Jan. 26, with a daily average of 2,600" (Deschin 1955).

In Steichen's words, the exhibit was designed to show "the essential oneness of mankind throughout the world" (1956, 195). The show, which consisted of photographs portraying how people from all over the world experience different life events and emotions in similar ways, was circulated by the Museum of Modern Art (MoMA) in cities throughout the United States, including Dallas, Cleveland, Philadelphia, Baltimore, and Minneapolis, where attendance numbers per capita surpassed New York's (Kramer 1955). In addition to the original display, several small-scale versions toured more than thirty-five U.S. cities, and six duplicates of the original exhibit traveled abroad under the auspices of the United States Information Agency (USIA). By 1968, "more than nine million people in sixty-nine countries" had seen *The Family of Man* (Steichen 1963, n.p.).[5]

The phenomenal success of *The Family of Man* extended beyond the exhibition. By 1978 at least five million people had purchased one of the three book versions of the show (Meltzer 1978).[6] Two hundred and fifty thousand were bought within three weeks of the first publication in June 1955. A bestseller both in the United States and abroad, *The Family of Man* was also used in many universities (Forsee 1968). The thirtieth-anniversary edition, published in 1986, went into its fifth printing in 1996. To Steichen (1958) the success of *The Family of Man* was irrefutable proof that photography was a universal language that could touch and deeply move people and that there existed a public eager to see the photographs.

When reviewing the exhibit for *Popular Photography,* Arthur Goldsmith, Jr., argued that the show would be "praised, damned, criticized, and discussed for a long time to come" (1955, 88). He was right. More than thirty years after its creation, critics and commentators were still discussing *The Family of Man,* and many photography encyclopedias or histories reference Steichen's accomplishment (see, for example, Barrett 1990; Beloff 1985; Gee 1989; Green

1984; Guimond 1991; Harley 1990; Lutz and Collins 1993; Ritchin 1989; Rosenblum 1984; Sandeen 1987, 1995; and Sekula 1984).

If many of these scholars agree that photographs are cultural artifacts that reflect the specific political, economic, and social contexts in which they are created and used, not all concur on the criteria by which to judge Steichen's production. While Beloff calls for new evaluations "to see how the taken-for-granted quality of humanism may be open to more complex interpretation" (1985, 124), Gee argues that "photography, tied irrevocably to the world, is a barometer of change, both sociopolitical and cultural. In order to place photography of the fifties in its proper historical perspective, it must be seen in the context of the times" (1989, 62). Pointing out the weakness of recent criticism that judges *The Family of Man* on the book version rather than on the exhibit itself, Sandeen (1995) also suggests that it is "too easy" to criticize Steichen's work from the perspective of the 1990s.

In order to assess the role that *The Family of Man* came to play in American culture, one must begin with the man behind the show, Edward Steichen, and the events that led him to create the photographic exhibit.

### Edward Steichen's Vision

Born in Luxembourg in 1879, Steichen was raised in the United States, where his family settled soon after his birth. A painter and a soft-focus photographer, it was not until after World War I that Steichen, disgusted by the atrocities of the war and displeased with the growing detachment of painting from representation, began to look for a visual medium that would make "an affirmative contribution to life," a medium that would enable him "to reach into the world, to participate and communicate" (Steichen 1963, n.p.). He turned to traditional photography, to which he had been exposed as director of the U.S. aerial photographic service during World War I.[7] Convinced that it was possible "to give abstract meanings to very literal photographs . . . if the symbols used were universal" (Steichen 1963, n.p.), he spent several months in his French country home mastering techniques that he believed would create maximum realism and enable him to reach a large number of people. Returning to the United States in 1923, Steichen worked for fifteen years as a portrait and fashion photographer for Condé Nast's *Vanity Fair* and *Vogue.* He also took photographs for the J. Walter Thompson advertising agency. In 1938, bored with the routine of his job, he closed his commercial photographic studio.

As World War II loomed, Steichen became increasingly convinced that "if a real image of war could be photographed and presented to the world, it might make a contribution toward ending the specter of war" (Steichen 1963, n.p.). He volunteered his services, and the U.S. Navy asked him to form a small team of photographers to document naval aviation. Steichen became director of the U.S. Navy Photographic Institute and was placed in command of all naval combat photography. In 1945 the sixty-six-year-old Steichen produced *Power in the Pacific,* a photographic exhibition based upon the *Road to Victory* show he had created in 1942. The highly successful exhibitions showed the country's march toward unity and gave people something to base their faith upon (Forsee 1968; Phillips 1982; Pollack 1969; Sandeen 1987; Steichen 1963).

In 1947 the New York Museum of Modern Art created a position for Steichen as director of the Department of Photography—"the one museum that . . . from its inception had given photography more recognition that it had ever been accorded by any other institution in the world" (Steichen 1963, n.p.).[8] Steichen wrote several articles, helped publish several books on photography, and organized forty-four photo exhibitions during his fifteen years with the museum. Capitalizing on photography's central role as a mass medium rather than as a unique, purely aesthetic art form, he considered photography:

> a great and forceful medium of mass communication. To this medium the exhibition gallery adds still another dimension. . . . In the exhibition gallery, the visitor sets his own pace. . . . [R]esources are brought into play that are not available elsewhere. The contrast in scale of images, the shifting of focal points, the intriguing perspective of long-and short-range visibility with the images to come being glimpsed beyond the images at hand—all these permit the spectator an active participation that no other form of visual communication can give. (1963, n.p.)

*The Family of Man* was the pinnacle of Steichen's life and career, both as a visual communicator and as photography director of the museum. Although he began working on the exhibition at seventy-three, he recalled the principle that supported the show as being rooted in an event that had taken place during his childhood in Milwaukee. Steichen recalled coming home from school one day and, closing the door of his mother's millinery shop, turning around and shouting "You dirty little kike!" to a boy in the street. When Marie Steichen asked what he had said, young Steichen repeated the insult "with innocent frankness." Excusing herself from customers, she locked the door of the store and took him upstairs to their apartment. There, she talked to him "for hours," explaining that all people were the same despite differ-

ences in race, creed, and color. She also told him about the villany of bigotry
and intolerance. The incident "was possibly the most important single moment in my growth towards manhood, and it was certainly on that day the
seed was sown that, sixty-six years later, grew into an exhibition called 'The
Family of Man'" (Steichen 1958, 1963, n.p.).

The exhibition also grew from the realization that the negative approach
he had previously taken in the war exhibits had failed to make a lasting impression on visitors:

> Although I had presented war in all its grimness in three exhibitions, I had failed
> to accomplish my mission.[9] I had not incited people into taking open and united
> action against war itself. This failure made me take stock of my fundamental
> idea. What was wrong? I came to the conclusion that I had been working from
> a negative approach, that what was needed was a positive statement on what a
> wonderful thing life was, how marvelous people were, and, above all, how alike
> people were in all parts of the world. (Steichen 1963, n.p.)

At first Steichen planned to focus on human rights, but he soon relinquished
that idea because "the subject of human rights was becoming an international
political football." One day, as he was leafing through Carl Sandburg's biography of Abraham Lincoln, he came across a speech in which Lincoln had used
the expression "family of man." The exhibition he had been planning for so
long had finally found a theme and a title (Steichen 1963, n.p.).[10]

In addition to showing "the relationship of man to man" and sharing his
belief in the oneness of humanity, Steichen also used *The Family of Man* "to
demonstrate what a wonderfully effective language photography is in explaining man to man" (Steichen 1958, 161). In his view, the best service photography could render history was to record human relations. Photography, a
universal language, required no translation because it communicated equally
to everyone throughout the world. "The camera may lie, but it can also tell a
lot of truth. What's more, it tells it in the most universal language of all—in
terms of birth, death, love, children, work, play, pleasure and pain, fears and
hopes, tears and laughter. And that was the purpose behind 'The Family of
Man' show—to demonstrate amid all possible diversity and variables those
universal constants of being that all humanity shares" (Steichen, quoted in
Weiss 1970, 50).

The search for photographs that would impart Steichen's timeless message began in 1952 when he made a survey trip to Europe to make certain that
he could supplement American resources with European materials. Convinced that the project was feasible, he and his assistant Wayne Miller sub-

mitted requests for photographs to photographers, camera clubs, picture agencies, libraries, newspapers, and magazines all over the world (Steichen 1963, n.p.).

From the very beginning Steichen was adamant about not placing *The Family of Man* into any specific historical context. The news release he sent in 1954 made that request very clear: "It is essential," he said, "to keep in mind the universal elements and aspects of human relations and the experiences common to all mankind rather than situations that represented conditions exclusively related or peculiar to a race, an event, a time or place" (quoted in Sandeen 1987, 373).

Steichen and Miller went through the extensive archives of *Life* and *Look* magazines, picture agencies such as Magnum and Black Star, and files of individual photographers, searching for photographs. As word of the exhibition spread, photographs began to pour in. From two million possible photographs, ten thousand were selected, a number then cut down to one thousand (Meltzer 1978; Sandeen 1987, 1995). The final reduction to 503 photographs proved to be most difficult and "heartbreaking" (Steichen 1963, n.p.). Although Steichen had the final say on images related to the world situation, Miller was in charge of those that pictured men and men's work, and his wife Joan made decisions on photographs that portrayed women, children, or women's work. Rather than being selected on grounds of technical or artistic quality, the 503 final photographs were chosen because of their ability to portray the themes of the exhibition and to develop a visual sequence (Sandeen 1987, 1995; Steichen 1963). Sixty-eight countries and 273 photographers were represented.

It is important to note that none of the prints used in the exhibit were provided by the photographers themselves. Instead, Steichen asked them to send him a negative or negatives for enlargement. If he could not obtain original negatives, new ones were shot from available images. In order to have total control over the prints, Steichen asked all photographers to sign release forms giving him permission to manipulate the images (Meltzer 1978; Sandeen 1987).

In addition to the photographs, Steichen used brief Bible quotations, folk-sayings, and text from world literature, including thoughts from Virgil, Homer, Lao-tse, Lui-Chi, Thomas Paine, Thomas Jefferson, James Joyce, Shakespeare, William Blake, Montaigne, and Anne Frank, as well as from the Bhagavad-Gita and from Native Americans, to keynote the exhibit's themes. A small credit line on the photographs indicated the photographer and the country where the picture had been taken.

If the choice of the photographs was a vital component in the creation of *The Family of Man* so was the way the final prints were shown. To ensure that the 503 photographs "collectively communicate a significant human experience," Steichen asked Paul Rudolph to help with the installation of the exhibit. He believed that the Bauhaus-trained architect would orchestrate the space on the second floor of the Museum of Modern Art to create a highly evocative and unified experience for viewers (Harley 1990; Steichen 1963). If photographs could be used as a force, he believed, people who ordinarily never visit museums would "flock" to see them (quoted in Phillips 1982, 43).

After three years of intense preparation, during which Steichen lost thirty pounds, *The Family of Man* opened to the public on January 26, 1955. As visitors entered the museum, they received a flier announcing "The Family of Man—an exhibition of creative photography, dedicated to the dignity of man, with examples from sixty-eight countries, conceived and executed by Edward Steichen, assisted by Wayne Miller; installation by Paul Rudolph" (Adams 1955, 69). The flyer also contained a prologue by Carl Sandburg that ended with the following words:

> There is only one man in the world
> and his name is All Men.
> There is only one woman in the world
> and her name is All Women.
> There is only one child in the world,
> and the child's name is All Children.
>                             (Adams 1955, 69)

The exhibit opened with a large panorama of water and sky accompanied by religious quotations. Visitors were then led to scenes depicting love and courtship, pregnancy, childbirth, mothers and children, children (learning, playing, and fighting), and fathers and sons. From there, they envisioned work, from ancient tilling of soil to nuclear physics. The focal point of the exhibit was a series of five family portraits. Work gave way to eating, dancing, music, drinking, and playing, which were followed by learning, teaching, and thinking. Then came photographs showing human relationships, death, loneliness, and compassion that served as a prelude for images representing thought and religion. The narrative continued with photographs depicting hard times, famine, inhumanity, revolt, and rebellion. Then came youth, justice, elections, and public debate. From there, visitors faced "faces of war," captioned with a quotation from Bertrand Russell warning against the danger of hydrogen bombs. Visitors confronted a photograph of a dead soldier before entering a darkened room in which there was a floor-to-ceiling color transparency of the hydrogen blast at Bikini Atoll. Leaving that room, visitors came face to face with ten photographs of couples, each labeled "we two form a multitude." A photograph of the General Assembly of the United Nations, the largest in the exhibit, followed. After a series of portraits of children, *The Family of Man* closed with Eugene Smith's "Walk to Paradise Garden" (Goldsmith 1955; Sandeen 1987; Steichen 1958).

Throughout the preparation of the exhibit Steichen insisted on selecting photographs that would "mirror the flaming creative forces of love and truth and the corrosive evil inherent in the lie" (quoted in Hughes 1989, 330). Shortly before the show opened, he told Miller that "unless we have the elements of love dominating this entire exhibition—and our lives—we'd better take it down before we put it up" (quoted in Forsee 1968, 50). Any time life was endangered or destroyed there followed hope and faith. Death did not appear at the end of the exhibit, but at mid-point. Hope was found in dream, religion, compassion, rebellion, justice, elections, the United Nations, and, above all, in children. To convey this optimistic mood, a photograph of a merry Peruvian flutist (fig. 9.1) was repeated throughout the display.

In addition to judiciously juxtaposing the photographs, Steichen used a wide variety of display techniques to guide visitors through the exhibit. In lieu of looking at a sequence of photographs that were carefully mounted, framed, placed behind glass, and hung at eye level, visitors were thrown into an elaborate three-dimensional photomontage that disregarded traditional "museum-esque" mise-en-scène. Angles, distances, and sizes were freely and

*Figure 9.1.* Photograph by Eugene Harris (© Violet J. Olsen)

extensively manipulated to create dramatic effects. Photographs were mounted at right angles to walls, against transparent panels, parallel to the ceiling,
on vertical posts affixed to the floor, on the floor, on circular metal construction, or back to back. Print dimensions varied from snapshot size to giant
mural enlargements. Some prints were isolated while others were grouped
in dynamic sequences. All these techniques made visitors walk through what
looked like "a three-dimensional version of a picture magazine" (Rosenblum
1989, 56).[11]

Like the exhibit, the book version of *The Family of Man* was a smashing
success. With fifteen or twenty exceptions it reproduced photographs used
in the exhibit. Missing, for instance, are a close-up photograph of the nude
stomach and breasts of Harry Callahan's "very pregnant" wife; the photograph of the H-bomb explosion; a Hungarian family portrait, one of the five
family portraits that served as central theme of the exhibit; three photographs
from the series "we two form a multitude"; a photograph of the execution
of prisoners during World War II; and a photograph of the lynching of a black
man. Due to the two-dimensional aspect imposed by book format, photographs were also arranged and sequenced slightly differently than in the original exhibit and their sizes sometimes varied. Prominent photographs in the
exhibit were sometimes reduced in the book and vice versa.

### Initial Critical Response

Sandeen (1995, 26) suggests that photographic production in the 1920s and
1930s had accustomed American viewers to interpreting events, both national
and international, through photographs. Not only did publications such as
*Ladies Home Journal, Life, Look, Saturday Evening Post,* and *National Geographic* help readers visualize what the world looked like, but—most important—they also provided a Western perspective from which to view it. Eventually, "picturing everyday life, both in the United States and abroad, became
one more way in which America laid claim to world dominion."

By the mid-1950s, not only had picture magazines conditioned the American public to explore the world via photographic imagery, but the public itself, tired of the wars and conflicts of the previous fifteen years, was also longing for reconstruction, reconciliation, and peace. Thus, except for a few
dissenting voices, *The Family of Man* exhibit and book, which reinforced the
commonality of life and epitomized the goodness of human beings around
the world, were critically acclaimed by the general public.[12] Among photography experts, critics, and photographers, however, opinions were divided.
Although reviews of the book ranged from favorable to excellent, opinions

about the form and the content of the exhibit varied from high praise to severe criticism.[13] Some critics had mixed feelings, whereas others remained noncommittal.

Among those who responded most favorably to *The Family of Man* were Leon Arkus (1956), who reviewed the show for *Carnegie Magazine,* and Barbara Morgan (1955), a photographer who selected captions for the photographs and whose work was represented in the exhibit. The most outspoken critic of *The Family of Man* was Phoebe Lou Adams, whose three-page satirical piece "Through a Lens Darkly" appeared in the April 1955 issue of *Atlantic Monthly.* Although recognizing the value and quality of some individual photographs, Adams ruthlessly attacked the exhibit theme by theme, sneering at Steichen:

> an Ice Age Hunter, . . . a warlock . . . [whose] choice is the surface of things, reproduced as clearly as possible with a nice moderate gloss. . . . the powers the display is designed to propitiate, whatever they are, are unimaginative and even a trifle myopic, with a weakness for the obvious example, the facile tear, and the literal meaning. . . . The shoulder-patting gesture is repeated so often . . . that it loses all meaning, and photographs that are first-class in themselves become faintly comic. . . . [M]ankind is back in the second grade and enjoying every minute of it. (69, 71, 72).

After comparing the hydrogen bomb explosion to a "splash of orange fire, not as stimulating as a good Fourth of July display perhaps, but a handsome thing in its way," Adams concluded that the show was unsuccessful because Steichen had not presented the differences that divide humankind and had forgotten "that a family quarrel can be as fierce as any other kind" (72).

One *Atlantic Monthly* reader suggested in a letter to the editor in June 1955 that Adams had been unfair to both the exhibit and Steichen. Reacting to her remark that "deliberate evil has been carefully excluded; there are dead men, but no murderers," the reader wrote: "If she [Adams] returns to the exhibit and looks carefully, she will find a series of photographs portraying 'deliberate evil' in most unsubtle terms. It includes two pictures of the destruction of the Warsaw Ghetto by the Germans during World War II, and one picture of a lynching victim taken in this country. In the former two pictures, the jack-booted murderers are clearly visible; in the latter, their existence is necessarily implied" (Albrecht 1955, 18).

Had Adams returned to the photo-exhibit, however, she would not have found the photograph of the lynched black man chained to a tree. Disliking the attention that the print was getting from MoMA visitors and the press, Steichen removed it after a week (Miller 1994b; Sandeen 1987).[14]

Other mid-1950s' critics attacked *The Family of Man* for its superficiality, lack of contextualization, vagueness, and inability to bear the weight of history, as well as for the sentimentality of its theme.[15] Positing that the most profound link between people is their political link, Kramer argued that the lack of photographs of political violence illustrated that *The Family of Man* was nothing but "a self-congratulatory means for obscuring the urgency of real problems under a blanket of ideology which takes for granted the essential goodness, innocence, and moral superiority of the international 'little man,' 'the man in the street,' the abstract, disembodied hero of a world-view which regards itself as superior to mere politics" (1955, 367). In his view, the exhibit had great appeal because it relieved critics and commentators of the necessity to think politically and confront the more troubling issues and problems of the era.

In addition to questioning the content of *The Family of Man,* critics debated its form, Steichen's use of photography as a medium "of the people for the people," and the uncommon display techniques employed. For instance, although Rosskam (1955) commended Steichen for his editorial skills and his effort to transform photography into a more popular medium, he also blamed him for using "stunts" in the installation of the prints. Concluding his description of the exhibit's installation techniques, McKenna stated that some photographs "happily, just hang" (1955, 30). Others, such as Goldsmith (1955), found the display techniques quite attractive and appropriate and suggested that other museums and galleries experiment with them.

Like any other artifact, *The Family of Man* must be placed and read within its specific cultural and historical context, and there is little doubt that the exhibit and the response to it exemplify a cultural debate concerned with the status of photography in American culture.[16] The debate, which had been seething for many years, considered the role of photography in society. Was it high art, low art, or no art at all? Was photography a mass medium? Ought it be shown in museums? If museums were to exhibit photography, what kinds of photographs should they show and how should they present them? What place should photography occupy in American society? While critics pondered these questions, the general public also reacted strongly to the display. "A stubborn lady" was reported to have "demanded her admission refunded on the grounds that there were no paintings on view" (Kramer 1955, 364).

Opinions among critics varied greatly as to the status of photography in American culture and society. Where some believed that the medium should stop being treated like painting (see, for example, Goldsmith 1955; Grafly 1955; and Rosskam 1955), others perceived the exhibit, and its phenomenal success, as part of a dangerous trend threatening high culture and art. They suggested that *The Family of Man* should be moved from the Museum of Modern Art to the Museum of Natural History (Goldsmith 1955, 148) or to the lobby of the United Nations (Adams 1978, 403; Gee 1989, 64; Wright and Wright 1955, 22).[17] Kramer was confounded that such a plebeian exhibition would be presented and promulgated by the Museum of Modern Art. "What is disheartening," he commented, "is to see the agency which claims to preside over the artistic values of photography tumble so easily into the vulgar ideological postures which, with less fanfare and less prestige, if also less taste, thousands of periodicals every day embrace as a matter of course" (1955, 367).

A series of letters sent to *New York Times* art editor Aline Saarinen following publication of her February 6, 1955, piece "The Camera versus the Artist"—in which she asked whether photography had replaced painting as the great visual form—testifies to the importance of this debate. Among the heated responses was that of painter-photographer Ben Shahn, whose work was also displayed in *The Family of Man:*

> Let us also note that it is not at all surprising that the public turns to the Steichen show with such undivided enthusiasm. The reason is, I am sure, that the public is impatient for some exercise of its faculties; it is hungry for thinking, for feeling, for real experience; it is eager for some new philosophical outlook, for new kinds of truth; it wants contact with live minds; it wants to feel compassion; it wants to grow emotionally and intellectually; it wants to live. In past times all this has been largely the function of art. If art today repudiates this role, can we wonder that the public turns to photography; and particularly to this vivid show of photographs that have, it seems, *trespassed* into almost every area of experience. (Shahn 1955, 15)

Shahn was not the only photographer who defended photography, Steichen, and *The Family of Man*. Nell Dorr, whose work also appeared in the show, responded to another condemnatory letter published in the May 1955 issue of *Popular Photography* in which a reader accused Steichen of personal flag-waving. Arguing that human beings are a biological family but differ tremendously in social, moral, and ethical values, the reader found the concept of the show "rather trite,—based on ignorance, if not a lie" (Ringel 1955, 6). Commenting that Steichen's own work was hardly featured in the show, Dorr suggested that photographic exhibits ought to depict and stand for something more important than just a "Who's Who in Photography."[18] "We love, we hate, and we fear," she noted. "We all are born, we suffer, and we die, and within that compass we all must walk. Doesn't the *Family of Man* stress those points? Doesn't it bring the world a little closer?" (Dorr 1955, 8).

Other photographers who contributed to the exhibit, such as Dorothea Lange and Homer Page, showed great enthusiasm for *The Family of Man*. Not surprisingly, some whose work had been turned down were not as supportive of the show or of Steichen.[19] Imogen Cunningham, for instance, referred to him as "a great commercial man" (Danziger and Conrad 1977, 44). Many photographers were also distressed to see the individual character of their work sacrificed to the requirements of the show, and "only those of philosophical disposition understood that the solution was artistically inevitable" (Szarkowski 1978, 17).

The harshest criticisms by a photographer came from Ansel Adams, who was revolted by the copy the museum had made of his Mount Williamson photograph. "I became ill when I saw the finished mural. He had transformed Mt. Williamson . . . into expensive wallpaper" (Adams 1985, 210). Earlier, he said, "[T]hey made a terrible copy, and then when they cut the prints, they trimmed off so the sections didn't match. There was an inch lost between each one. And here was this thing on display!" (1978, 322). According to Adams, the quality of the prints was so "disgracefully bad" that the show "put photography back twenty years!" Calling *The Family of Man* "one of the worst catastrophes that ever happened to creative photography," he said he was sorry to have been included (1978, 209, 322).

Not all photographers felt like Adams and, as Deschin's last review indicates, there was general support for the exhibit:

> The overwhelming chorus of yeas from a general public to whom the show was an excitingly new experience had one outstanding effect: it 'sold' photography to the public as nothing had ever done before on a scale so grand and effective, and Mr. Steichen emerges as photography's most convincing salesman. People who came to see the show were impressed and deeply moved. They told others, and the visitors came in crowds. They lined up outside the museum, as at movie theaters, waiting for the doors to open.
>
> Even if the show did nothing else than achieve this response to a medium which can be, above all mediums, the most articulate form of visual communication to the man in the street, it was remarkably successful. (1955)

The public probably did not consider the role of photography in the culture debate when they visited *The Family of Man;* the success of the exhibit in 1955 was primarily due to the accessibility, the apparent transparency, and the appeal of the message delivered. The commonality of human life and hope for the future was a message people wanted to hear.

The majority of the general public was not concerned with issues dealing with the technical quality of final prints, the effacement of the individual photographer behind the message, or the threat the exhibition posed art photography. Unlike critics or photographers conversant with the ambiguity of photographic imagery, they viewed the photographs as perfect, transparent, and authentic visual records and trusted their ability to document life truthfully. Because they did not know Steichen personally, their like or dislike of him, his persona, or what he stood for did not influence their assessment of his show. As a result, they remained unaffected by the controversy surrounding the physical display of the exhibit, their readings of the show were based on its message rather than on its form, and the positive response they gave to *The Family of Man* was emotional rather than critical or analytical.

## Critical Reappraisal

Between 1955 and 1962 some nine million people saw *The Family of Man* as it toured the United States and numerous countries.[20] The success of Steichen's enterprise did not go unnoticed in the intellectual milieu. Over the years the show has been reappraised by a variety of critics, some of whom have come to suspect that, perhaps, Steichen did more than just sell photography to the public.

Echoing past criticisms are scholars such as Beloff (1985), Berger (1980), Green (1984), Ritchin (1990), Sontag (1977), and Westerbeck (1976) who blame *The Family of Man* for its simplistic approach, use of clichés, complacency, manipulation of images, exploitation of human feelings, disregard for the photographers' original intents, and denial of the weight of history. Positing that "most photographs taken of people are about suffering, and [that] most of that suffering is man-made," Berger, for instance, faults Steichen for treating a class-divided society as if it were a united family (1980, 57). Westerbeck (1976) argues that although Steichen did not invent the mythic appeal of the united family he permanently installed it in the public's expectations of photography. *The Family of Man* had led to the creation of "photographic anthropology" books designed to make readers believe that the people of the world are far more similar than they are different.[21] In Westerbeck's view, the exhibit served as a prelude to yet another myth, that of the global village, which McLuhan proposed in the 1960s.

Unlike commentators in the 1950s, Westerbeck and other contemporary critics have the benefit of hindsight, including the history of the exhibit, its traveling duplicates, and its book version, and the political, cultural, economic, and social history of the United States on which to base their judgments. With time, some critics concluded that *The Family of Man* was more than just an exhibit or a book in praise of the essential goodness of humanity and its oneness throughout the world.

According to Sekula, *The Family of Man* symbolized and reinforced the concept of the bourgeois nuclear family, capitalism's prime target since the 1920s.[22] Just as families portrayed in Steichen's commercial photography were always dominated by a corporate authority, Sekula argues that "The Family of Man [has] to be understood as a profoundly corporate image of the world, as a Cold War utopia" (1984, 50). Because of its expansionist nature, capitalism aims at unifying the world into a unique system of commodity production and exchange. By celebrating the family as "the exclusive arena of all desire and pleasure," Sekula suggests that *The Family of Man* glorified and legitimized family-based consumerism in advanced capitalist societies (90).

While Sekula sees the symbol of the bourgeois nuclear family in *The Family of Man,* Green views Steichen's exhibition as a recreation of "the social realism of the thirties, which shunned the bourgeois in favor of the noble proletariat" (1984, 48). To him, the show is a "programmatic, socialistic statement" whose hero is "not the family, but the common man, the common worker" (1984, 48). Prosperity, freedom, and peace are not dependent on the unity of the family but on workers' health, brute strength, sanity, and common sense. In order for as large an audience as possible to understand his message, Green argues that Steichen used a variety of techniques, including simple, vague images that avoided the personal and the private, "predigested" text that spared viewers any effort at thought, and the photo-essay format that left viewers with little room for personal reactions and feelings. Because *The Family of Man* "played to and for the very people it idolized," Green contends that the exhibit gave no sense of intellectual endeavor, nor did it portray the possibilities of the contemplative or speculative mind.[23] Quoting Sandburg's prologue to the show, he writes that the exhibit is made up of lovers, eaters, drinkers, workers, loafers, fighters, players, gamblers, ironworkers, bridgemen, musicians, shandhogs, miners, builders, jungle hunters, landlords, the landless, saints, sinners, winners, and losers, "not a catalog of the most notable human accomplishments . . . but it is sufficiently vague and archetypal for every viewer to recognize some aspect of himself in the photographs" (1984, 47).

Unlike Green, who sees in the exhibition the exaltation of the common people to the detriment of the elite, Guimond (1991) argues that the show unified society by emphasizing the values that united its members while playing down the differences that separated them. In his view, the exhibit was not meant to celebrate the working class solely. Rather, it was produced to salute the triumph of national unity over racial, social, cultural, political, or economic diversity.

Whether Steichen's family stood for the bourgeois, the worker, both, or neither, many recent critics have castigated the show for being deeply rooted in the values of Western civilization. To some, the exhibition was nothing but "an exercise in Western/Northern self-congratulation" (Beloff 1985, 38) manufactured to comfort a public weary of national and international conflict (Gee 1989). Like Kramer in 1955, Beloff and Gee attribute the success of *The Family of Man* to the public's lassitude regarding political and social vexations and its longing for a world where people are all the same, merry, and of goodwill. The early 1950s had been a bleak era for the United States. The Korean war had illustrated that World War II had failed to bring lasting peace, and the country was caught up in McCarthyism, desegregation conflicts, and the fear caused by atomic and hydrogen bombing experiments. By 1955, with the end of the Korean war and McCarthy's reign of terror and the election of Eisenhower, the country was ready for a change. The exhibition not only enabled people to forget about the disheartening recent past but also helped them believe in the essential goodness of humanity, giving them hope and allowing them to think that the final choice between world destruction and world salvation was theirs.

Gee (1989), Green (1984), and Sekula (1984) also suggest that several institutions used and turned the exhibition to their advantage. It was held during the height of abstract expressionism, when many people felt a great aversion to abstract and modern art. Green suggests that the Museum of Modern Art used *The Family of Man* to show that an institution which usually catered to a sophisticated elite could also reach out to the public. The museum regarded photography as a sociopolitical instrument, and by certifying mass cultural values as fine art it hoped to win the sympathy of the masses.

Looking beyond the national scene, critics also claim that *The Family of Man* served as cultural weapon in the international politics of the cold war (Gee 1989; Sekula 1984). The phenomenal success of the exhibit at home did not go unnoticed by the U.S. government. During the cold war, art was considered a precious weapon that could help to win the minds and hearts of people (Gee 1989).[24] As a result, *The Family of Man*, which was originally to be circulated by the museum's International Circulating Exhibitions Program, received a new sponsorship, that of the United States Information Agency.[25] Intended and expected to have enormous popular appeal, the duplicate versions of the exhibit were more extensively circulated and publicized than any previous MoMA production (Sekula 1984). The USIA produced two *The Family of Man* films, one of which was translated into twenty-two languages, and published a variety of special brochures, pamphlets, and posters for distribution abroad (Sandeen 1995).

The exhibition toured Canada, Europe, Japan, Australia, and the developing nations, where it "tended to appear in political 'hot spots'" (Sekula 1984, 94). *The Family of Man* showings abroad were cosponsored by U.S. corporations that deemed the exhibit a valuable marketing and public relations tool (Sekula 1984). The Coca-Cola corporation, for instance, described the showing of the exhibit in Johannesburg in 1958 in the following terms: "At the entrance of the hall the large globe of the world encircled by bottles of Coca-Cola created a most attractive eye catching display and identified our product with Family of Man sponsorship" (Sekula 1984, 95).

Commenting upon this last example of what he calls "Cold War extravaganza," Sekula writes, "In the political landscape of apartheid, characterized by a brutal racial hierarchy of caloric intakes and forced separation of black African families, sugar and familial sentiment were made to commingle to the imagination" (1984, 95). In his view, the beautiful world created by the exhibit was only part of an international market economy where economic bonds had been transformed into artificial, sentimental ties and former racism had been replaced by "'the humanization of the other' so central to the discourse of neo-colonialism."

Sandeen also addresses the commodification of *The Family of Man*. To him, the commercial-cultural approach to international persuasion reached its peak with the 1958 World's Fair in Brussels, where "visitors would see all facets of American life without leaving Belgium" (127). By the time the exhibit arrived in Moscow a year later, "It was subsumed into a larger text, crafted for a new audience that both echoed and transcended the construction of *The Family of Man*" (Sandeen 1995, 133). Where Steichen and Miller had gone through millions of photographs in search of those that would transcend ideology by presenting universally understood symbols, the American staff of the Moscow exhibition examined millions of products in search of goods that would embody American ideology so the items would represent a specific national culture. "With *The Family of Man* the United States had portrayed itself as humane, understanding, cultured. With the American National Exhibition in Moscow, the United States declared itself to be the winner of a battle of abundance" (Sandeen 1995, 153).

In addition to claiming that *The Family of Man* was used to promote corporate liberalism, bourgeois values, and American commodities, Sekula also argues that the exhibition may be viewed as an implementation of the structural-functionalist family model of sociologist Talcott Parsons, where "instrumental" male roles are clearly differentiated from "expressive" female functions. Sandeen (1995) refutes that argument, however, and claims that the 503 photographs in the exhibition were selected for reasons of common sense rather than to support a then-dominant sociological theory. What mattered to Steichen, Sandeen argues, was that the final product would portray the family as a unit rather than as a combination of different gender-based roles.[26]

No study has investigated why people in the 1970s and 1980s continued buying the book commemorating Steichen's exhibit, and therefore one can only speculate about their motivations. Like photography critics and other commentators whose views have been outlined earlier, the public's readings of *The Family of Man* are based on the book rather than on the exhibit. But where historical insights, with the benefit of hindsight, drastically influenced critical assessment of Steichen's project, the public remains riveted by the "photographic truths" they persist in seeing in the images. As a result, their approach to the imagery remains uncritical.

*The Family of Man* may be seen to have brought a message of hope to people in the 1960s, 1970s, and 1980s. These were times marked by racial conflicts, the assassinations of Martin Luther King and John and Robert Kennedy, and a war in Vietnam. But longing for national and international peace and harmony may not have been the only motive that led people to buy *The Family of Man* and other look-alike publications.[27] Whether it is the history of the human race that is reflected in the history of the individual family or vice versa, readers felt emotionally connected with the visual narrative presented to them. Unlike critics who judged the imagery by its ability to document and explain political facts and other historical happenings, the public focused on the book's timeless feelings and emotions, which they could apply to their own life histories.

Although it is not known whether the intensity of these readers' responses would have changed had they seen *The Family of Man* in its exhibition form, Sandeen (1995) suggests that the negativism present in recent critiques of Steichen's work is in part because commentators have relied on the book version rather than on the original photographic exhibition. Could it be, in the manner of McLuhan, that the form of the message itself influenced the meanings and readings of *The Family of Man*? Would a revival of the photographic exhibit bring new readings of Steichen's endeavor?

## A Permanent Home for the Exhibit

On a rainy day in June 1994, a crowd gathered in Clervaux, Luxembourg, for the official opening of *The Family of Man* museum in the small town's medieval castle. For the first time the Luxembourg public and others would be able to see Steichen's visual legacy. Steichen had originally planned to honor his native country by making it the first stop on the exhibit's worldwide tour, but when the Luxembourg government showed no interest in *The Family of Man* project in 1953 he changed his mind and broke off all ties with the grand duchy. Not a single photograph from Luxembourg was found among the ten thousand images from which the final 503 prints would be selected, and although *The Family of Man* toured many European countries during the late 1950s and early 1960s it never stopped in Luxembourg.

By the mid-1960s, however, Steichen's relationship with his homeland had improved sufficiently enough for him to urge the U.S. government to donate one of the original displays to Luxembourg (Krieps 1994). The request was rapidly granted, and in 1966 Steichen returned home with the European version of *The Family of Man*.[28] Clervaux Castle was chosen as repository site but, due to lack of space, only half the images were kept there; others were stored in the attic of a nearby school. In 1989, as the grand duchy was celebrating 150 years of independence, its government decided to restore both the prints and the castle. After four years of work, including two thousand hours spent restoring the photographs, *The Family of Man* finally reopened on June 3 (Back 1994, 1996).[29]

While some of Steichen's visual artifices have been abandoned, other strategies are used to better integrate viewers into the rhetoric of the photographic display (Back 1994). For instance, the white gauze and green neon used in the 1955 "temple of pregnancy" to recreate the atmosphere of a maternity hospital have been disposed of in Luxembourg. The H-bomb explosion has also been stripped of color.

The photograph that now symbolizes *The Family of Man* is that of a Palestinian woman raising her hand in a gesture of despair, revolt, and indignation (fig. 9.2). Riwkin-Brick's image was chosen because it reiterates the compelling humanism of the former exhibit. By raising her hand to the sky, the woman cries out against the calamities and injustices that exist throughout the world. The gesture of survival also illustrates the history of the photographic exhibit itself, because it has outlived appalling traveling and storage conditions since 1955. Finally, the fact that the photograph lends itself well to a cinematographic poster makes it a good choice (Back 1996).

*Figure 9.2.* Photograph
by Anna Riwkin-Brick
(© Museum of Photography,
Stockholm)

Ethnologist Martine Segalen (1994) forecast that the European public
would be more demanding than the public of the previous decades. Her
prediction has been proven wrong. Before being permanently displayed in
Clervaux Castle the restored *Family of Man* went on a mini-tour during
which thousands saw the exhibit in Toulouse, Tokyo, and Hiroshima. Reviv-
ing the popular success of thirty years earlier, the daily average number of
visitors in Tokyo reached 1,500; in Hiroshima three thousand attended during the show's final week. In Clervaux, where the exhibit receives a smaller
but more international audience, Steichen's images keep stirring viewers'
emotions.[30] While the Japanese public was most deeply touched by the imagery picturing maternity, childhood, and the family, Bauret suggests that
many viewers saw in the exhibit a moral call for dialogue, respect for life,
world peace, and unity (1994c, 1994d). Although Clervaux visitors like to
rediscover what they have lost since the exhibit was first shown in the 1950s,
they remain deeply moved by its humanism and continue to support
Steichen's ideal of brotherhood (Back 1996).

To Jean Back and Sebastião Salgado, the choice of photographs by Steichen and his team is critical to the success of *The Family of Man* now. Very few of the 1955 images have become obsolete (Back 1996). The exhibit works, Salgado argues, because "all of its images are great images. One by one, they tell a story. If they did not, they would not be there; they would not have withstood time" (translation by author, quoted in Bauret 1994a, 138).

The current success of *The Family of Man* also shows that a body of photographs can be read as a text and that photography can be used to define an international discourse. Although enthusiastic comments unquestionably predominate in the visitors' book and most viewers interpret the imagery similarly, not all endorse Steichen's views.[31] After seeing the show in June 1996, a Luxembourg woman wrote in the book, "How lucky we are to be a part of this vast 'Family of Man'! I believe that despite all the differences we really form a big family. If only we would stop destroying one another!" In stark contrast, a British visitor commented ten days before: "The exhibition wants us to believe that we are all the same fundamentally. But we are not. We all are born, have children, and die. But there the similarity between me and an African, a Chinaman, or a Muslin living in Saudi Arabia ends. We all have very different morals and attitudes—we are not a 'family.'"

## Conclusion

Since its first showing in 1955, Steichen's united family has been the source of controversy among photographers, commentators, historians, and others. Although some criticisms have been expressed toward *The Family of Man*, many grievances have also been directed against Steichen himself. The most frequent concern the sentimentality of the show, its naïveté, and its ahistoricity, of which the most flagrant example is Steichen's removal of the photograph depicting the lynching of a black man. While such deletions raise the issue of contextualization and provide ground for heated argumentation, it should be remembered that Steichen's intention when compiling the exhibit was expressly not to make a historical statement or show the evilness of humanity. Although love and unity pervade the exhibit, Steichen was aware that differences, intolerance, hate, and fear are omnipresent. His approach, therefore, was the production of a show and a book that was not too controversial or provocative. However romantic or ahistorical, his show was an overwhelming success and introduced photography to the general public like no photographic event had ever done.

Another criticism raised by recent scholars is that *The Family of Man* was used as a tool in the cold war fight for cultural hegemony. The role Steichen played in this surreptitious battle, he who had abandoned the idea of producing an exhibit on human rights because the subject "was becoming an international political football," has yet to be established. In an interview published in a special issue of *Les Beaux-Arts* he claimed that *The Family of Man* was not propagandistic (Mellquist 1956).[32] Miller further recalls that as Steichen was making the final photographic selection he refused to discard an image showing physicist Robert Oppenheimer interacting with students because "we cannot let a politician [McCarthy]—or anybody else—dictate us what must or must not be in the exhibit" (translation by author, quoted in Miller 1994a, 48).[33] His reaction when he found himself confronted with accusations of political involvement and propaganda was to "shrug his shoulders and proceed with what he was doing" (Miller 1994b). To be sure, had he been involved in cold war politics and the U.S. fight for cultural hegemony it would have been unlikely that he would have advertised his role. "If the exhibit participated in the cultural cold war, it was as an ingenuous conscriptee" (Sandeen 1995, 119). Steichen's profound humanism made him a perfect draftee also.

Several reasons have been offered to explain the objections of some viewers to Steichen's exhibition. Most recently, commentators have suggested that part of the controversy raised by *The Family of Man* may be explained by the changing status of the photographic medium over the years as well as by the personality of those who have reviewed the exhibit and its book version. Photographer Roy DeCarava argues that many people now devote too much attention to photography as a form and an individual creative process and too little to the content and meaning of the photographic message. For DeCarava, contemporary societal values and attitudes have become so limited and superficial that human beings are being dehumanized or simply ignored (quoted in Burg 1994). In a similar vein, Sandeen writes, "Over the past thirty years we have become cynical. . . . Some of those who saw the exhibition in the mid-1950s now distrust the strong impressions of their more youthful sensibilities, having been inundated by images, many of them horrific rather than embracing" (1987, 382, 389). Could it be, as Sandeen proposes, that some of the contemporary observers of *The Family of Man* have become so "hardened to the socially constructive uses of emotions" (389) that they miss what Steichen thought to be the strength of his message?

In seeking to make sense of the varying, if not contradictory, readings of *The Family of Man* it is necessary to go back to notions of history, photography, and meaning-making. One could say that with *The Family of Man* Steichen constructed a visual grand narrative of humanity similar to *The Uprooted* (1951), in which historian Oscar Handlin presented the typical immigrant experience. Like Steichen, Handlin was criticized for his tendency to overgeneralize the human experience of immigration and minimize ethnic attachments. Like Steichen, Handlin was commended for his use of "poetry" and his ability to portray feelings and emotions, hopes and yearnings. Like Steichen's *Family of Man,* Handlin's piece became a best-seller and eventually won its author a Pulitzer Prize for history. Steichen introduced a new use of photography to the public while Handlin introduced a new kind of history to his readers. But that is not to say that the productions mirrored one another. While Steichen's work reflected a mood that was largely optimistic, Handlin's did not. If criticisms of these two works have grown over time, Handlin's piece has generated a variety of immigration studies focusing on the diversity of immigrant experiences while Steichen's exhibition has produced a multiplicity of books displaying human commonality.

Both Steichen's exhibit and Handlin's book raise the issue of the nature of historiography and history as a negotiated, intellectual construction of an event and its place in the social, political, or cultural context of the time. Following Fiske (1987) in the context of history and historiography, the meanings of historical facts or documents (including photographs) are not found in the facts or documents themselves but in how readers or viewers are socially, culturally, politically, and intellectually situated.

While critics judged *The Family of Man* primarily in terms of its relationship with art and its place in U.S. culture and then in terms of its relationship with political and social situations, the general audience paid almost sole attention to the timeless truths, feelings, and emotions that they found in the imagery and to which they could relate on a personal basis. In other words, the general audience integrated *The Family of Man* into their popular culture because they were able to see and/or create connections between it and their own social experiences.

One could therefore say that, to some extent, *The Family of Man* also resembles a family photo-album. Like many albums, it lacks references such as dates, names, specific places, and historical contexts. Like a family album, it is "a construction of communicative statements and interpretations of life . . . a pictorial version or rendition of life" that serves specific purposes and reveals how the author orders and thinks about the world (Chalfen 1991, 11–12). Unlike a family album, which typically only shows the good times of family life, however, Steichen's *Family* includes scenes of fight, misery, and death. Like some family albums that are thrown away once younger generations are unable to recognize the older generations portrayed in the pictures, *Family* books are sometimes disposed of by their buyers. But like some family albums that are cherished across several generations, Steichen's *Family* has become the "reference family (book)" to which an emotionally connected audience faithfully returns.

Steichen was fully aware that the family camera could be used to record history, and he strongly believed that all photographs were historical documents.[34] Addressing members of the Wisconsin State Historical Society in 1958 about the exhibition, he exclaimed, "Here is a great historic tour. Here is an exhibition that is making history" (Steichen 1958, 167). Indeed, *The Family of Man* was and still is a historic exhibit in the sense that it remains the most successful photographic show of all times and the only photographic display of that scope that has been restored and given a permanent resting place in a museum. *The Family of Man* also makes history through its ability to appeal to members of a social group well known for its lack of interest, indeed, its lack of trust, in photography: peasants and farmers.[35] In his autobiography, Steichen remarked on the success of the show among peasants in Guatemala.[36] Although the Clervaux visitors' books contain little information on the social background of those who sign them, informal interviews I conducted with farmers who have seen *The Family of Man* in Luxembourg indicate that they are enthusiastic about it. To them, the show is not just a photographic display; it is a narrative that expresses "the seasons of life" and its "simple" yet "most important values."

But *The Family of Man* is more than a historic exhibit. It is a historical document whose multifaceted readings reflect specific moments and perspectives in the political, social, and cultural history (including the history of taste) of the United States and elsewhere. Paradoxically, the historicity of the document could only be acquired by stripping all of its 503 components of their individual historical attachments. In the end, there is an ensemble of photographs that lasts not on the basis of each of its individual images but rather as a whole, a visual text that people can read and to which they can relate. It is an exhibit that was able to achieve popularity even when critical feelings ran high against it; an exhibit with a message so strong and so heartfelt that it was used in a brochure about hospital coronary care; and an exhibit that serves as evidence of the versatility of meaning-making, culture, and history.

## Notes

I would like to thank Hanno Hardt, whose generous advice and comments have been incorporated into this chapter, and Jean Back, who provided a variety of sources as well as insights into the revival of *The Family of Man* in Clervaux.

1. As I was going through documents given to me by project director Jean Back after the reopening of *The Family of Man* photographic exhibit and the creation of

the museum of the same name in Clervaux Castle (Luxembourg) in June 1994, I noticed a brochure entitled "The Coronary Care Team" (Seifert and Seibert 1973). Pictured on the cover was an obviously distressed woman looking toward the back corner of a hospital room where a man, presumably her husband, lay on a hospital bed surrounded by medical staff. I wondered why this brochure was included with documents for the exhibition. The booklet included some well-known images: "Migrant Mother" (Dorothea Lange); a farming couple (Alfred Eisenstaedt); a drum major and his mimics (Alfred Eisenstaedt); and a young couple in Paris (Robert Doisneau), along with some startling captions: "'When one of us is sick, our whole family is sick'" ("Migrant Mother"); "every team needs a leader" (drum major); "the spouse is an important and valuable member of the coronary care recovery team" (farming couple); and "a little sex is good for the heart" (Parisian couple).

It is not clear whether Edward Steichen ever saw the brochure or if he was aware of the medical treatment given some of the photographs he had used in his 1955 photographic exhibit, *The Family of Man*. The use of photographs in the sixteen-page booklet, published the year of Steichen's death in 1973, is striking not only because it exemplifies one of the uses of the photographs from the exhibit but also because it shows the impact the exhibit had on domains far remote from photography.

2. Etymologically speaking, photographs also are 'written documents' because the word *photography* comes from the Greek *Øws* (light) and *ypáØw* (write), hence, to write with light.

3. Exceptions include: Borchert (1981, 1982), Levine, ed. (1987, 1989), Schlereth ed. (1980), and Schlereth (1982, 1985).

4. Tagg (1988) offers an example of how photographic meaning is negotiated and how it can change the course of history. Between 1896 and 1901, the Leeds City Council used photographs of the Quarry Hill area of that city to secure appropriations from Parliament for slum clearance. The photographs, taken by the local medical officer of health, became the sole basis on which parliamentary committee members relied in their decision to raze parts of the neighborhood. The photographs, Tagg claims, never spoke for themselves. The committee members accepted a reading that had been proposed by those who supported the slum clearance proposal. The decision to raze therefore came through a process of negotiations where photography became part of an institution of power. Had the interpretations of the photographs been different, the neighborhood might not have been razed and the course of history for that particular neighborhood might have changed.

5. "The largest attendance in any one day was in Calcutta where twenty-nine thousand people crowded into the exhibition hall on a hot, blistering day" (Steichen 1958, 167).

6. While a deluxe edition was published by Simon and Schuster, a paperback edition was published by the Maco Press, and a still smaller edition was published by Pocket Books (Steichen 1963).

7. Steichen's assignment was to prepare reconnaissance photographs of enemy-occupied areas. In order to reveal as much detail as possible, the photographs had to be extremely sharp (Tausk 1980).

8. Phillips argues that by offering Steichen the director's position museum trustees were hoping to "retrieve photography from its marginal status among the fine arts, and to attract . . . a substantial popular following" (1982, 39). By presenting photography as a medium rather than the theme, trustees hoped to put an end to some members' open hostility to the photographic press who accused the department of being "snobbish," "pontifical," and "shrouded in 'esoteric fogs.'" They also hoped to gain much-needed financial support from the photographic industry and those interested in the medium (1982, 40).

9. In addition to *Road to Victory* and *Power in the Pacific,* Steichen also curated *Korea,* a photographic exhibit about the Korean War. The three shows were successful, but he felt that visitors forgot the ugliness and aberration of war as soon as they left the museum (Steichen 1963, n.p.).

10. Some critics suggest that the concept for *The Family of Man* was inspired by "People Are People the World Over," a series of photo-essays conceived by Robert Capa and John G. Morris and published in the *Ladies Home Journal* in 1948 and 1949. Each month for a year the magazine ran a two-page spread showing the similar ways in which farming families from twelve different countries worked in the fields, did housework, worshipped, cooked, raised their children, and performed other chores (Phillips 1982; Sandeen 1995; Whelan 1985). Morris maintains that he and Steichen discussed "People Are People" and suggests that the series must have influenced *The Family of Man,* even though Steichen never mentions the magazine in his autobiography (Bauret 1994b).

11. Another unusual display technique was the placement of a mirror in the center of the "faces of war" sequence so viewers would see their reflections and implicate themselves in the display. Following visitor reaction and critics' caustic remarks, however, the mirror was taken down after a few weeks (Sandeen 1987).

12. As a result of its huge popular success, *The Family of Man* won the Newspaper Guild's Front Page Award for the museum, and Steichen received citations and awards from the National Urban League, the American Society of Magazine Photographers, the Philadelphia Museum School of Art, and Kappa Alpha Mu, the professional honorary fraternity for photographers ("American Magazine" 1955; "Cited by Urban League" 1955; Forsee 1968).

13. The book was hailed for its "excellent reproduction and superb layout" (Kenney 1955, 7) and for its ability to show "man in relation to his environment, to the beauty and richness of the earth" (review, *New Yorker* 1955, 175). If some reviewers were disappointed it was because they missed the dramatic three-dimensional design of the exhibit itself. Writing for *Commonwealth,* John Stanley noted: "This drama, this poem, this song has been turned into a book which is much less dramatic than what appeared at the Museum, but is still touching, stirring. . . . [T]hrough the lyricism, there is enough laughter and astringency and ashes to make an appeal sufficiently broad and deep to communicate with many" (1955, 333).

14. The lynching was not the only photograph removed from the show. Considered too daring, the photograph depicting the nude stomach and breasts of Harry

Callahan's pregnant wife was also removed from the U.S. exhibit. As mentioned earlier, neither photograph appeared in *The Family of Man* book version (Green 1984).

15. See, for instance, Barthes (1972), Kramer (1955), McKenna (1955), and Rosskam (1955).

16. Dwight MacDonald's writing constitutes an excellent example of this debate. For MacDonald, Steichen's show was a perfect example of "Midcult," the dreadful thing that corrupted High Culture and passed "itself off as the real thing" (1962, 38). Midcult was dangerous because it pretended to obey the standards of High Culture although it actually debased them. MacDonald wrote (1962, 45): "The Midcult mind aspires toward Universality above all. A good example was that "Family of Man" show of photographs. . . . There were many excellent photographs, but they were arranged under the most pretentious and idiotic titles. . . . The editorializing was insistent—The Midcult audience always wants to be Told—and the photographs were marshaled to demonstrate that although there are real Problems (death, for instance), it's a pretty good old world after all" (see also Sandeen 1995).

17. For a particularly telling example of the fight over photography (and control over the museum's photography department), see Newhall (1993, 127–28, 146–50), particularly the discussion of his opposition to Steichen and his perspectives on the uses of photography.

18. Only two of Steichen's photographs (one depicting his mother—the smallest print in the exhibit—and one depicting one of Miller's children) were used in the exhibit, whereas some eleven of Miller's images were used.

19. Elliott Erwitt thought the show was good, "incredibly, brilliantly produced, exploited, and advertised by the man who was master of it all, Steichen," but thought the content was "OK, but . . . kind of sentimental and soupy" (quoted in Danzinger and Conrad 1977, 87). As to Minor White, after first comparing *The Family of Man* to a Cecil B. DeMille production (1961, 41) he later said that he had "all kinds of feelings about it—good, bad, and indifferent!" The hanging of the photographs, however, "was a very exciting experience. I really felt that it was a magnificent show" (quoted in Hill and Cooper 1979, 357). Herbert Bayer found the exhibit retrogressive, sentimental, and somewhat pompous. Bayer, who had designed Steichen's *Road to Victory* exhibit in 1942, was somewhat surprised that Steichen did not come back to him for *The Family of Man*. Like Cunningham and others, his disappointment may have influenced his perceptions of the show. Speaking about the preparation of *Road to Victory*, Bayer also commented, "We always spread photographs on the floor to look at them and he [Steichen] always became sentimental about America" (Hill and Cooper 1979, 125). That sentimentality became ground for some of the criticism against *The Family of Man*.

20. *The Family of Man*'s imagery was often adapted to the country where it was shown. When the exhibit was presented in Tokyo, for instance, Steichen increased the number of Japanese photographs and added images of Nagasaki after its destruction in August 1945 (Bauret 1994c, Kuramochi and Watanabe 1994). The Nagasaki images,

however, were not included in any other *Family of Man* traveling exhibit, and they were "discreetly veiled" when the emperor visited the show in 1956 (Bauret 1994c). When preparing the show for a European audience, for instance, Steichen decided not to eliminate Callahan's photograph of his pregnant wife, he increased the number of photographs by Henri Cartier-Bresson, he enlarged a print showing the Warsaw ghetto, and he eliminated a photograph depicting the execution of World War II prisoners (Back 1996). Thus, Gabriele and Helmut Nothhelfer assert, when the exhibit was shown in Berlin in 1955, "Germans [could] walk through the exhibit with no fears, the photographs [were] not accusing them, they [did] not confront them with the horrible crimes of Nazi Germany" (1994, 143, translation by author). Although the Warsaw ghetto was represented in the exhibit, the image did not show what had really happened and barely gave a glimpse of the atrocious reality (Nothhelfer 1994).

21. Westerbeck cites as examples of photographic anthropology books Ken Heyman and Margaret Mead's *World Enough,* Mary Ellen Mark's *Passport,* and Abigail Heyman's *Growing Up Female.* Other books published since 1976 that are in keeping with the family theme are *The Family of Children* (1977), *The Family of Woman* (1979), and *The World's Family* (1983), all edited by Jerry Mason, the first editor of *The Family of Man.* The lucrative aspect of the "family business," the publication of these books, and the fact that the 1986 commemorative edition of *The Family of Man* went into a seventh printing may be seen to provide support for Westerbeck's thesis.

22. Looking for new domestic markets, capitalism started a monumental ideological campaign in the 1920s that was aimed at recreating the family as a "bottomless receptacle for goods" (Sekula 1984, 49).

23. "In The Family of Man there are no poets, painters, writers, philosophers, craftsmen, or social scientists . . . and there are very few representatives of the highest civilized activities" (Green 1984, 47). Green fails to consider the teachers, students, professors, theologians, researchers, and various religious personalities as well as the scientists who are proportionally well represented in the exhibit. Considering the numerous musicians portrayed in the show (from street musicians to symphony orchestra players and conductors), one might also wonder why Green denies music the status of "highest civilized" activity.

24. During the cold war, exhibitions of contemporary American art, primarily abstract expressionism, were circulated abroad by the Museum of Modern Art in an effort to demonstrate "especially in Europe that America was not the cultural backwater that the Russians, during that tense period called 'the cold war,' were trying to demonstrate it was" (Lynes, quoted in Cockcroft 1974, 40 and in Sekula 1984, 93; see also Gee 1989). By exhibiting its art abroad the United States aimed to promote high culture and show that people in a free country were able to think, work, and create as they pleased (Gee 1989).

25. The USIA was established in 1953 to promote, through communication media, a better understanding abroad of the United States and its foreign policies.

26. One unique commentary is Marvin Heiferman's exhibition, *The Family of*

*Man: 1955–1984* at P.S. 1 in New York in 1984. In Heiferman's words, the new exhibit was a "casual reconsideration of the earlier exhibition," in which he examined its great themes by displaying photographs culled from newspapers, magazines, publicity files, and pornography. He also showed postcards, handbills, cereal boxes, movie publicity stills, and original works by artists and photographers. The visual narrative was accompanied by citations from Brecht ("there is little one can do with children, except to be photographed with them") and from Yiddish proverbs ("if God lived on earth, people would break his windows") (Phillips 1984, 10). According to Phillips, Heiferman's exhibition was more rooted in time and history than Steichen's show. By considering how cultural channels had transmitted and shaped attitudes about such themes as birth, death, family, body, and sex, viewers could "chart the slow metamorphosis of a certain range of social conventions as filtered through a similarly shifting set of pictorial conventions" (Phillips 1984, 10).

27. Of the three "family picture" books I own, all of which were secondhand purchases, one was originally offered as a Valentine's gift and one was a Christmas present.

28. With fewer than ten images missing (lost or destroyed), the European traveling exhibit was the most complete version in existence. All the other *Family of Man* displays have been dismantled, lost, or damaged beyond repair.

29. The total cost of the renovation project was 90 million LUF (around $3 million), of which 2.5 million LUF (around $85,000) was used to repair the photographs (Back 1996). Production of the 1955 MoMA exhibition had cost more than $100,000 (Sandeen 1995).

30. By October 1996 some sixty-two thousand people had visited *The Family of Man* exhibit at Clervaux Castle. According to Back (1996), that number reflects the fact that cultural tourism is not (yet) well developed in Luxembourg. Although most visitors are from Europe (Belgium, Germany, France, Holland, and Luxembourg), there are also those from South America, the United States, Japan, and India who make a special trip to Europe to see the Clervaux exhibit.

31. Visitors find the exhibit "moving," "overwhelming," "so beautiful and so right," *"fantastich,"* and "thought-provoking."

32. "You see, we do not follow any kind of propaganda. You won't find an Iron Curtain here," he told reporter Jérôme Mellquist (1956, 16, translation by author).

33. However determined Steichen was to be the master of his own show, he nevertheless occasionally yielded to objections made by the public and critics, as the removal of the mirrors and the removal of the lynching and the Callahan photographs show. Potential public reaction also influenced his treatment of the visual narrative, as the veiling of the Nagasaki photographs in Japan and the removal of the POWs' execution in the European exhibit indicate. Although these changes could have been made in an effort not to hurt the public's feelings, they could also have reflected Steichen's attempt to reinforce the ahistoricity of his narrative. He was determined that no single photograph should become the focus of the exhibit and that the final

message should be positive rather than negative. The changes could also have reflected his desire to keep out of trouble by raising as little controversy as possible.

34. "There are said to be forty million homes in the United States that have at least one camera. . . . That means there are at least forty million photographers, forty million potential historians," he argued. "Any photograph that is made . . . becomes a historical document. Its use as such will depend largely on historians" (Steichen 1958, 159).

35. For a discussion of the social uses of photography in rural milieu, see Bourdieu, ed. (1965).

36. "On the final day of the exhibition, a Sunday, several thousand Indians from the hills of Guatemala came on foot or muleback to see it. An American visitor said it was like a religious experience," Steichen wrote. "Regardless of the place, the response was always the same. . . . The people in the audience looked at the pictures, and the people in the pictures looked back at them. They recognized each other" (1962, n.p.).

## References

Adams, Ansel. 1978. *Conversations with Ansel Adams* [interview by Ruth Teiser and Catherine Harroun in 1972, 1974, 1975]. Berkeley: University of California, Regional Oral History Office.

————. 1985. *Ansel Adams: An Autobiography.* Boston: Little, Brown.

Adams, Phoebe Lou. 1955. "Through a Lens Darkly." *Atlantic Monthly* 195(4): 69–72.

Albrecht, Peter L. 1955. Letter to the editor. *Atlantic Monthly* 195(6): 18.

"American Magazine Photographers Society Awards to Steichen and W. Miller for Family of Man Show." 1955. *New York Times,* April 17, X19.

Arkus, Leon Anthony. 1956. "The Family of Man." *Carnegie Magazine* 30 (May): 185–86.

Back, Jean. 1994. "Itinéraire d'une mission culturelle." In The Family of Man: *Témoignages et documents,* ed. Jean Back and Gabriel Bauret, 207–13. Luxembourg: Artevents/CNA.

————. 1996. Personal communication, Nov. 14, 19.

Barrett, Terry. 1990. *Criticizing Photographs.* Mountain View: Mayfield Publishing.

Barthes, Roland. 1972. *Mythologies.* Translated by Annette Lavers. New York: Hill and Wang.

Bauret, Gabriel. 1994a. "*The Family of Man* et la main de l'homme de Sebastião Salgado." In The Family of Man: *Témoignages et documents,* ed. Jean Back and Gabriel Bauret, 133–38. Luxembourg: Artevents/CNA.

————. 1994b. "John G. Morris. "1948, dans le *Ladies' Home Journal.*" In The Family of Man: *Témoignages et documents,* ed. Jean Back and Gabriel Bauret, 189–95. Luxembourg: Artevents/CNA.

————. "Tokyo et Hiroshima 1994." 1994c. In The Family of Man: *Témoignages et documents,* ed. Jean Back and Gabriel Bauret, 197–203. Luxembourg: Artevents/CNA.

————. 1994d. "Toulouse, 1993, Jean Dieuzaide." In The Family of Man: *Témoignages et documents,* ed. Jean Back and Gabriel Bauret, 189–95. Luxembourg: Artevents/CNA.

Beloff, Halla. 1985. *Camera Culture.* New York: Basil Blackwell.

Berger, John. 1980. *About Looking.* New York: Pantheon.

Berlo, David K. 1960. *The Process of Communication.* New York: Hold.

Bloch, Marc. 1953. *The Historian's Craft.* New York: Knopf.

Borchert, James. 1981. "Analysis of Historical Photographs: A Method and a Case Study." *Studies in Visual Communication* 7(4): 30–62.

————. 1982. *Alley Life in Washington: Family, Community, Religion and Folklife in the City, 1850–1970.* Chicago: University of Illinois Press.

Bourdieu, Pierre, ed. 1965. *Art moyen: Essai sur les usages sociaux de la photographie.* Paris: Editions de Minuit.

Burg, Jean-Philippe. 1994. "Roy DeCarava." In The Family of Man: *Témoignages et documents,* ed. Jean Back and Gabriel Bauret, 81–87. Luxembourg: Artevents/CNA.

Chalfen, Richard. 1991. *Turning Leaves. The Photograph Collections of Two Japanese American Families.* Albuquerque: University of New Mexico Press.

"Cited by Urban League." 1955. *New York Times,* May 1, 78.

Cockcroft, Eva. 1974. "Abstract Expressionism: Weapon of the Cold War." *Artforum* 12(10): 9–11.

Danziger, James, and Barnaby Conrad. 1977. *Interviews with Master Photographers.* New York: Paddington Press.

Deschin, Jacob. 1955. "'Family's' Last Day: 270,000 Have Visited Steichen Exhibition." *New York Times,* May 8, X17.

Dorr, Nell. 1955. "*The Family of Man:* A Rebuttal" [letter to the editor]. *Popular Photography* 37(1): 8.

Fisher, David Hackett. 1970. *Historians' Fallacies.* New York: Harper and Row.

Fiske, John. 1987. *Television Culture.* London: Routledge.

————. 1989. *Understanding Popular Culture.* London: Routledge.

Forsee, Aylesa. 1968. *Famous Photographers.* Philadelphia: Macrae Smith.

Gee, Helen. 1989. "Photography in Transition: 1950–1960." In *Decade by Decade,* ed. James Enyeart, 62–71. Boston: Little, Brown.

Goldsmith, Arthur A., Jr. 1955. "The Family of Man." *Popular Photography* 36(5): 80–88, 147–49.

Gottschalk, Louis. 1969. *Understanding History.* New York: Knopf.

Grafly, Dorothy. 1955. "The Camera, Friend or Foe." *American Artist* 19(5): 42.

Green, Jonathon. 1984. *American Photography.* New York: Harry N. Abrams.

Guimond, James. 1991. *American Photography and the American Dream.* Chapel Hill: University of North Carolina Press.

Hall, Stuart. 1993. "Encoding, Decoding." In *The Cultural Studies Reader,* ed. Simon During, 90–103. London: Routledge.

Handlin, Oscar. 1951. *The Uprooted: The Epic Story of the Great Migrations That Made the American People.* Boston: Little, Brown.

Harley, Ralph L., Jr. 1990. "Edward Steichen's Modernist Art-Space." *History of Photography* 14(1): 1–22.

Haskell, Francis. 1993. *History and Its Images: Art and the Interpretation of the Past.* New Haven: Yale University Press.

Hill, Paul, and Thomas Cooper. 1979. *Dialogue with Photography.* New York: Farrar, Straus, and Giroux.

Hughes, Jim. 1989. *W. Eugene Smith: Shadow and Substance.* New York: McGraw-Hill.

Kenney, H. C. 1955. Review of *The Family of Man. Christian Science Monitor,* June 23, 7.

Kramer, Hilton. 1955. "Exhibiting *The Family of Man.*" *Commentary* 20(4): 364–67.

Krieps, Rosh. 1994. "Luxembourg 1966: Un émigré en quête de patrie." In The Family of Man: *Témoignages et documents,* ed. Jean Back and Gabriel Bauret, 163–73. Luxembourg: Artevents/CNA.

Kuramochi, Goro, and Yoshio Watanabe. 1994. "Tokyo 1965." In The Family of Man: *Témoignages et documents,* ed. Jean Back and Gabriel Bauret, 147–53. Luxembourg: Artevents/CNA.

Levine, Robert M., ed. 1987. *Windows on Latin-America: Understanding Society through Photographs.* Coral Gables: North-South Center, University of Miami.

———. 1989. *Images of History: Nineteenth and Early Twentieth Century Latin American Photographs as Documents.* Durham: Duke University Press.

Lutz, Catherine A., and Jane L. Collins. 1993. *Reading National Geographic.* Chicago: University of Chicago Press.

MacDonald, Dwight. 1962. *Against the American Grain.* New York: Random House.

Malmsheimer, Lonna M. 1987. "Photographic Analysis as Ethnohistory: Interpretive Strategies." *Visual Anthropology* 1(1): 21–36.

Mason, Jerry, ed. 1977. *The Family of Children.* New York: Ridge Press.

———. 1979. *The Family of Woman.* New York: Ridge Press.

———. 1983. *The World's Family.* New York: Pound Press.

McKenna, Rollie. 1955. Review of *The Family of Man. New Republic,* March 14, 30.

Mellquist, Jérôme. 1956. "Edward Steichen." *Les Beaux-Arts.* Brussels: Palais des Beaux-Arts de Bruxelles, 6, 15.

Meltzer, Milton. 1978. *Dorothea Lange: A Photographer's Life.* New York: Farrar, Straus and Giroux.

Miller, Wayne. 1994a. "1953–1955." In The Family of Man: *Témoignages et documents,* ed. Jean Back and Gabriel Bauret, 45–54. Luxembourg: Artevents/CNA.

———. 1994b. Personal communication, June 3.

Morgan, Barbara. 1955. "The Theme Show: A Contemporary Exhibition Technique." *Aperture* 3(2): 24–27.

Nevins, Allan. 1963. *The Gateway to History.* Chicago: University of Chicago Press.

Newhall, Beaumont. 1993. *Focus: Memoirs of a Life in Photography.* Boston: Little, Brown.

Nothhelfer, Gabriele, and Helmut Nothhelfer. 1994. "1955 'Nous tous—*The Family of Man* à Berlin.'" In The Family of Man: *Témoignages et documents,* ed. Jean Back and Gabriel Bauret, 141–45. Luxembourg: Artevents/CNA.

Phillips, Christopher. 1982. "The Judgment Seat of Photography." *October* 22 (Fall): 27–63.

———. 1984. "In a Family Way." *Afterimage* 11(10): 10–11.

Plaut, A. S. 1955. Review of *The Family of Man. Library Journal,* Dec. 1, 2783.

Pollack, Peter. 1969. *The Picture History of Photography.* New York: Harry N. Abrams.

Review of *The Family of Man.* 1955. *New Yorker,* Sept. 17, 175.

Ringel, Fred. 1955. "'The Family of Man': A Minority Report" [letter to the editor]. *Popular Photography,* May 8, 6.

Ritchin, Fred. 1989. "What Is Magnum?" In *In Our Time: The World as Seen by Magnum Photographers,* ed. William R. Manchester, 417–44. New York: American Federation of Arts.

———. 1990. *In Our Own Image.* New York: Aperture.

Rosenblum, Naomi. 1984. *A World History of Photography.* New York: Abbeville.

———. 1989. "From Protest to Affirmation: 1940–1950." In *Decade by Decade,* ed. James Enyeart, 48–61. Boston: Little, Brown.

Rosskam, Edwin. 1955. "Family of Steichen." *Art News* 54 (March): 34–37.

Saarinen, Aline R. 1955. "The Camera versus the Artist." *New York Times,* Feb. 6, X10.

Sandeen, Eric J. 1987. "*The Family of Man* at the Museum of Modern Art: The Power of the Image in 1950s America." *Prospects* (11): 367–91.

———. 1995. *Picturing an Exhibition: The Family of Man and 1950s America.* Albuquerque: University of New Mexico Press.

Schlereth, Thomas J., ed. 1980. *Artifacts and the American Past.* Nashville: American Association for State and Local History.

———. 1982. *Material Culture Studies in America: 1876–1976.* Nashville: American Association for State and Local History.

———. 1985. "Social History Scholarship and Material Culture Research." In *Material Culture: A Research Guide,* ed. Thomas J. Schlereth, 155–95. Lawrence: University Press of Kansas.

Segalen, Martine. 1994. "*The Family of Man* ou la grande illusion." In The Family of Man: *Témoignages et documents,* ed. Jean Back and Gabriel Bauret, 117–28. Luxembourg: Artevents/CNA.

Seifert, Milton H, Jr., and Sandra J. Seibert. 1973. "The Coronary Care Team." Minneapolis: Minnesota Heart Association.

Sekula, Allan. 1984. "The Instrumental Image: Steichen at War." In *Photography against the Grain.* Halifax: Press of the Nova Scotia College of Art and Design, 1984.

Shafer, Robert Jones, ed. 1980. *A Guide to Historical Method.* Homewood: Dorsey Press.

Shahn, Ben. 1955. Letter to the editor. *New York Times,* Feb. 13, 15.

Smith, Maryann Yodelis. 1989. "The Method of History," in *Research Methods in Mass Communication,* ed. Guido Stempel and Bruce H. Westley, 316–30. Englewood Cliffs: Prentice-Hall.

Sontag, Susan. 1978. *On Photography.* New York: Farrar, Straus and Giroux.

Stanley, John. 1955. "Love and Praise" [review of *The Family of Man*]. *Booklist,* July 1, 333–34.

Steichen, Edward. 1956. "The Family of Man." *Carnegie Magazine* 30 (May): 185.

———. 1958. "Photography: Witness and Recorder of Humanity." *Wisconsin Magazine of History* 41(3): 159–67.

———. 1963. *A Life in Photography.* New York: Doubleday.

Szarkowski, John. 1978. *Mirrors and Windows.* New York: Museum of Modern Art.

Tagg, John. 1988. *The Burden of Representation: Essays on Photographies and Histories.* Minneapolis: University of Minnesota Press.

Tausk, Petr. 1980. *Photography in the Twentieth Century.* London: Focal Press.

Weiss, W. 1970. "Happy Birthday, Mr. Steichen." *Saturday Review,* March 28, 49–51.

Westerbeck, Colin L., Jr. 1976. "How Others Live: Some Recent Photography Books." *Artforum* 15 (Sept.): 40–45.

Whelan, Richard. 1985. *Robert Capa.* New York: Alfred A. Knopf.

White, Minor. 1961. Review of *The Family of Man. Aperture* 9(1): 41.

Wright, George, and Cora Wright. 1955. "One Family's Opinion." *Aperture* 3(2): 19–23.

# ■ 10

## Photographing Newswork: From the Archives of the *New York World-Telegram & Sun*

*Hanno Hardt*

The history of American photography reflects the social struggle for place and identity in U.S. society. When photography replaced painting and daguerreotype in Western culture with its ability to reproduce "a slice of life," the photographic eye wandered beyond the portrait and the still life to catch sight of modern preoccupations: the city, urbanization and technology, immigration, and the conquest of the West. Photographers began to visualize the human condition of nineteenth and early twentieth century life while an emerging documentary tradition raised the social consciousness of society.

At the same time, however, American photography also shaped a dominant vision of the other—minorities and working-class segments of an immigrant society who rose to prominence as aestheticized objects of public curiosity or social reform. Although their photographic presence may have helped raise social or spiritual concerns among social and political elites, it also legitimated visual exploitation and confirmed class differences in the process of introducing photo-documentation to social issues.

Thus, photographs about work, the work place, and working-class environments contain the authorial bias of outsiders whose individual or collective interests dictated place, time, or perspective without regard for the inclinations or reservations of their anticipated (and pre-visualized) subjects. While works ranging from those of Jacob Riis (1970 [1890]), Lewis Hine (1932), or Farm Security Administration photographers (Stryker and Wood 1977) to the photographs of Walker Evans (1938) or Robert Frank (1958) capture the existence of the other, they also represent examples of completely different efforts to put photographs to specific ideological uses. The result are visions of U.S. society that claim cultural affinities with their subjects while expressing the calculated distance of the photographer as observer. This problematic of documentary work has been addressed powerfully by James Agee:

> It seems to me curious, not to say obscene and thoroughly terrifying, that it could occur to an association of human beings drawn together through need and chance and for profit into a company, an organ of journalism, to pry intimately into the lives of an undefended and appallingly damaged group of human beings, an ignorant and helpless rural family, for the purpose of parading the nakedness, disadvantage and humiliation of these lives before another group of human beings, in the name of science, of "honest" journalism (whatever that paradox may mean), of humanity, of social fearlessness, for money, and for a reputation for crusading and for unbias which, when skillfully enough qualified, is exchangeable at any bank for money . . . and that these people could be capable of meditating this prospect without the slightest doubt of their qualification to do an "honest" piece of work, and with a conscience better than clear, and in the virtual certitude of almost unanimous public approval. (1970 [1941], 7)

An involvement of the traditional subject as the other in the production of a visual record of society, however, emerges when still cameras become an accessible means of fast and inexpensive reproduction in the hands of virtually everyone. Still cameras do not replace but join the practice of professional documentation, not for money or for "a reputation for crusading" but for establishing individual and collective identities and responding to a search for immortality.

An increase in family photography among middle-class consumers, initiated particularly by women, for example, began with the accessibility of camera equipment. Also, worker-photographers in Germany during the 1920s bought cameras and carried them into their workplaces and into the streets to document the conditions of work and the struggle for workers' rights. The camera became a weapon in the fight against injustice and oppression, and worker-photographer movements were reported in other countries, including the United States. The results are revealing documentary photographs of not only middle-class existences but also the daily lives of working-class individuals and their families. These images are characterized by an amateur aesthetics that expresses a particular sense of immediacy when the other becomes the self. The visual exploration of the familiar as a project of self-discovery provides a sense of community and legitimates the struggle for recognition. In either case, an understanding of the dominant gaze or the liberating stare rests on understanding the ideological in the production and conventional reading of photographs that are cultural constructions of reality that challenge the critical imagination to make meanings and establish truths.

Press photographers who have photographed their colleagues and their working environments, including editorial offices, engage in a process of self-discovery. They are insiders responding to a need for realizing a particular vision of themselves and are well served by their familiarity with institutional rules, labor relations, and working conditions as well as with individual newsworkers, who are defined as participants in the editorial process. They are also trusted with their work within their organizations. For these reasons, images of newswork are of particular interest; they reveal an insider's perspectives on workplaces and the people in them. The result is a collective self-portrait of newsworkers, often over time, and a visual construction of their relations to each other, their bosses, and their public. It is also a form of self-expression, articulating how they want to be seen or remembered because many newsroom photographs are never published. They survive only in the archives of their respective newspapers—pages from a public diary whose content reveals the hidden details of a working life.

Specifically, the context of the following archival photographs is the *New York World-Telegram & Sun,* an institution that suffered the results of mergers and consolidations over several decades. Its lengthy title (in the 1950s) reflects the passing of an era of significant daily newspapers that helped shape the tradition of urban journalism in the United States. Thus, when the *New York World* folded in 1931, the evening *World* was merged with the *Evening Telegram* into the *World-Telegram.* In 1950 the *New York Sun* was combined with the *World-Telegram* and was published as the *World-Telegram & Sun* until it was merged into the *World Journal Tribune* in 1966. That newspaper collapsed in 1967 and "with it went the shades of Pulitzer, Greeley, Bennett, Dana, Scripps, Howard, Hearst, and a dash of Munsey" (Emery and Emery 1988, 625).

The photographs in the following series are representative of the type of images found in this particular collection. They span the mid-1940s to 1950s and range from informal to formal, or from the casual to the newsworthy, in their approach to photographing colleagues in a variety of work environments. In many instances these photographs add a human face to the untold stories of newswork and labor relations. They bear witness to the existence of specific individuals at a specific time in the history of this particular newspaper and are reminders of the potential of an alternative history of journalism that honors labor and the contributions of individuals rather than the existence of institutions and their owners. These photographs suggest the possibilities of constructing a portrait of urban newswork in America with the aid of archival photographs and original captions that add detail and authenticity to each image.

## References

Agee, James, and Walker Evans. 1970 (1941). *Let Us Now Praise Famous Men.* Boston: Houghton Mifflin.

Emery, Michael, and Edwin Emery. 1988. *The Press in America.* Englewood Cliffs: Prentice-Hall.

Evans, Walker. 1938. *American Photographs.* New York: Museum of Modern Art.

Frank, Robert. 1958. *The Americans.* New York: Aperture.

Hine, Louis. 1932. *Men at Work.* New York: Macmillan.

Riis, Jacob. 1970 (1890). *How the Other Half Lives.* New York: Scribner's.

Stryker, Roy, and Nancy Wood. 1977. *In This Proud Land: America 1935–1943.* New York: Galahad Books.

*Figure 10.1.* "City desk: seated (clockwise)—Paul Havely, picture desk; Herb Kamm, assistant city editor; Bob Prall, staff; William D. (Bill) O'Brien, city editor, and Joe Janoff, assistant city editor. In right background, Frank Kappler, picture desk, talks to Len Falkner, news editor," September 9, 1949. (Library of Congress, Prints and Photographs Division, NYWT&S Collection [reproduction number LC-USZ62-113838])

*Figure 10.2.* "Armed with pads and pencils and warm, comfortable clothing, the ladies of the press toured Fort Meade on December 8 to learn at first hand, how Uncle Sam's soldiers are prepared for combat duty. Shown many phases of Army life, the women were also permitted to fire the heavy guns, and they had their lunch, Army style, in outdoor bivouac. They interviewed military men in rank from private to brigadier general and observed the thorough training Army men must undergo before they serve in combat areas. The highlights of their visit are shown in the following series. First stop was the office of Brigadier General John E. Dahlquist, acting commander of the 70th Division. After a brief interview, the tour got under way," 1942. (Library of Congress, Prints and Photographs Division, NYWT&S Collection [reproduction number LC-USZ62-119982])

*Figure 10.3.* "New York: News cameramen struggle for a chance to photograph Valentine Gubitchev as the Soviet engineer is rushed into a police van after being found guilty of conspiracy to commit espionage. Co-defendant Judith Coplon, U.S. government girl, also was found guilty. Sentence will be pronounced Thursday," March 7, 1950. (Library of Congress, Prints and Photographs Division, NYWT&S Collection [reproduction number LC-USZ62-119981])

*Figure 10.4.* "A picket line thrown around the offices of the *New York World Telegram and the Sun,* June 13, marks the first day of the Newspaper Guild of New York (CIO) strike against that publication. The Guild, representing 540 editorial and business office employees of the newspaper, called the strike after negotiations to resolve the dispute over union demands for wage increases and other benefits broke down," June 13, 1950. (Library of Congress, Prints and Photographs Division, NYWT&S Collection [reproduction number LC-USZ62-119983])

# Contributors

**Kevin G. Barnhurst** is associate professor at the Department of Communications, University of Illinois at Chicago, and author of *Seeing the Newspaper* (1994). He was founding head of the International Communication Association Visual Communication Interest Group. His research looks at visual communication as a social phenomenon and examines the political implications of media form.

**Monique Berlier** holds a license in Germanic philology from the Catholic University of Louvain, Belgium, an M.A. in communication from Northeast Louisiana University, and a Ph.D. from the University of Iowa School of Journalism and Mass Communication. Her dissertation explores the social uses of photography by immigrants in rural America during the late nineteenth and early twentieth centuries and looks at how photographic imagery can be used as historical evidence.

**Bonnie Brennen** is an associate professor at the University of Missouri School of Journalism in Columbia. She has published several articles focusing on a cultural history of the media and recently completed an oral history project, *For the Record,* that deals with former newsworkers in the Rochester, New York, area. Her first book, *Newsworkers: Toward a History of the Rank and File,* edited with Hanno Hardt, was published in 1995.

**Robert L. Craig** has a Ph.D. in mass communication from the University of Iowa. He has taught at Dublin City University, the University of Minnesota, Marquette University, the University of Ulster, and Syracuse University. He is professor and chair of the Department of Journalism and Mass Communication at the University of St. Thomas in St. Paul, Minnesota. He has published in *Design Issues,* the *Journal of Advertising, Communication, Visual Sociology, Discourse and Society, American Journalism History,* and other communication research journals.

**John Erickson** is an associate professor of journalism and mass communication at the University of Iowa. His research interests lie in the history of mass communications in the United States, specifically the intellectual history of inquiry into news and the cultural history of reporting. He is also conducting research on the social meaning of news.

**Michael Griffin** is a visiting professor at the University of St. Thomas in St. Paul, Minnesota. He has taught mass media studies and journalism for sixteen years at the University of Minnesota and has taught as a visiting faculty member at the University of Amsterdam and the University of Pennsylvania. He specializes in research on visual media production and representation, relationships of media and culture, and the implications of global media systems across cultures. His most recent publication is *International Media Monitoring* (1999), edited with Kaarle Nordenstreng. The work for this volume was an outgrowth of an Annenberg Scholars Program Fellowship on "The Future of Fact" at the University of Pennsylvania (1995–96).

**Hanno Hardt** is John F. Murray Professor of Journalism and Mass Communication at the University of Iowa, with a joint appointment in the Department of Communication Studies; he is also a professor of communication at the University of Ljubljana, Slovenia. His recent books include *Interactions: Critical Studies: Essays on Communication, Media, and Journalism* (1998), *Newsworkers: Toward a History of the Rank and File* edited with Bonnie Brennen (1995), and *Critical Communication Studies: Communication, History, and Theory in America* (1992).

**John C. Nerone** is a research professor in the Institute of Communications Research at the University of Illinois at Urbana-Champaign. He is the author of *Violence against the Press: Policing the Public Sphere in U.S. History* (1994); editor of *Last Rights: Revisiting Four Theories of the Press* (1995); and coeditor of the History of Communication series for the University of Illinois Press.

**Dona Schwartz** is an associate professor of journalism and mass communication at the University of Minnesota. She is an active member of the International Visual Sociology Association and the International Communication Association's Visual Communication Interest Group. Her principal area of interest is the ethnography of visual communication. She is the author of *Waucoma Twilight: Generations of the Farm* (1992) and *Contesting the Super Bowl* (1997).

**David R. Spencer** is an associate professor in the faculty of information and media studies at the University of Western Ontario. He is the past president of the American Journalism Historians Association. Interested in alternative press and visual communication, he has written articles and book chapters on journalism history for publications in both Canada and the United States.

**Barbie Zelizer** is an associate professor of communication at the Annenberg School for Communication at the University of Pennsylvania. A former reporter, she has published widely on journalism as a cultural practice and is the author of *Covering the Body: The Kennedy Assassination, the Media, and the Shaping of Collective Memory* (1992) and *Remembering to Forget: Holocaust Memory through the Camera's Eye* (1998), for which she was designated both a Guggenheim Fellow and a research fellow at the Freedom Forum Center for Media Studies at Columbia University during the 1994–95 academic year.

# Index

# The History of Communication

Typeset in 10.5/13 Adobe Minion
with Adobe Minion display
Composed by Jim Proefrock
at the University of Illinois Press
Manufactured by Cushing-Malloy, Inc.